CW00594993

SUPPLY NETWORK STRATEGIES

The IMP (Industrial Marketing and Purchasing) Group was formed in 1976 by researchers from five European countries. The group's first work was a large-scale comparative study of industrial marketing and purchasing across Europe. Results from this study were published by John Wiley in 1982, edited by Håkan Håkansson, under the title *International Industrial Marketing and Purchasing: An Interaction Approach*. The group's 'interaction approach' is based on the importance for both researchers and managers of understanding the *interaction* between *active* buyers and sellers in continuing business *relationships*. The group has since carried out a large number of studies into business relationships and to the wider networks in which they operate. This work is published in numerous books and articles. A selection of this work can be seen in *Understanding Business Markets (Second Edition)*, edited by David Ford, Dryden, 1997. *Managing Business Relationships*, also by David Ford and a team of IMP authors was published in 1998 by John Wiley & Sons, Ltd. This is book encapsulates the teaching, research, consulting and writing experience of the IMP Group. The group hosts an international conference in September of each year which attracts a large number of researchers working in the areas of business marketing, purchasing and inter-company networks.

SUPPLY NETWORK STRATEGIES

Lars-Erik Gadde

Chalmers University of Technology

Håkan Håkansson

Norwegian School of Management

JOHN WILEY & SONS, LTD

Chichester • New York • Weinheim • Brisbane • Singapore • Toronto

Copyright © 2001 John Wiley & Sons Ltd,
             The Atrium, Southern Gate, Chichester,
             West Sussex PO19 8SQ, England

             Telephone   (+44) 1243 779777

Email (for orders and customer service enquiries): cs-books@wiley.co.uk
Visit our Home Page on www.wileyeurope.com or www.wiley.com

Reprinted June 2005, February 2006

All Rights Reserved. No part of this publication may be reproduced, stored in a retrieval
system or transmitted in any form or by any means, electronic, mechanical, photocopying,
recording, scanning or otherwise, except under the terms of the Copyright, Designs and
Patents Act 1988 or under the terms of a licence issued by the Copyright Licensing Agency
Ltd, 90 Tottenham Court Road, London W1T 4LP, UK, without the permission in writing of
the Publisher. Requests to the Publisher should be addressed to the Permissions Department,
John Wiley & Sons Ltd, The Atrium, Southern Gate, Chichester, West Sussex PO19 8SQ,
England, or emailed to permreq@wiley.co.uk, or faxed to (+44) 1243 770571.

Lars-Erik Gadde and Håkan Håkansson have asserted their right under the Copyright, Designs and
Patents Act, 1988, to be identified as the authors of this work.

This publication is designed to provide accurate and authoritative information in regard to
the subject matter covered. It is sold on the understanding that the Publisher is not engaged
in rendering professional services. If professional advice or other expert assistance is
required, the services of a competent professional should be sought.

Other Wiley Editorial Offices

John Wiley & Sons Inc., 111 River Street, Hoboken, NJ 07030, USA

Jossey-Bass, 989 Market Street, San Francisco, CA 94103-1741, USA

Wiley-VCH Verlag GmbH, Boschstr. 12, D-69469 Weinheim, Germany

John Wiley & Sons Australia Ltd, 33 Park Road, Milton, Queensland 4064, Australia

John Wiley & Sons (Asia) Pte Ltd, 2 Clementi Loop #02-01, Jin Xing Distripark, Singapore 129809

John Wiley & Sons Canada Ltd, 22 Worcester Road, Etobicoke, Ontario, Canada M9W 1L1

Library of Congress Cataloging-in-Publication Data
Gadde, Lars-Erik, 1945-
    Supply network strategies / Lars-Erik Gadde, Håkan Håkansson.
       p. cm.
    ISBN 0-471-49916-1
    1. Industrial procurement. I. Håkansson, Håkan, 1947 - II. Title.
    HD39.5 .G333 2001
    658.7′2–dc21   2001026252

British Library Cataloguing in Publication Data

A catalogue record for this book is available from the British Library

ISBN-10 0-471-49916-1 (P/B)
ISBN-13 978-0-471-49916-9 (P/B)

Typeset in 10/12pt Palatino by C.K.M. Typesetting, Salisbury, Wiltshire.
Printed and bound in Great Britain by Antony Rowe Ltd, Chippenham, Wiltshire.
This book is printed on acid-free paper responsibly manufactured from sustainable forestry in
which at least two trees are planted for each one used for paper production.

CONTENTS

PREFACE

This book is about the supply side of companies—what historically has been identified as purchasing. This function has gone through a remarkable change over recent decades. Purchasing has developed from being regarded as something that had to be done towards something that is central for the whole functioning of the modern company. We have had the pleasure of following this development and the book summarizes our experience of 25 years of research in the purchasing area. The main emphasis of this book is on the key issues that purchasing is faced with today, which to a large extent are about developing appropriate relationships with suppliers and combining these relationships into efficient supply networks.

In the process of writing this book we have benefited from co-operation with a large number of colleagues from practice and research. We are grateful to SILF Competence in Stockholm and its CEO Svante Axelsson, who organized and participated in a round-table discussion concerning the current procurement challenges in Swedish companies. In particular, we want to thank Klas Frisk, Nordic Construction Company, Gunnar Ivansson, Ericsson Mobile Systems, and Gösta Hulthén, Inköp & Logistik for valuable contributions. We also want to acknowledge the input from interaction with many practitioners during the research projects in which we have been involved.

We have the good fortune to be part of an extensive network of researchers in the Scandinavian countries, which is also connected to the rest of Europe, the US and Australia. In particular, we want to mention five persons: Alexandra Waluszewski, Uppsala University, Ivan Snehota, Stockholm School of Economics, Anna Dubois and Jens Laage-Hellman from Chalmers University of Technology in Gothenburg, and David Ford, University of Bath. They have all been highly involved in the research that the book builds on, and at times we place considerable reliance on things they have written. Many other people have also influenced us. The most important ones to mention are the following: Virpi Havila, Torkel Wedin, Anna Bengtsson, Susanne Åberg, Bertil Markgren, Jan Johanson and Enrico Baraldo, all at Uppsala University; Kajsa Hulthén, Lennart Bångens, Daniel Hjelmgren and Oskar Jellbo at Chalmers; Lars-Gunnar Mattsson,

Stockholm School of Economics; Ann-Charlott Pedersen, Tim Torvatn and Elsebeth Holmen in Trondheim; Göran Persson and Marianne Jahre in Oslo; Christian Grönroos and Carl-Johan Rosenbröijer in Helsinki; Anu Söderlund in Vaasa; Luis Araujo, Geoff Easton and Debbie Harrison in Lancaster; Ariane van Raesfeld in Twente; and Annalisa Tunisini and Roberta Bocconcelli in Urbino.

We have also benefited from comments received from reviewers engaged by our publisher. These comments were both encouraging and challenging and gave us new insights. Thanks to Asta Salmi, Thomas Johnsen and Martin Spring. Linda Schenck was a very efficient proof-reader and improved the English considerably.

Last, but not least, we gratefully acknowledge the economic resources provided by Humanistisk-Samhällsvetenskapliga Forskningsrådet, Axel och Margaret Axson Johnsons stiftelse för allmännyttiga ändamål, and Riksbankens Jubileumsfond. We are indebted also to the Swedish School of Economics in Helsinki, which provided both intellectual and financial support in terms of a visiting professorship for one of the authors.

Lars-Erik Gadde
Håkan Håkansson

Oslo and Gothenburg
February 2001

Part I

PURCHASING CHALLENGES

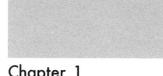

Chapter 1

THE ROLE OF PURCHASING IN THE COMPANY

> In the past when you could do nothing else at IBM we made you a buyer,
> when you couldn't design anything,
> when you couldn't build anything,
> when you couldn't carry anything,
> when you couldn't deliver anything,
> we put you into the purchasing organization.

This quote is a representative illustration of the way purchasing operations and purchasing departments were regarded not long ago. The statement was made by IBM's purchasing director in an interview where the company's new approach to purchasing is presented (Carbone 1999). Since the procurement re-orientation of the company, purchasing and purchasers are now perceived as 'an incredibly competent dedicated group of professionals' (ibid. p. 45). This distorted attitude to the role of purchasers is not unique to IBM. On the contrary, the changed perspective is representative of a fairly general development in which the strategic significance of purchasing and purchasers has been substantially enhanced.

A New View of Purchasing

Traditionally, purchasing has been considered a clerical and administrative function mainly expediting orders, where others have specified the content. Today, however, this perspective has shifted considerably. Studies of purchasing in a number of companies revealed, among others, the following perceptions of purchasing and purchasers (Fitzgerald 1999, p. 57):

> Skills for purchasing are much more multifaceted and sophisticated as the game changes. There's more emphasis on the ability to discover, link and manage supplier resources with our appetite for technology. There's also greater need for leadership talent.
> (Maytag Corp., appliance manufacturer)

> Skill sets have been redefined for all purchasing pros in order to be consistent with our supply management strategy.
> (Harley Davidson, motorcycle manufacturer)

> Need for technical skills has increased in importance. Traditional buying and selling does not occur anymore, but strategic technical sourcing does.
> (Donelly Corp., supplier of window systems and mirrors)

These quotes clearly indicate both new attitudes towards purchasing and new requirements imposed on purchasers. The main reason for these changes is the increasing strategic importance of the supply side in any company's operations. We discuss the reasons for this enhanced significance in the second section

These new attitudes to purchasing and purchasers are also a reflection of a change in the view of what is supposed to be efficient purchasing behaviour. A traditional emphasis on optimizing single transactions now is supplemented with a long-term view of procurement efficiency and effectiveness. This, in turn, affects the perception of what role suppliers can play for the buying company. Historically, buying and selling transactions were considered 'zero-sum-contests'—what one stands to gain the other stands to lose. Selling firms were thus considered adversaries rather than collaborators. However, numerous examples show that win-win situations do exist and that suppliers can contribute substantially to the fulfilment of the new requirements imposed on purchasing. Achieving this support from suppliers requires reconsideration of the view of efficiency in customer–supplier relationships. The prevailing attitude, stressing the need to avoid dependence on individual suppliers, was modified when the potential advantages of close collaboration were discovered. Recent developments in industrial operations have thus brought the interfaces with other companies into focus. Concepts and techniques such as 'just-in-time' (JIT), the zero-defect principle and TQM (total quality management) have had substantial impacts on the way firms operate. All this means that relationships between a firm and its suppliers are now regarded as of crucial importance. It also means more careful consideration of the benefits and costs associated with different types of relationships.

One natural consequence of these developments is that the competitiveness and profit-generating capacity of the individual firm is highly dependent on its ability to handle the supply side. Firstly, there is a direct effect on profitability, because purchasing accounts for a substantial portion of company costs. Secondly, there is an indirect impact because 'internal' costs are greatly affected by what goes on at the interface between a company and its suppliers. Thirdly, as the above quotes from three buying companies pointed out, there is a role for suppliers as providers of resources and technology in general. Therefore, suppliers also impact on the revenue side of company accounts.

The Increasing Significance of Purchasing and Suppliers

For most companies the costs of purchased goods and services represent the dominant portion of total costs. An American study revealed that these costs

TABLE 1.1 The extent of outsourcing in American industry. Based on *Purchasing* 1999a.

High extent of outsourcing	(%)	Low extent of outsourcing	(%)
Textiles	62	Utilities, gas and electric	17
Motor vehicles and parts	61	Petroleum refining	21
Chemicals	57	Food manufacturing	38

amounted to 50% or more in 16 industries out of 32 (*Purchasing* 1999a, p. 52). In a Swedish study it was found that purchasing, on average, accounted for 51% of total costs. However, the figures presented indicate huge variation among industries (Table 1.1).

As Table 1.1 illustrates, there is wide variation between industries, ranging from 17% outsourcing in gas and electric up to over 60% in textiles and automotive. It is important to observe that, according to this survey, 'most if not all industries' have increased their spending on suppliers. Figures from Sweden indicate similar patterns. At Volvo Car Corporation purchased goods and services amount to 70% of total costs. According to company representatives, this share will increase to 80% in a few years' time. For contractors in the construction industry it is not unusual for the figure to exceed 75%.

The most prominent driving force underlying these figures is the strong reliance on outsourcing. During the last few decades firms have increasingly concentrated their operations in order to become more specialized. In doing so, they have attempted to focus on a limited set of activities. This, in turn, means that they rely more and more on purchasing, and thus on suppliers. The figures presented clearly indicate the importance of the supply side relative to other company functions. For large corporations these figures mean that the monetary value handled by purchasing is substantial. For example, Ford Motors spent USD 76,540 million on suppliers in 1999 (Purchasing 1999a, p. 56). Corresponding figures for the next three largest spenders in the US were 62 billion dollars (General Motors), 41 (IBM) and 34 (General Electric). The larger the portion of outsourcing, the larger the financial importance of purchasing. This relationship is the background for the significant changes in the IBM attitudes to purchasing, as illustrated by Carbone (1999, p. 45):

> Ten years ago when IBM was vertically integrated, purchasing was not that important to IBM because it was basically an administrative function. Purchasers executed the buying transactions after being told what to buy.

However, in 12 years the costs of purchased goods and services increased from 28% to 51% of the company's total costs. These changes increased the attention to the operations on the supply side and made purchasing a strategic function.

In this way, IBM has been through a development similar to most large, vertically integrated companies. These companies (e.g. car manufacturers, producers of white goods, etc.) used to rely on 'Fordism', an approach where any problem was supposed to be solved through vertical integration—anything that was important should be done by the company itself. The task of purchasing was then to handle the rest, which, by definition, was not so important! The role of the purchasing function is thus reduced when vertical integration increases. Consequently, the importance of purchasing is enhanced when firms disintegrate. The recent attention paid to the activities on the supply side can be explained by the changes in the reality of the large companies. When they reduce their extent of vertical integration, purchasing attracts more interest and come into focus, because the large companies tend to set the agenda for what is considered important—by practitioners as well as by consultants and researchers.

In small companies purchasing has probably never been treated in the same way as in large companies, the main reason being that in these firms 'purchasing' is normally not defined as a specific and particular task. In many cases it has been an integrated part of business in general and the owner of the company (or the CEO) has been responsible for all strategic deals. Suppliers have always been important to these companies. One example is the way the Swedish car manufacturer Volvo approached the supply side during the first three decades of its operation. When the company was set up in the 1920s its resource base was very limited. Volvo lacked most of the crucial resources and therefore had to work together with suppliers that produced vital components and systems, such as the engine. Suppliers had to be regarded as strategic partners and were not handled by a separate purchasing department, but by top management. The design of products and the way they were delivered were jointly discussed and decided. Top management even used the expression 'the larger Volvo' to characterize the structure including 'the smaller Volvo' and its important suppliers (Kinch 1987).

The Volvo example illustrates an important difference between small and large companies. It is much easier for small companies to develop a coherent way of working with suppliers. Large companies have to organize this kind of behaviour. However, small companies have other problems in purchasing. They may have problems in gaining interest from suppliers because they buy in small volumes and normally lack the management resources to find and develop different alternatives and solutions. In the coming discussion of the development of the purchasing function and the way purchasing problems have been approached we use the large companies' perspective, because this has dominated. However, now and then we examine the view of small companies.

It is not only the relative financial importance of purchasing and the monetary value of the throughput that makes the supply side of strategic significance. The changing character of the content of the input from suppliers is important as well. Over time, outsourcing of manufacturing activities has been followed by outsourcing of design and development work. To an increasing extent, suppliers contribute to the technical development of the buying company. A study in the US revealed that about 50% of the companies in the sample used suppliers as sources of technical knowledge. Purchasing plays an important role in these ambitions because this function represents the interface with suppliers. For a long time, purchasing staff argued that they would be able to improve performance in this respect if they were allowed to bring in suppliers early in the product development process. Present experience indicates that this is true, as is exemplified in the following Box where the effects of supplier involvement in design are illustrated.

How Suppliers Improve Design

- By getting involved early in the design process, Rittal Corp., Springfield, Ohio, saved a computer manufacturer money by adapting its standard, modular, free-standing enclosure to include provisions for thermal management. The solution: A special door that facilitated ventilation. Previously, the company would choose a separate climate-control system after getting its enclosure.
- Honeywell credits Mentor Graphics and Hewlett-Packard with helping it complete development of its space computer, intended for space-borne and avionics data processing. 'HP showed us how to migrate to our new systems gradually without losing productivity,' says Honeywell staff engineer Lee Dreger. 'Without their technical assistance, we would never have hit our milestones.'
- For designers unsure of whether their application calls for a proximity sensor or switch, Virtual Sensor Specialist Software (VS3) from Square D Co. presents users with multiple decision paths that quickly narrow the number of available selections. 'Not only are questions presented to the user based on a profile of the user's applications,' says Thurston Horton, solid-state sensors product specialist, 'but they take into account the user's level of expertise.' VS3 software is available through Square D's Web site.

Source: *Purchasing* 1997, p. 32S13.

The increasing significance of suppliers is recognized in other fields as well, as is shown in many studies. For example, between 1990 and 1997 executive perception of supplier importance changed from 3.10 to 3.83 (on a scale of 1 to 5) according to Trent and Monczka (1998, p. 5). The companies in the sample projected that this importance would rise to 4.64 in the early 2000s, thus indicating a strongly enhanced reliance on suppliers. In particular, the executives in these surveys highlighted supplier importance in product development. This figure increased from 4.5 in 1990 to 5.9 in 1997 (7-digit scale).

The new views of suppliers and purchasing go hand-in-hand with a revised perspective on purchasing efficiency. Traditionally, optimization of single transactions was considered the primary driver of purchasing efficiency. Therefore, the most relevant cost item to focus on was the price paid in each transaction. However, the price tag of an item is only one of the costs affected by the operations on the supply side. Purchasing behaviour may have a strong impact on other costs as well, as is illustrated in Figure 1.1 with examples of what is usually known as indirect purchasing costs. These costs are affected by the purchasing operations and may sometimes be more relevant targets for cost reductions than price.

The increasing interest in collaboration with suppliers is a reflection of the fact that buying firms have reconsidered efficient purchasing. Attacking the various types of indirect costs calls for joint activities of buyer and supplier in terms of mutual adjustments of equipment, systems and working methods. Achieving economic benefits from these investments requires that buyer and supplier have a shared view of one another and what they can gain from co-operation. This broadened vision demands a long-term perspective, contrasting the short-sighted view favouring the lowest price in single transactions. The coming

FIGURE 1.1   Costs affected by purchasing. Source: Gadde and Håkansson 1993, p. 47.

section includes a number of examples of the effects that may be gained from such co-operative efforts.

Two Strategic Roles of Purchasing

The contributions from purchasing to the strategic development of a company may be summarized in two strategic roles: rationalization and development (Axelsson and Håkansson 1984).

The Rationalization Role

The rationalization role of purchasing comprises all the numerous day-to-day activities performed to decrease costs successively. This may include changes in the technical specification of the solution used and/or changes in the way the solution is produced and delivered. The quote below illustrates the rationalization role played by some of the suppliers of Boeing (Stundza 1999, p. 71):

> Replacing a pattern of spot competitive purchases of aluminium of varying alloys our Portland plant has firmly committed to fixed purchases of precisely defined blocks over a two-year period from two suppliers based in the Los Angeles area. They have also completely overhauled the transportation system linking the Oregon plant with three key California-based suppliers. The payoff for Boeing: The people who are doing the final assembly of the 777 are now getting all the flap supports they want, exactly when they want them, and at a unit cost that is 30%–35% lower than it was just a year ago.

There are three main types of rationalization roles. The first is related to discovering what needs to be purchased. This includes decisions of whether to purchase or manufacture in-house, as well as the specification of the products, components, and systems to be purchased. It is possible for purchasing to contribute to increased effectiveness in these processes through co-operation with internal functions such as design, development and production, and through qualified awareness of what different suppliers have to offer.

Rationalization of logistics comprises the second opportunity for efficiency improvements. The automotive industry is well known for efficient just-in-time deliveries (see, for example, Womack *et al.* 1990 and Lamming 1993). Less spectacular, but no less significant, examples have been reported elsewhere. One and the same issue of an American magazine presents three interesting illustrations (Minahan 1995). Frito Lay is a major producer of snacks who encountered problems associated with transportation from suppliers to its plants. A logistics provider was made responsible for supplying all input to Frito Lay's 38 plants. The service provider was able to reduce costs of transportation by 12%, and improved delivery reliability substantially. Another case shows how a specialized firm improved materials handling at the Miami Herald. By making use of more sophisticated equipment, loading time was reduced from 5 hours to 20 minutes, and costs decreased. A supplier of electronics had difficulties in meeting customer demands for spare parts. When serving customers from its 135 distribution centres all over the country, delivery times were on average 3 to 4 days—mainly because only a fraction of the total product range could be stocked at each of the warehouses. The service function was outsourced to a logistics provider. This firm reduced delivery times to 24 hours at the most. The main change was a reduction in the number of distribution centres—from 135 to 7. In these remaining warehouses the complete assortment could be stocked at reasonable cost, and deliveries were made overnight. Transportation costs increased because the number of warehouses was reduced. Total costs, however, were reduced substantially because both capital cost and inventory cost decreased even more.

Even in their administrative routines, buying firms experience problems. This brings us to the third type of rationalization in which purchasing should be involved. Each business transaction is associated with a number of administrative operations from preliminary inquiries to invoices. Especially where it comes to frequent purchases of low-value items these costs may be the most important ones to tackle. A study in the US estimated the costs for handling a single purchase order for uncomplicated items like MRO-supplies to be at least 20 dollars. For procurement of more advanced products the costs were calculated to be in the range of 75–150 dollars. In the construction industry it has been estimated that the cost of handling an invoice is around 40–50 dollars for the buying company. One of the main primary contractors in Sweden receives an average of 1.5 million invoices per year—in Sweden alone. From these figures it is obvious that one of the most important determinants of efficiency in this type of procurement is to find effective routines for dealing with a huge number of transactions rather than optimizing single purchasing decisions. It thus becomes more a matter of developing procurement routines that secure long-term efficiency. Because each purchase is in itself relatively marginal in financial terms, many companies have neglected to undertake these rationalization efforts. Consequently, they are struggling with a large number of fragmented purchases from a large supplier base, imposing an unnecessary administrative burden.

The Development Role

The second strategic role of purchasing is the development role. The reason for its significance is that suppliers can be important resource providers for the technical development of the customer firm. The development role has been enhanced owing to the increasing specialization of the actors in industrial networks. Most firms today make use of products and services based on a variety of technologies. Over time, it has become increasingly difficult for a firm to develop and maintain its own capability in each specific area of technology relevant to its operations. Therefore, buying firms more and more rely on suppliers as sources of technical development. This means that the internal R&D activities of the customer need to be co-ordinated with those of suppliers. One important mission for the purchasing function is to become involved as early as possible in the R&D process to be able to bring in suppliers. Early supplier involvement makes it possible to make use of vendor capabilities in product development, which is important because estimates have shown that up to 80% of the total costs of a new product are determined in the design phase. Furthermore, early supplier involvement is a means of shortening lead times in the development of new products. For these reasons suppliers become involved much earlier in these processes today than they used to be. The article about Boeing also illuminated the development role (Stundza 1999, p. 71):

> One of the suppliers suggested that high-speed machining could be greatly facilitated, even revolutionized, if the aluminium blocks were made in a new way that reduces residual stress—the theory being that blocks forged the old way had greatly complicated the machining process. In effect the machine operators were being forced to whittle away at the sides of the block rather than sculpting it. Working closely with its suppliers, Boeing tested and confirmed the approach that the machine operators could carve straight into a new kind of block. It proved to be a key insight leading to a whole series of changes between our Portland plant and its suppliers.

The examples of supplier involvement in design operations reported in the box on page 7 represent further illustrations of the development role.

The Position of Purchasing in the Company

The chapter began with recognition of the substantial attention purchasing operations are given today at IBM and other large companies. It was also indicated that attitudes towards purchasing and purchasers have changed quite dramatically in recent decades. In Chapter 2 we present a historical overview of the purchasing field, from which it is clear that the somewhat negative attitudes towards the function have been accompanied by a fairly weak position in the organizational hierarchy. Over time, this position has successively improved, as is indicated by the fact that in 1990 a study in the US showed that in 50% of companies the purchasing department was involved in strategy presentations with the executive committees of the firms. The 1990s were then characterized by a rapid increase in the importance of purchasing, and in 1997 the corresponding figure was 83%. The portion of companies where the purchasing department was involved in strategy presentations with the board of directors increased from 18% to 32% (Trent and Monczka 1998, p. 4).

It is thus clear that issues related to purchasing have become of greater strategic importance and have other characteristics today than in the past. This development was discussed in the round-table session with Swedish purchasing managers mentioned in the preface of the book. They characterized the main tasks in the clerical and administrative era of purchasing as being mainly related to *expediting orders*. This ordering function was later supplemented with increasing involvement in *negotiating* with suppliers. In many cases the purchasing department was provided with a list of approved vendors. The task of purchasing staff was then to secure that the supplier presenting the best financial deal was chosen. Over time, the potential strategic contributions from purchasing were recognized. Making full use of this potential required that purchasing became involved in the procurement operations before the list of approved vendors had been laid down. Therefore, purchasing increasingly became involved in *strategic sourcing* issues. Finally, as revealed in the analysis of purchasing's rationalization role, logistics and material supply have become increasingly important issues on the supply side of companies. Just-in-time deliveries have replaced established activity structures where huge inventories served as buffers. The new supply systems relying on more or less continuous flows of materials require substantial synchronization. In most cases, purchasing staff are responsible for these operations related to *supply chain management*.

Altogether, this means that what began as a clerical and administrative function has developed into a strategically significant profession. This profession includes four sub-functions with different characteristics and requirements: ordering, negotiating, sourcing, and supply chain management. Against this background the enhanced requirements on purchasing staff indicated in the introductory section are easily understood. These requirements have affected the purchasing departments considerably. The changing conditions are described as follows by a Swedish purchasing director:

> In 1983 the average age of people at the purchasing department was fairly high—only two people were younger than thirty. In 1997 purchasing staff, on average, were twenty years younger than in 1983. The educational background of the people also changed dramatically. In 1983 only two had an engineering background while in 1997 there were more than one hundred engineers.

According to this purchasing director, people with a technical background were important to purchasing for three reasons. Firstly, the engineering background was a necessary competence for the new tasks imposed on purchasing. Secondly, it helped improve the status of the purchasing function. Thirdly, when technicians were involved both in purchasing and production/design the conditions for interaction among these functions were substantially improved. This change was important for IBM as well. When people with a technical background were recruited to purchasing it became possible for IBM procurement to change 'from being guardians of secret information to facilitators of communication between IBM's manufacturing and engineering people and its suppliers' (Carbone, 1999, p. 42).

The opportunities for purchasing to act as a link between the engineering functions and suppliers are determined not only by the educational background and the competence of purchasing staff. The organizational design of the buying company is important as well. Like other company functions, purchasing may either be centralized or decentralized. Centralization of purchasing implies that procurement operations of the different business units of a company are handled by a common headquarter function. Decentralization means that the different business units—or even individual manufacturing sites—are responsible for their own purchases. Most companies rely on a combination of centralization and decentralization, as illustrated by the following example from Compaq.

Centralized and Decentralized Purchasing at Compaq

In 1993 procurement at Compaq was re-engineered from top to bottom. The corporate procurement group was established to manage strategic commodities. Cross functional teams were formed and more emphasis was placed on the sites...

Strategic issues are handled by the corporate management group, which manages mass storage, mechanical devices, ASICs and flat panels, memory, microprocessors and micro-peripherals on a world-wide basis. Each commodity is managed by a procurement functional team comprised of a director and key business and technical support people. The teams develop and implement strategic business plans and sourcing strategies. The director is also in charge of a cross-functional team that includes design engineers and marketing people, representatives from each of the manufacturing sites, and a financial analyst.

While the corporate procurement group is strategic, the site purchasers are tactical. They do the day-to-day purchasing for their sites. They are working more on a 90-day window pulling material into the factory working under the umbrella of strategic plans.

Source: *Purchasing* 1995, p. 36.

The working conditions and purchasing issues change depending on the organizational design, as is illustrated by the two examples below. The first deals with a centralized purchasing organization. Mr Anderson, purchasing manager, is in his office at company headquarters in Stockholm. He has just concluded a conversation with a supplier in Gothenburg, and he has lodged a serious complaint. The supplier was delayed with a delivery, failed to notify the company, and the result was production disturbances at the Wermland plant. Yesterday, Anderson was roundly lectured by the plant manager, and now he has passed the message along. He is very familiar with the supplying firm, and turned to someone high up in the corporate hierarchy to emphasize his statement that if this happens one more time his company intends to change suppliers. He is certain that he has made himself understood, and now hopes he will never hear from Wermland again regarding this supplier.

The second example relates to a situation in a decentralized purchasing organization. Mr Pettersson, purchasing manager of a completely different company, has just rung off after a similar telephone conversation. Pettersson's office is in Örebro, in the same building as the production unit whose purchases he manages. That unit is part of a large company with a central purchasing co-ordinator, who has no operative responsibility. Pettersson is having problems with a supplier in Sundsvall who has trouble keeping his deadlines, mainly because he gets contradictory messages from different units within the purchasing company. Several units use the same product, and owing to a shortage in recent months, tough 'competition' has evolved regarding volumes. Pettersson and the supplier agree by phone to try to develop a routine together with the other units within the buying company in order to solve the problem.

As these examples show, purchasing is affected by the organizational structure a company has chosen. A central purchasing department makes it easier to specialize in relation to different supplier markets. On the other hand, a centralized purchasing unit makes it more difficult to keep in touch with the plants that are using the products. In a highly decentralized firm, it is easy to keep up internal contacts in each of the local units and also to stay in close contact with suppliers used frequently. It is more difficult to co-ordinate between the different units belonging to the same firm and to have a clear external overview. These are some of the main factors impacting on the design of the organizational structure of the buying company. We return to this important issue in Chapter 6.

Finally, we need to bring up the difference between large and small companies and also the divergence between US companies and European ones. We have very consciously chosen to start with the recent situation for large companies in the US, mainly to show that some problems and strategies that have long been regarded as typically European are now being observed and considered important in the US as well. We belong to the IMP-tradition, which is based on research on how European companies approach one another. The importance of close business relationships has been the main theme since the first book was published (Håkansson (ed.) 1982). Some of the problems faced by IBM and other large companies—and also some of the ways they solve them—are analysed in the case studies from the 1970s. However, this does not imply that European companies are more advanced than their US colleagues, or that they have been cleverer in developing supply strategies. The main reason for the differences relates to the contexts of the companies—there is clearly not only a difference between the size of the markets but also in the perceptions of markets and efficiency.

There is no reason to believe that the 'average' relationship has been less developed in the US than in Europe. However, in the US there has been a clear focus on large vertically integrated companies which, in turn, leads to a particular view of purchasing and suppliers. This view is of general interest because it has influenced the perception of purchasing in Europe as well. For example, in the 1950s Volvo changed its supply strategy and turned to a more American way of buying. In Chapter 2 we describe how companies—American and European—have developed their supply strategies over time.

Another distinction needs to be made between large and small companies. The organizational problems discussed above are clearly related to large companies. In a small company there is no need to separate purchasing problems from production or marketing issues. In small companies top management prefer keeping them together. Generally, small companies have approached suppliers in a more co-operative way. Most often suppliers have been considered strategic business partners, vital in relation to both day-to-day operations and to the development of new products and technologies. Again, there are considerable differences between companies, partly owing to their sizes but also related to their extents of vertical integration.

Entirely New Roles for Purchasing

A recent cover story about IBM's purchasing activities in Carbone (1999) revealed some innovative characteristics of procurement today. In particular, two non-traditional purchasing activities are identified. One of them is Customer Solution Procurement, the other the IBM Procurement Services Group.

Customer Solutions Procurement (CSP) is an organization with about 200 buyers that was formed to support IBM's Global Services division. CSP provides IT solutions for corporate customers. In 1998 Global Services did about USD 29 billion worth of business, and its business is growing by about 20% per year. CSP is the fastest growing segment of IBM purchasing. The idea of Global Services is to provide one-stop shopping for a company buying IT. The company hires IBM to determine its corporate computing needs. The customer may need a few thousand PCs, software, several hundred printers, someone to install the equipment, and computer programmers. The customers may buy IBM computers but want Hewlett-Packard printers and Microsoft software. Customer Solutions Procurement buyers buy the printers and software and hire the installers and the programmers on behalf of the customer. The manager of the CSP-operations explains the way of working (Carbone 1999, p. 40):

> If Lucent wants HP printers, we are going to give them HP printers. We'd rather give them our own, but if they want HP, my guys will go out and buy them. The value that the customer sees is he doesn't have to go out and buy it and make sure it is going to be compatible with their applications. They say: 'IBM, you put the whole solution together. We want you to do it all.'

For IBM this is a completely new type of procurement. It is unique because purchasers specify and buy, but it's delivered to the customer. They also hire temporary help to assist at the customer's doorstep to install equipment or train people on how to use it. It's also different because purchasers work with IBM's marketing people even before a sale has been finalized. Buyers work on proposals together with the marketing team. They are involved early because they need to understand the customer's requirements. This is important because it is an ambition of the purchasing department to influence which suppliers are used. Purchasing wants to rely as much as possible on the pre-negotiated leveraged contracts they have with suppliers. IBM has pre-negotiated deals with many suppliers, and bid-team buyers try to direct as much business as possible to them. For example, a potential customer would really like to use Ricoh copiers, while IBM may have a deal with Canon. In such a case the purchaser would pull the salesperson away and say: 'we can save you 15% on this if you convince them to use Canon instead of Ricoh' (Carbone 1999, p. 40).

CSP procurement changes the relationship to competitors as well. In CSP the IBM buyers often have to negotiate and buy from competitors. According to the manager of CSP this means they have the unenviable task of sitting at a desk across from Microsoft, Dell, Computer Associates, and Compaq and talking about the need to make deals. But in most cases this represents no major problem because even if they are competitors to some extent they also need to collaborate. The manager states that 'we may be competitors, but none of us is stupid. We need them to complete our solution, and they need us to sell their hardware.' The reason for this changed perception about what used to be identified as competitive relationships is the increasing specialization and, consequently, a greater need for collaboration with others.

IBM Procurement Services Group (PSG) is an organization that can be used by other OEMs to buy MRO, office supplies, capital equipment, business equipment, human resources, and temporary-personnel services. PSG was established when other firms were coming to IBM and doing benchmarking sessions. The manager of PSG explains that 'they saw we did a good job and asked if we would do the same for them'. Initially, IBM declined, saying it was not in that business. But IBM saw that Global Services was the fastest growing part of its business and saw an opportunity to provide another innovative service. Procurement Services Group uses the same procurement system, software, and purchasing strategies that IBM uses internally to buy non-production materials and services. OEMs outsource non-production purchasing for the same reason they may outsource manufacturing or information-technology services, at lower cost. Most companies recognize that the non-production area is quite significant to their business, but it is an area that has not been focused on. In some cases, a company will outsource part of its non-production purchasing, such as office supplies, to IBM. In one case, United Technologies Corp. outsources all of its non-production purchases to IBM for one of its divisions and expects to eventually roll it out to all divisions. After one year the system has saved the company millions of dollars and helped UTC to dramatically reduce its number of suppliers. Key to the system are pre-negotiated deals that IBM procurement buyers make with suppliers on behalf of customers. Purchases are then made from those contracts.

This section makes clear that the established view of purchasing as a department mainly procuring items from suppliers to support manufacturing operations in their own company needs to be changed. The PSG organization illustrates that purchasing operations can be undertaken for other firms. The same is exemplified by the CSP-department, which also shows that procurement may sometimes be conducted from firms that were traditionally considered competitors. This is further illustrated by the fact that IBM's own component manufacturers today supply IBM's competitors. The Microelectronics division used to be 'the de facto source of IBM' (Carbone 1999, p. 45). However, they were challenged by IBM's efforts to find external suppliers as alternative sources. According to a purchasing representative this helped the microelectronics division to become a more competitive supplier. Today, the division supplies a number of other customers—previously identified as competitors. The component business to external customers has expanded considerably. Sales to other firms such as Dell, Compaq and Gateway have grown from nothing to USD 6.5 billion in a few years' time.

However, it may be of interest to note that what is new to IBM and some other large companies is not so new for industry in general. Developments at IBM have made the company similar to a distributor. Purchasing in distribution companies has always been dominated by efforts to make the purchasing/marketing interface as close and direct as possible. Industrial distributors often support their customers in finding the most appropriate product or supply source, similarly to IBM. Therefore, while the problems perceived by IBM and others are new to them, they have earlier been experienced by other firms. These changes also explain why networks have become so important. Through the combined effects of reduced vertical integration and increasing specialization, companies have become more unique and traditional roles such as producer, distributor and buyer/user are less clear than they used to be. All firms are becoming nodes in networks of relationships with different characteristics.

A Supply Network View of Purchasing

This chapter points out the increasing importance of purchasing issues in the company. From being primarily an inward-directed operation with administrative characteristics, procurement operations are now strategic. This shift has changed the perspective on the purchasing activities. When purchasing is more important, then suppliers are more important—not only in financial terms. Attaining the strategic potential residing in more efficient purchasing requires a reorientation in the view of suppliers and their resources. Forming close relationships with suppliers is a means of gaining access to these resources. For this reason purchasing issues increasingly cross the boundaries of the buying firm. However, in many cases these efforts need to be further extended. A buying company might benefit substantially from encouraging co-operation among its suppliers, for example in terms of joint activities in product development. Efficient supply chains require not only the involvement of the direct supplier. Even suppliers to the suppliers must be integrated in these activities to avoid sub-optimization. Therefore, efficient and effective purchasing requires a supply network perspective.

Figure 1.2 illustrates a highly simplified supplier network, based on a mechanical engineering firm manufacturing a certain type of equipment. In order to do so,

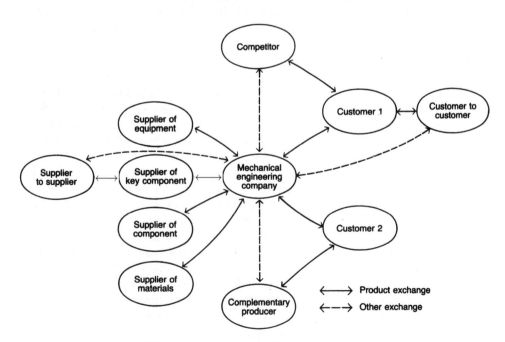

FIGURE 1.2   An example of a supplier network.

the firm purchases components, one of which is particularly critical to the functioning of the equipment. The firm also purchases other materials of different kinds. Last but not least, the firm also buys some production equipment. Figure 1.2 illustrates the most relevant actors in this network.

Even this highly schematic figure illustrates the interdependencies that exist among the actors in a network. When the buying firm tries to improve its operations on the supply side, it might take advantage of these dependencies. For instance, to find new solutions to better satisfy their customers, the buying firm could activate its suppliers as much as possible. They might even be able to affect their suppliers' subcontractors or use those firms to affect the direct suppliers. Alternatively, there may be good reason to co-operate with the complementary producer. If the buying firm wants to increase the effectiveness of its relationship with a given supplier, the firm may have to convince its customers to make some adaptations either in terms of the technical design of a product, or in relation to time or capacity constraints. Similarly, an agreement with a competitor as to some standardization of the end product can make possible producing on larger scale which, in turn, may lead to benefits in terms of effectiveness of supplier relations. Moreover, changes in one supplier relation enable improvement of another. Figure 1.2 gives a brief indication of the variety of possibilities for affecting/changing one relationship by acting in relation to another. Irrespective of which relationship we examine, it is always possible to find ways to indirectly affect it. A network perspective on purchasing substantially enhances the opportunities for improving efficiency and effectiveness on the supply side of companies.

Aim and Scope of the Book

The aim of this book is to launch a framework for supply network strategies. The first chapter gives some preliminary insight into the most important issues to handle on the supply side of companies. Activities traditionally identified as purchasing have become increasingly important and, therefore, subject to re-orientation. In this process, relationships with suppliers have been reconsidered. The present development of industry—often described in terms of the new economy—is characterized by enhanced specialization and sub-division of activities in combination with developments in information technology. Most firms focus their operations and try to develop a more specialized competence. This means that the resources available in a network become increasingly scattered, implying that firms are dependent on access to the resources of other firms. Overall, this means that reality has become more and more network-like. It does not mean that relationships are a new phenomena. But it means that it has become a much more focused phenomenon. This is the main argument for our call for a supply network perspective.

The structure of the book is as follows. In Chapter 2 we discuss the dynamics and challenges of the purchasing function. The chapter consists of a historical overview of purchasing and an analysis of its current challenges. The conclusion of the chapter is that the identification of important issues for purchasing depends on the overall strategic considerations of companies. Therefore, Chapter 3 is devoted to an analysis of what the ongoing developments in 'the new economy' mean to the view of the company. Our argument is that in the network economy the individual firm needs to be analysed from different perspectives. The company is looked upon as a production unit, a knowledge unit, a communicative unit and a capital-earning unit.

The second part of the book introduces a network perspective on purchasing issues. The industrial network model (Håkansson 1987) makes a distinction between three layers in a network structure—activities, resources and actors. In Chapters 4–6 the analytical framework for supply network analysis is developed. Chapter 4 deals with purchasing and the activity structure, while Chapter 5 is devoted to an analysis of purchasing and the resource structure. In Chapter 6 we discuss the actor structure of the network and how purchasing can play an important role in influencing other actors in a desired way.

The third part of the book launches the supply strategies. In Chapter 7 we bring up the issue of what activities and resources should be internal in the buying company and to what extent to rely on other companies. In Chapter 8 we discuss the ways in which different types of relationships impact on the benefits and costs of dealing with suppliers. Chapter 9 is an analysis of the total supply base of the company. In particular, we discuss supply network issues. Chapter 10 concludes the book with an analysis of purchasing's role in network strategizing and 'networking'.

Chapter 2

PURCHASING DYNAMICS AND CHALLENGES

Chapter 1 illustrates the changing role and the significance of purchasing in the corporation of the 21st Century. In this second chapter we bring up the changes of the function over time and its main current challenges. We introduce the chapter with a short historical overview of important issues in purchasing and how the function has developed in a long-term perspective in the US. This overview both shows that the importance of different purchasing issues change over time, and illustrates that what become significant issues for purchasing is determined by the overall strategic situation of the buying firm. In the second section we describe the recent reorientation of purchasing at IBM, where the purchasing strategy and purchasing behaviour have changed quite considerably during the second half of the 1990s. Most of the changes undertaken by IBM are representative of changes conducted, or under way, at other large vertically integrated companies and are therefore of a general interest. The third section is an overview of current issues facing companies in general. Even these cases mainly involve US corporations. Therefore, the fourth section illustrates how these issues are approached by European companies and also brings up the situation for small and medium-sized companies. Both these sections are based on a review of the literature combined with interviews with company representatives. In the final section we present the conclusions of the analysis.

Historical Development of the Purchasing Function

Purchasing as a separate company function has existed for roughly one hundred years, according to a recent historical review (Morgan 1999). The review starts by describing the 'Genesis period' in the early 1900s. According to the author, the job of a purchasing agent at that time 'was not exactly a prestige position'. Purchasing was a latecomer as a specialized corporate function and the responsibilities were not well established (Morgan 1999, p. 73).

Indeed at the beginning of the 20th century, in many corporate purchasing departments, major responsibilities involved observing rules, regulations, and procedures put in place by accountants to establish paper trails and satisfy concerns about taking prudent action to discourage larceny.

Furthermore, few purchasing managers had control of all or even the majority of their companies' purchases. At that time even many large corporations were still run by their founders. Often, purchasing was one of the last hands-on responsibilities to be abandoned by top corporate managers. Therefore, even in many large corporations the most important purchases continued to be handled by top management while the purchasing department dealt with the paperwork processing. When the more important procurement tasks were transferred to purchasing specialists, it was done 'reluctantly, grudgingly, and with a large number of protections created to keep these purchasing people honest'.

Many of the attitudes towards purchasing and purchasing professionals that caused problems in the reorientation of the function in the 1990s were apparently established 100 years earlier. According to Morgan, the attitudes of non-purchasing personnel towards purchasing specialists at that time were often a mixture of 'amusement, indifference, hostility and contempt'. The general perception was that (ibid., p. 73):

purchasing offices were staffed by huge cadres of clerks who possessed little practical knowledge of company supply needs. Among purchasing's most brutal antagonists industrial buyers were mainly portrayed as dullards who concerned themselves with squeezing vendors for rebates and kickbacks.

Thus, at the beginning of last century the importance of purchasing was much less significant than it is today. At that time purchasing departments often accounted for barely 20% of corporate expenditures.

In the coming decades purchasing professionals succeeded in improving their position. They did so by extending their operations into areas in which they had not traditionally been involved. By demonstrating significant insights into the economies of goods and services they were gradually able to win the respect of and co-operate with other corporate functions. By around 1920, purchasing had become involved in a wide variety of corporate affairs 'involving areas as inventory management, transportation, source selection, even make/buy decisions' (ibid., p. 75). In these efforts purchasing had also developed towards greater professionalism and become more 'scientific'. For example, inventory control was improved by the use of economic-order-quantity models. In the mid-1920s, the first attempts were made to develop schemes for evaluation of prospective vendors as well as models for establishing performance measures for present suppliers.

The prosperous situation for purchasing changed significantly during the great depression in the 1930s. In this period purchasing professionals played an important role but they had returned to the behaviour and the attitudes from the beginning of the century. Purchasing was important because it was recognized as a centre for cost reduction and was considered 'a reservoir of price cuts, rebates, and discounts' (ibid., p. 79). According to the review, purchasing in many industries fell back into 'old charges of penny-pinching and clerkism'. However, World War II saw a rebirth of professionalism in purchasing. Buyers extended the scope of many of the ideas developed during the 1920s on measuring supplier performance. In doing so, they made plant visits to suppliers and potential vendors, instead of being 'chained to their desks'. Inventory control was still an important issue and increasingly buyers were becoming deeply involved in solving logistics problems.

The late 1940s marked the entrance of purchasing into the realm of strategic thinking and planning. For example, General Electric 'revolutionized purchasing participation in product development with its pioneering of value analysis and value engineering'. Basically, both value analysis (VA) and value engineering (VE) are studies of the trade-off between the costs of various solutions and their functionality. VE is concerned with function during the design stage, while VA relates to function in products that are already being manufactured. The following Box illustrates a checklist useful for value analysis. Both VE and VA investigate the relationships among design, function, method of manufacture, use of materials, and sources of supply. To contribute in these operations buyers had to analyse function, cost, fabrication, how goods were handled on the shop floor, design features, special requirements, cost of doing business and inventory requirements (ibid., p. 83).

Elements of Value Analysis

1. Can the item be eliminated?

2. If the item is not standard, can a standard item be used?

3. If it is a standard item, does it completely fit the application or is it a misfit?

4. Does the item have greater capacity than required?

5. Can the weight be reduced?

6. Is there a similar item in inventory that could be substituted?

7. Are closer tolerances specified than necessary?

8. Is unnecessary machining performed on the item?

9. Are unnecessarily fine finishes specified?

10. Is commercial quality specified?

11. Can the item be manufactured more cheaply in-house than purchased? If it is being manufactured in-house, can it be bought for less?

12. Is the item properly classified for shipping to obtain lowest transportation rates?

13. Can cost of packaging be reduced?

14. Are suppliers being asked for suggestions to reduce cost?

Source: Webster 1991, pp. 54–55.

During the following decades purchasing gradually reinforced its position in the company hierarchy. In the 1950s the most significant dimension of procurement strategy to emerge was the development of system contracting. Originally, it was considered a way to reduce costs associated with MRO-procurement (maintenance, repair and operating supplies). Over time, it was found to have wider applications in the purchase of production goods and services. System contracting committed the supplier to furnish a whole family of goods 'at specified service levels, for a specific time period, at specified prices, with little day-to-day involvement by the purchasing department in the transaction'. The buying company, in turn, was committed to buying a line of items exclusively from the supplier. The main objectives of the agreement were 'elimination of paperwork and transaction processing, reduction of inventory, improved material flow, and best overall pricing for the goods' (ibid., p. 84).

In the 1960s and 70s materials management (MM) was a concept greeted with enthusiasm. The principles of materials management were supposed to improve the competitiveness of companies. In essence, the call for MM was a call for the creation of a new functional centre in the company headed by a vice president of materials or the equivalent. The main objective of the MM-function was to improve the integration of such activities as production scheduling, purchasing, transportation and distribution. The need for integration among these activities was enhanced, since buying firms had increasingly come to rely on external suppliers. At that time it was estimated that 'most of the dollars that a company spends are for goods and services (35%–65%)' (ibid., p. 85). One important instrument in integration of the activities was systems for materials requirement planning (MRP). These systems were 'means to improve material planning, reduce plant downtime through the comprehensive use of computer power'. The proponents of MRP argued that these systems should make it possible to establish precise control over scheduling production and vendors owing to the vast speed and memory resources of the computer. The optimists declared that it might even be possible to 'convert scheduling information into dollars to make a company game plan' (ibid., p. 88).

Unfortunately, neither of the new approaches worked according to expectations. The main problem with MRP was that the complex computerized systems could not satisfactorily deal with bloated inventories, long lead times, shortage lists and expediting. The materials management approach failed to drive integration in the desired way. Instead MM seems in many cases to have resulted in little more than the creation of more 'functional silos'. According to one practitioner few companies were ever able to get beyond the creation of positions and departments of materials management. There are two explanations for these problems (ibid., p. 85):

Many—maybe most—companies have never mastered the knack of using multi-functional teams to effectively solve flows of materials ... Key measures and systems were, in most cases, inwardly focused. Few individuals or organizations were concerned or focused on chains of suppliers for their products.

Again, the position of the purchasing function had been weakened. However, a more prosperous era was also again to emerge. Around the 1980s 'purchasing was beginning to take on a whole new role in corporate thinking and planning' (ibid., p. 88). The reason for this recovery was that purchasing could make substantial contributions to solving some severe problems in US corporations at that time. One of these problems was that companies were spending too much in manufacturing their products and therefore tended to be at price disadvantages compared with producers from other countries (in particular Japan). In spite of these high costs the quality of US-made products was often found to be inferior, which constituted the second problem. Thirdly, the production processes suffered from huge amounts of waste. Excess inventories were choking production facilities and soaking up scarce investment capital. In the efforts to tackle these problems, purchasing was able to play an important role 'by looking for causes of non-competitive pricing, bad quality, and unacceptable waste' (ibid., p. 90). In these processes the tools for value engineering and value analysis developed in the 1940s turned out to be useful once again.

Furthermore, it became increasingly important to deal with the drawbacks experienced in the implementation of the materials management concept. The objective of MM was to enhance integration among the functional departments in the buying company and with suppliers. Three reasons explain why this succeeded in the 1980s although it had failed in the 1960s. Firstly, when purchasing departments tried to tackle the problems of the 1980s they were forced to work more closely with other functions. The causes of, and the solutions to, many problems crossed the borders of different functions, which called for the combined efforts of cross-functional teams. Secondly, cost-reductions, quality improvements, and elimination of waste required the prevailing inward focus to be abandoned. Successful outcomes of these change efforts required the active involvement of suppliers and 'more and more sourcing teams began working with preferred suppliers to assure the quality of purchased parts and systems' (ibid., p. 90). In these efforts the systems for evaluation of supplier performance came into use again. Thirdly, the MM-concept was unsuccessful at the first attempt to introduce it because the systems were too complex. Therefore, companies now turned to simpler, more visual approaches. In many cases firms adopted versions of the Japanese JIT-approach (just-in-time) according to which 'a major reason for manufacturers' bloated inventories is not their lack of good sales forecasting, but their lack of good control over in-plant processes'. Instead of being dependent on complicated computer programming JIT concentrates on 'squeezing the time from when an order comes in the door and goes out the door' (ibid., p. 88).

In the first chapter we mentioned that the two last decades have been characterized by substantial changes in purchasing reality. This book is an analysis of the prerequisites for these changes and an interpretation of their consequences. Therefore, at this point we do not go more deeply into details about recent developments. However, to make the history complete we conclude this section with mentioning the two main trends in purchasing during the 1990s, according to the review. The first is 'outsourcing', which is described in the following way (ibid., p. 90):

Loosely defined, outsourcing involves the taking of an operation or function traditionally performed in-house and jobbing it out to a contract manufacturer or third-party service

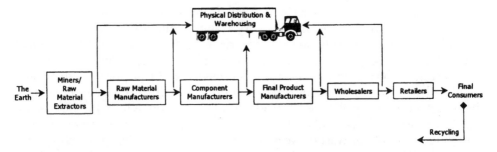

FIGURE 2.1   Activities and firms in a supply chain. Source: Tan 2001, p. 40. Copyright © 2001, with permission from Elsevier Science.

provider. Outsourcing gets down to conserving corporate resources for use where they are most effective. Most companies no longer have the resources to be the best at what they do, so they look for suppliers that are strong where they are weak.

The second main trend affecting purchasing is what has been identified as supply chain management. Essentially, it is an effort to win economic advantage by expert deployment of sourcing resources. In its simplest form a supply chain (see Figure 2.1) is a connected series of organizations, resources, and activities involved in the creation and delivery of value. There are numerous attempts to define what supply chain management is about. The following description is a representative view of what normally is included in these definitions (Morgan 1999, p. 94):

> Supply chain management deals with the integration of the processes required to deliver value to the external customer. Integration of processes involves linking the many steps along the way from determination of the product or service that the customer wants and needs to the creation of that new product or service. It does that through the use of a new product development process, which is linked to an order fulfilment process.

The Re-orientation of Purchasing at IBM

IBM was the 1999 winner of Purchasing Magazine's Medal of Professional Excellence for the transformation of its purchasing operations. In the same issue of the magazine where the winner is announced the re-orientation of the company is described. In this section, we reproduce some of the most interesting characteristics of the transformation. In particular, we focus on the changes representative of purchasing trends in general.

This section builds completely on Carbone (1999) and deals with the following issues:

— outsourcing
— supplier relationships
— consolidation of the supply base
— electronic commerce

Outsourcing

IBM's transformation began several years ago when top management realized it had to turn its long practised approach to purchasing upside down. Instead of doing nearly everything in-house IBM's leaders decided the company needed to find outside companies that could help IBM maintain its leadership. In the early 1990s, IBM was a highly vertically integrated company that made most of its own components. Until 1995, IBM built 100% of its printed circuit boards (PCBs). Now it makes only about 10% of its boards and those are the leading edge, big, complex PCBs. Furthermore, IBM used to make 85% of the memory chips used in its computers; in 1999 this figure was about 15%. Keyboards and power supplies were built in-house in the past, now they are outsourced. IBM used to assemble all its own computers. Now, contract manufacturers build most of them.

A company representative describes the breeding ground for the transformation as follows (ibid., p. 39):

What happened was we woke up. We realized that we couldn't be expert in everything.

IBM became aware of the fact that outside suppliers had the technology that IBM needed. Furthermore, competitors were reducing their costs by outsourcing. While IBM could make many of its own critical components for IBM computers, so could other suppliers—often at lower costs. Consequently, IBM began buying more from outside suppliers thus outsourcing more. In the ten-year period after 1986, the proportion of IBM's revenues spent on outside suppliers increased from 28% to 51%. In 1999, the company was outsourcing to the tune of $3–$3.5 billion per year to contract manufacturers. Suppliers conducted PC-assembly, manufactured notebook computers, lower-end servers and workstations, and mass-storage devices. IBM continues to build high-end products likes its System 390 enterprise server, because it is a complex product that requires unique components and a sophisticated manufacturing process. The strategy adopted is to be involved in activities 'where we make a difference'. In these cases IBM does the manufacturing. 'Where we don't, we will buy them,' argues a company representative (ibid., p. 42). The economic outcome of the transformation is that IBM has reduced its costs by about 20% through outsourcing.

While IBM outsources manufacturing, it has kept control of the purchasing of components used by its contract manufacturers. This is in contrast with many firms that let contract manufacturers buy the parts for boards and systems that are outsourced. IBM believes it can get lower prices than the industry average for many commodities. If it lost its leverage it would have to pay more for parts for the equipment it manufactures in-house. This would also mean a higher cost for the parts the contract manufacturers have to buy. This cost, in turn, would be passed on to IBM. Therefore, the strategy is to continue to control component sourcing, thus directing contract manufacturers to specific suppliers. According to one company representative, the difference between the prices for which IBM contracted the components and the prices contract manufacturers were quoting differed to the tune of $65 million.

Relationships With Suppliers

The focus of IBM production procurement is to develop 'enterprise relationships' with suppliers. IBM uses vendors who supply multiple commodities such as memory and monitors. So far these transactions have been managed as individual purchases, but the intention is to develop an enterprise relationship with these suppliers. The idea is to manage the overall relationship between IBM and the supplier who is providing multiple commodities. A purchasing representative of IBM illustrates the advantages of this approach in the following way (ibid., p. 48):

> We think that drives efficiencies for them and for us and also drives a level of certainty for them in terms of the kind of business overall they can expect from IBM over a period of time.

For an IBM supplier, it is important to have multiple component capacities up to finished product level. All else being equal, IBM would source with a supplier who has multiple capabilities. A key competence for an IBM supplier is technology leadership. IBM purchasers look for suppliers who are going to be tomorrow's technology leaders. In this process the technology road maps of IBM's suppliers are evaluated and compared with the technological direction in which IBM is going. It is important for the company to give meaningful feedback to suppliers so they know where IBM is technically. The idea is to communicate the upcoming technical requirements with suppliers so that IBM is guaranteed a supply of the parts it needs.

   The activities directed towards suppliers indicate a major change in the nature of relationships. This collaborative atmosphere contrasts sharply with the situation before the transformation. At the time when most activities were conducted in-house the characteristics of supplier relationships were quite different. A purchasing representative portrayed the general attitudes towards suppliers as described in the following Box.

Illustration of 'Arm's Length Relationships' at IBM

There was also a feeling that everybody in the industry was trying to steal our technology and ideas, which was true 20 years ago. Everything at IBM was a secret. In procurement we were the guardians of confidential information, the guard at the door who didn't let suppliers know anything.

   You couldn't have effective collaboration with suppliers because IBM didn't want suppliers to know what product their parts were going to be used in.

   You couldn't develop volumes very well because the volumes planned were a secret.

   You couldn't say which plant would build the product that the part was going to be used in. Parts would be shipped to central locations like Kansas City or St. Louis and then we shipped it from there so suppliers wouldn't know what plant it was going to.

Source: Carbone 1999, p. 39.

Today, IBM frequently has 'brainstorming' sessions with suppliers to communicate its future technical needs and to listen to what the supplier has to say about those requirements. IBM also works with emerging suppliers who might provide

IBM with a competitive edge in the future. IBM put huge resources into these efforts. One example described concerns the development of a Taiwanese supplier of memory. IBM sees Taiwan as becoming a significant force in memory over the next several years. Today, however, these suppliers are considered to be '12–18 months behind in terms of technology, as well as quality' according to purchasing people at IBM. The aim is to push the supplier to the forefront of technology by giving feedback on where they fall short as well as providing design support and manufacturing expertise. IBM wants to avoid memory technology developing in a direction that is beneficial to someone else. By being engaged in the operations of this supplier IBM can be involved in steering the technological direction.

Consolidation of the Supply Base

IBM is buying more and more from outside suppliers. At the same time, the number of production suppliers is declining. About 85% of IBM's total spending is on about 50 suppliers. The supply base has been reduced for two main reasons. The first is that developing collaborative relationships is resource demanding. It is not possible to have close relationships with too many suppliers. Therefore, beyond the core of 50 suppliers IBM is significantly reducing the supply base. For example, IBM used to have two dozen mechanical parts and cable suppliers; now it has one for each of these commodities. There is a second reason for the decreasing number of suppliers. Before the transformation a collection of divisional purchasing groups made entirely independent procurement decisions. IBM wanted to take advantage of its huge purchasing volumes globally, because there were great benefits to be gained from increasing purchasing leverage. The means was to set up commodity councils to buy parts rather than having individual sites who bought components on their own. The councils combined the requirements of all the divisions and negotiated long-term contracts with suppliers, resulting in lower prices and major reductions of IBM's supplier base, with accompanying cost savings.

IBM established commodity councils for different supply items, such as microprocessors, logic cards and monitors. IBM has one global contract with a supplier of each item. So, a logic chips supplier would supply logic to all IBM divisions. At the same time, IBM will commit to buying a percentage of its component requirements from this supplier. The contracts are usually for three years with various re-openers for pricing issues. These figures represent a dramatic change for IBM: five to ten years ago they had virtually no long-term agreements with suppliers.

The commodity councils are also responsible for reducing the number of suppliers. This has been a challenge because the various IBM sites have had their favourite suppliers. Commodity councils are populated with buyers from various IBM facilities around the world. The problems and challenges are illustrated by this quote concerning the reduction in the number of suppliers (ibid., p. 41):

> They have battles over narrowing the supply base. We may want to have three suppliers in the world for a given commodity. The question is always: which three? In deciding, the

council has to take into account technology, price, quality and delivery. The weight of each criterion can vary depending on the commodity. We have some things where price is 80% and everything else is 5%, or technology may be 80% and price is not important.

Electronic Commerce

Doing business with the 'right' suppliers is crucial to IBM, as is the way IBM does business with these suppliers. In 1999, about 90% of IBM's purchasing transactions were handled by electronic data interchange (EDI). EDI is a complex means of information exchange requiring companies involved to standardize their operations and procedures. IBM, like most other companies, foresees the potential of the Internet, which is less complicated than EDI. The Internet is important to IBM as a procurement tool because it makes it possible to automate the transactional part of purchasing and allows buyers to make better use of their working time. While some firms consider the Internet as an instrument to reduce the number of people in the purchasing department, this is not the case with IBM. Rather, they view the Internet as a way to free buyers from the transactional part of purchasing, giving them more time to work on strategic issues. For example, the order and offering processes can be managed much more efficiently than before. Another form of rationalization gains is related to the handling of the paper flow which 'has always been the Achilles heel of the procurement function', according to an IBM representative. In 1999, IBM processed no less than 5 million pieces of paper per year (ibid., p. 60).

Suppliers have been told that doing business with IBM via the Internet is a requirement, not an option. However, IBM works closely with suppliers, especially medium-sized and small suppliers, offering them advice and technical services on implementing electronic commerce. Through their Web investments IBM wants to reduce procurement expense and lower the cost of buying. The Web can be instrumental in finding new sources of supply and for finding data that can help buyers when they are negotiating. In particular, it is supposed that e-procurement will make MRO buying more efficient.

There is more to IBM's Internet initiative than making purchasing transactions more efficient. While it may save millions of dollars, it will also be an essential tool to manage and communicate with suppliers with which they are deeply involved in collaboration. According to IBM's production procurement chief (ibid., p. 60):

> I believe that the Web creates the platform upon which these truly strategic relationships can be built. [the Web] can create a 'virtual organization' linking IBM engineers with suppliers' engineers and IBM buyers with suppliers' logistics people.

Supply Challenges for the 21st Century

These changes in IBM's purchasing activities are reflective of general developments on the supply side of companies in recent decades. Most firms have increasingly come to rely on outsourcing; they have enhanced co-operation with suppliers; and they have reduced the number of vendors in the supply base. Furthermore, most companies today emphasize the potential for efficiency improvements through e-procurement. There is no reason to believe that these strategic issues will become less significant in the future. On the contrary, it is most likely that they will remain at the top of the agenda. In this section we discuss some additional challenges facing buying firms in the early 2000s by presenting the findings from two US studies. One is analysing the 'competitive supply strategies for the 21st century' (Monczka and Morgan 2000). The other deals with the main purchasing and supply management trends in the 1990s (Trent and Monczka 1998). In the next section we relate these findings to the situation in Europe and also include small companies.

Monczka and Morgan (2000) analyse the impact of environmental factors on procurement operations and how these factors may determine the conditions for the coming decades. Based on this analysis the authors identify six areas ot utmost importance for the future. These 'critical six' are presented in the following box.

The Critical Six Strategic Issues

1. Increasing efficiency requirements.

2. Making use of information technology.

3. Integration and consolidation.

4. Insourcing and outsourcing.

5. Strategic cost management.

6. 'Network' management.

Source: Monczka and Morgan 2000, pp. 50–53.

There are obvious similarities between the critical six and the factors discussed in the section about IBM. Although the labels differ somewhat it is clear that factors 2, 3, 4 and 6 correspond to those discussed above. Factors 1 and 5, on the other hand, represent the underlying driving forces. Below, we discuss these two issues.

According to Trent and Monczka, the most important strategic factor for any buying firm is to achieve the 'absolute linkage of sourcing, purchasing, and the supply chain—to the financial plan or the economic-value-add contribution of the business' (ibid., p. 50). It is argued that there must be a clear connection between everything that goes on in sourcing and the supply chain processes and the results that show up as the financial performance of the firm. Considering the economic impact of the activities on the supply side this demand comes as no surprise. 'Performance improvement requirements' was also one of the strategic trends of the 1990s, according to Trent and Monczka (1998). These requirements, in turn, were the basis of another trend—'increasing reliance on performance measurements'. In the 1990s, the measurement area mainly emphasized purchasing efficiency (ibid., p. 7). For example, in 1997, more than 83% of the firms used performance measurements for cost reduction, supplier delivery performance, and adherence to standard, while indicators related to purchasing effectiveness were less common. In 1993, only 26% of the companies declared that they had introduced measures to analyse 'total cost of ownership'. The corresponding figures for two other effectiveness-oriented variables were:

— introduction of new technology from suppliers   18%

— concept-to-customer cycle-time reduction for new products   16%

However, for the coming decade the effectiveness related performance measurements are expected to gain most in importance. For example, in 1997, 85% of the firms declared that total ownership cost measurements were on top of the agenda. In the same vein, around 60% of firms stated that measurement of supplier technology provision and cycle-time reductions must be developed.

There is an old saying that 'what is measured will be done'. The plans above reflect the companies' ambitions to develop the rationalization and development roles of purchasing. Concerning rationalization, the 1990s were characterized by efforts to emphasize lower costs rather than lower price. In Chapter 1 we introduced the notion of direct and indirect costs that are affected by purchasing activities. The most obvious direct cost is price, i.e. what appears on the invoice from the supplier. The buying firm can affect price through its purchasing behaviour (for example, by buying large volumes and/or skilful negotiations). But not only price may be affected by the purchasing strategy and the purchasing behaviour adopted. As argued in Chapter 1, indirect costs are also dependent on the approach of the buying company. However, these costs are less obvious than the price tag. In some situations and for some firms, these costs represent a much greater potential for rationalization benefits. Kodak is one of the companies that have tried to detect the 'hidden' costs that are affected by its procurement strategy and behaviour (see Figure 2.2). Kodak's analysis reveals some other dimensions of indirect costs than those brought up in Chapter 1 (see Figure 1.1). Kodak estimates the hidden costs to be 250% of the direct costs. The

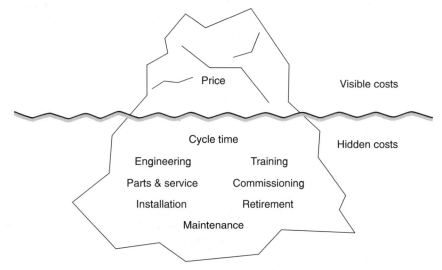

FIGURE 2.2   Kodak's visible and hidden costs. Source: Avery 1996, p. 45. Reproduced by permission of Purchasing Magazine (www.purchasing.com). All rights reserved. © Purchasing.

most significant determinants of the indirect costs are installation, engineering and maintenance, which together account for 90% of what is 'hidden'. It goes without saying, therefore, that in many cases buying firms stand to gain more by trying to affect these costs than chasing the lowest price. The prescriptions offered by Kodak for the reduction of these costs include both standardized and customized solutions requiring adaptations and integration with some suppliers.

With these figures in mind, it comes as no surprise that buying firms have devoted considerable resources to coming to grips with their indirect costs. In practice, however, these efforts have been only marginally successful in most cases. Monczka and Morgan argue that increasing attention to strategic cost management is the most important of the critical six strategic factors. The underlying motivation is that (ibid., p. 55):

> [And] regardless of all the talk about strategic cost management, most companies are only at the tip of the iceberg in terms of actual practices—in terms of looking at where costs reside, looking at cost drivers, building cross-enterprise strategies, and sharing the results. All of these practices are going to need to be refined. Cross-enterprise cost management is, and will increasingly be, critical to a firm's success.

Thus, from a cost management perspective increasing reliance on co-operation with suppliers seems to be a prerequisite for successful implementation of the rationalization role. The same strategy is relevant when the development role is emphasized. During the 1990s, increasing supplier involvement in product development has been one important means of achieving performance improvements. Both in terms of product and process technology, suppliers have come to play an enhanced role, and it is expected to be further strengthened (Trent and Monczka 1998). These contributions from suppliers are to a large extent explained by increasing ambitions of buying firms to develop supplier performance. Table 2.1, showing the results from three consecutive surveys, illustrates the changes of customer efforts in this respect during the 1990s.

We began this section with six critical strategic factors. The discussion of factors 1 (increasing efficiency requirements) and 5 (strategic cost management) has revealed that the role of suppliers will probably be strengthened when buying firms try to make use of purchasing's rationalization and development roles. This, in turn, implies that insourcing-outsourcing decisions (factor 4) will become increasingly important. Chapter 7 discusses this issue. The impact of information

TABLE 2.1   Buyers' supporting activities in supplier development. Source: Trent and Monczka 1998, p. 9.

Buyer activity	% of firms conducting the activity		
	1990	1993	1997
Conducting education or training programs	47	62	75
Providing technology	15	38	64
Providing personnel	12	34	55
Providing equipment	3	30	49
Providing program payments	3	36	42
Providing capital	6	23	38

technology and e-business (factor 2) is analysed in Chapter 4, where we discuss how the activities of different firms in a supply network are co-ordinated.

The third of the six critical factors identified by Monczka and Morgan (2000) is 'integration and consolidation', which represents the 'ability of firms to global-ize purchasing, sourcing, and supply management' (ibid., p. 52). This issue relates strongly to the question of whether to centralize or decentralize purchasing operations. Therefore, it is relevant not only to companies that are truly global. Even national and regional companies need to analyse the advantages and dis-advantages of different actions in this respect. It is possible to observe a shift in the perceptions of the pros and cons of different organizational arrangements when today's attitudes are compared with those of the mid-1990s. At that time the advantages of decentralization were highlighted. During the 1980s, the general trend of organizing developed towards smaller profit centres and more decentra-lized responsibilities. These developments impacted on purchasing as well, and the 1980s were characterized by the virtual disappearance of the large central pur-chasing departments. When the various business units were made responsible for their own financial situation it became impossible to decide centrally which suppliers to use. In 1993 we wrote (Gadde and Håkansson 1993, p. 132):

> The trend towards increased decentralization of purchasing decisions we have described goes hand-in-hand with our previous finding of changed relations with suppliers. The wider contact interface on which relations are now built is simpler and more natural for a decen-tralized organization to deal with.

In the same book we also concluded that the choice between centralization and decentralization is always a compromise. To attain the benefits at the one extreme of the scale, one has to sacrifice the benefits at the other. Therefore, companies' strategies concerning this issue have been characterized as a 'pendulum swing'. A company exploiting the centralization advantages to the maximum will soon realize the advantages of moving in the decentralization direction, and vice versa. Developments today indicate that the pendulum is swinging again—this time away from full decentralization. Listening to company representatives and reading purchasing magazines gives the impression that consolidation is a hot issue in most companies in the early 2000s. The advantages of consolidation on the business unit level have been shown to be substantial (Avery 1999a, 1999b, Milligan 1999, and Fitzgerald 1999). What can now be seen is that buying companies try to reap the benefits that can be attained from joint efforts on a group level. The 1990s were characterized by increasing horizontal integration, with numerous mergers and acquisitions. The larger the companies grew the more some of the centralization benefits increased, for example in terms of discounts and rebates and negotiation power. However, merging companies often used different suppliers. Therefore, the total supply base of the group was substantially extended, implying considerable potential for rationalization by reducing the number of suppliers. Altogether, this means that group headquarters of large companies today are more active in influencing sourcing decisions in different business units than they were in the 1980s and early 1990s. This doesn't mean, however, that purchasing decisions are centralized today. The pendulum is thus swinging—but not back to the same position as before. What it means is that it has become increasingly important to encourage co-operation among the various business units in large groups, in order to try to combine the benefits of centralization and decentralization. The conditions for the most appropriate combinations change all the time. We return to this issue in Chapter 6.

Finally, Morgan and Monczka (2000) argue that all the changes in procurement activities and the impact of external factors substantially increase the complexity on the supply side of companies. As a consequence, buying firms have to adopt the sixth of the critical strategies. This strategy has no specific label in the article, but we define it as 'network management'. What Monczka and Morgan consider important in this dimension is to realize the changing requirements for performance improvements owing to the increasing complexity of the operations (ibid., p. 55):

> The key to uncover such advantages gets down to first develop a much more refined strategic definition of these goods/services/technologies that make up the strategic supply chain or value chain—extending from paying customers back to tier 1-2-3 suppliers and differentially managing them.

The complexity entailed in combining a number of supply chains within one company is illustrated in Figure 2.3, presented in an analysis of current issues in supply chain management (Lambert and Cooper 2000).

The core of this book is in line with these thoughts. The book is about increasing understanding about the connection between procurement operations and other activities in the buying company and how these, in turn, are related to the activities and resources of other companies. However, our intention is to take the analysis one step further than is suggested in the quote and the figure below. Performance improvements in supply chains depend not only on the conditions among the companies making up a specific chain. To a large extent, the conditions

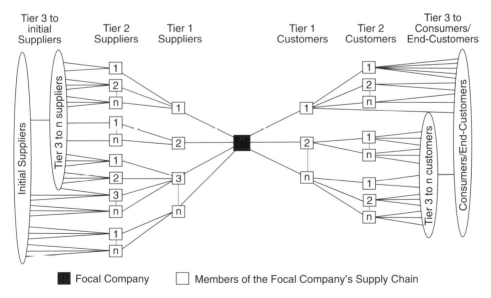

FIGURE 2.3   The individual company involved in different supply chains. Source: Lambert and Cooper 2000, p. 68. Copyright © 2000, with permission from Elsevier Science.

for efficiency and effectiveness in single chains are determined by the way activities and resources are related to those in other supply chains. For example, the efficiency of the focal company in Figure 2.3 is also dependent on what is going on in the other supply chains in which tier 1-suppliers are involved. In the same way, tier 1-customers have other suppliers than the focal company, which must also be taken into consideration. The conclusion of the analysis is that a network approach is necessary to reveal the complexity on the supply side of companies and how different strategies and actions may impact on performance.

Purchasing Issues in Other Firms

The second and third sections above mainly describe the situation for large firms in the US. Most of the examples that are used later in this book deal with European companies—especially firms from Scandinavia. By using some recent studies of the purchasing situation in large US companies we want to achieve two things. One is to demonstrate that some important changes that have been observed for some time in Europe now also take place in the US. Another reason is to illustrate that the issues we are dealing with are relevant to all companies, small and large, and independent of their locations. However, in Chapter 1 we showed that the situation for large US firms is different in some respects both from small and medium-sized companies and for the typical European firm. In this section, we analyse the extent to which the discussion in the above sections is representative also of such firms.

Returning to the 'critical six' issues, we argue that the requirements for increasing purchasing efficiency and strategic cost management apply to any company. The more the buying company depends on suppliers, the more it needs to improve its operations on the supply side. This means that the pressure for performance enhancement is even greater for firms that are less vertically integrated than the large US firms described. When it comes to outsourcing and consolidation, we think most large companies in Europe are in much the same position as US firms. Both these issues are outcomes of the dissolution processes in vertically integrated companies. Large European firms have also been through this process and their situation is similar to that of IBM. It has been shown that such firms are involved in the same types of changes (see, e.g., van Weele 2000).

The round-table discussion with Swedish purchasing managers focused to a large extent on issues similar to the critical six. For example, Ericsson, a manufacturer of telecom products, explained the increasingly important role of close relationships with key suppliers. Forty vendors account for a considerable share of Ericsson's total procurement and are crucial to its future development. These supplier relationships are considered 'virtual business units' of Ericsson and are subject to joint activities in product development, logistics and information systems. Consolidation is also important. Currently, local suppliers play a key role in the Swedish operations of Ericsson. A number of projects have been initiated with the common objective of reducing the supplier base and increasing the use of global sources.

Consolidation of the supplier base is also a top priority for primary contractor NCC—the Nordic Construction Company. This firm, like most contractors, is highly decentralized, and site managers are responsible for project procurement. When each project selects its own vendors, the supplier structure of the entire company becomes scattered and includes numerous suppliers. Therefore, reducing the supply base and consolidating purchases with fewer suppliers provides substantial opportunities for improving economies of scale. The strategic issue then is to identify the appropriate combination of centralization and decentralization.

Both Ericsson and NCC increasingly make use of information technology to improve efficiency in supplier relationships. In particular, standardized exchange of information is a way of rationalizing the buying of non-production materials— i.e. office equipment, transportation, stationery, packaging, consumables, etc. Both companies perceive these items as representing substantial potential for rationalization. By concentrating these purchases to fewer suppliers and standardizing administrative routines the costs for these purchases can be dramatically reduced. As part of these efforts Ericsson has developed a system for electronic purchasing —'Click to Buy'.

There might be a difference between the large US firm and the average European firm in their perspectives on supplier relationships. While the potential contribution from close relationships in the US seems to have become apparent only when the hierarchies were dissolved, developed supplier relationships seem to have been used by European companies in a more extensive way. In the first IMP-study (Håkansson (ed.) 1982) including buyer—seller relations in five European countries, the crucial role played by suppliers was found to be a common phenomenon for all buying companies. On average, these business relationships had lasted for 15 years but many were as old as the companies involved. The companies had evolved together in symbiotic ways. Relationships seem in this way to be of particular importance to the development of small companies.

Small firms and non-integrated companies have often been closely related to suppliers. This was shown in a Swedish study of the potential contribution of purchasing to company competitiveness (Axelsson and Håkansson 1984). In that study engineering companies such as Asea (now ABB), Alfa Laval (now Tetra Laval) and Sandvik were compared with automotive companies like Volvo and Saab-Scania and firms in the telecom industry such as Ericsson and IBM-Sweden. The main finding was that companies were well aware of the importance of purchasing and the significant opportunities residing in well-developed supplier relationships. Still, it was difficult to identify conscious strategies to handle suppliers and proactively develop them. This might be explained by prevailing attitudes to close and long-term relationships at the time. Such relationships were seen by purchasers as signs of inefficiency and should therefore be avoided. Today, this view has changed considerably, as illustrated in Chapters 1 and 2.

The situation of small and medium-sized companies is described in a survey of 123 Swedish companies (Håkansson 1989). The main findings are presented in the following Box, showing the significance of purchasing in company operations and the importance of the main suppliers. Table (a) shows the distribution of firms concerning the relationship between the costs of purchased goods and the turnover of the company. For 25% of the companies purchasing accounted for 60% or more of turnover. Only 29% reported that purchasing accounted for less than 40% of the turnover.

The Importance of Purchasing and Suppliers in Small and Medium-sized Companies

(a) The importance of purchasing

Purchasing cost as % of turnover	% of firms
0–24	7
25–39	22
40–49	30
50–59	16
60–79	19
80–100	6

(b) The importance of the main suppliers

% of total purchases with ten suppliers	% of firms
0–29	8
30–49	21
50–79	18
80–100	52

Source: Håkansson 1989, pp. 76, 79.

Table (b) illustrates the crucial role played by the main suppliers of a buying company. The firms in the study reported the proportion of total purchases accounted for by ten suppliers. For more than half the sample (52%), the ten largest suppliers accounted for 80% or more of total purchases. Only 8% of the companies reported this share to be less than 30%. On an average, the ten main suppliers accounted for no less than 70% of the purchasing value. Some other results of this study may be of interest. The average supplier relationship involving technical development had lasted for 13 years. The average number of ongoing projects including technical co-operation with suppliers was three to four, with each project involving some four people on each side. These figures seem to be representative not only for Swedish conditions, as similar findings are reported in a Danish study (Madsen 1999).

In this section we have shown that there are both similarities and dissimilarities in the development of purchasing and the role of suppliers. There is a large variation in the supply situations of different companies, which makes it impossible to identify a universal development of purchasing. The supply challenges presented in the third section are important to many companies. Our examples in this section show that some companies have experienced these challenges at an earlier stage than others. However, the main conclusion of the third section is that the recent challenges on the supply side require companies to apply a network perspective to their operations. This need is even more accentuated for buying firms already relying on supplier input to a large extent.

Implications for Understanding Purchasing

The historical review revealed the dynamics of the purchasing function over time. The importance of procurement activities seems to change radically with time— depending on the general business conditions. Sometimes, purchasing has been used as a reactive cost saver while in other periods it has been proactively involved in supplier development. The common perception that the strategic importance of purchasing was realized only in the 1980s is, however, misleading.

Purchasing operations have been a top priority for certain periods, followed by periods when other functions received greater strategic attention. It is the overall situation and context of the company that determines the importance of the various company functions.

It is also interesting to observe that the significance of the various purchasing issues changes over time. The historical survey at the start of this chapter showed that supplier development was important in the early part of the 20th century. It was considered less relevant in the 1950s and the 1960s but again became a hot issue in the 1980s. Value engineering and value analysis have been important for certain periods and less so in others. It is well known that the principles of quality management were developed in the US and then re-exported from Japan in the late 1970s. What is probably less well known is that the just-in-time system is not a Japanese invention. As shown by Schwartz and Fish (1998) the just-in-time approach was applied as early as the 1910s and 1920s in the Detroit car factories. The authors argue that although there are differences between that type of delivery system and the Japanese keiretsu the similarities are even greater, particularly when it comes to the relationships between customers and suppliers. However, the most significant aspect is that Detroit's system of reduced inventory levels—known as 'hand-to-mouth'—was almost indistinguishable from the just-in-time systems developed by Toyota many years later (ibid., p. 50).

There are two major conclusions to be drawn from the overviews in this chapter. The first is that understanding purchasing and its role and importance in the company requires an understanding of the general situation of the company and its business. Morgan (1999) concludes that (ibid., p. 72):

> as the tale of purchasing's rise to prominence in corporate America unfolds, it very quickly becomes apparent that the function is a mirror of US business in the 20th century

Depending on the overriding strategic driving forces, the operations related to purchasing take various forms and paths. Therefore, what will be important purchasing issues in the coming decades depends on the strategic situation facing companies. This, in turn, is to a large extent determined by changes outside the traditional boundaries of the individual firm. It has been claimed that we have entered 'the new economy'. Sometimes, this concept is used as a business buzzword. However, upon closer examination it becomes clear that some of the ingredients of this new economy have a profound impact on the way firms behave and how they do business. Therefore, a careful exploration of the implications of the new economic conditions with relevance for purchasing is required. In Chapter 3 we describe the most significant of these implications.

The second conclusion of the chapter is that as the importance and role of purchasing changes over time so do the significance of various purchasing operations. This explains why just-in-time systems, value engineering, system contracting, etc. tend to be important in some periods and almost neglected in others. Therefore, to identify and reveal the complexity of purchasing and procurement we need a holistic view of the corporation and its business context. Both in Chapter 1 and in the second section of this chapter we found a network perspective to be appropriate. As described in the first chapter, we return to the network model in Chapters 4–6.

Chapter 3

PURCHASING AND THE NEW ECONOMY

Chapter 2 indicates a strong relationship between the overall strategic situation of companies and the attention and priority given to purchasing issues. The chapter also brought up the recent challenges facing the purchasing function. If the historical connection still holds, these challenges for purchasing are likely to reflect the impact of changing conditions for companies. For some years, it has been argued that business is facing 'a new economy'. There seems to be general agreement about this change, but few interpretations of what the new economy is and what implications this shift imposes on business. To be able to develop supply network strategies we need to explore what is new in the economy and what this means for companies and, particularly, for purchasing.

   We begin the chapter by analysing some changes in the business situation of companies—i.e. exploring the main aspects of the new economy. The analysis shows that the general notion of a company as a production unit needs to be supplemented with three other perspectives: the company as a knowledge unit, the company as a communicative unit and the company as a capital-earning unit. The second section deals with purchasing issues in the production unit. The three following sections bring up purchasing issues in the knowledge unit, purchasing in the communicative unit, and purchasing in the capital-earning unit. The conclusion of this discussion is that both companies and their purchasing operations are continuously changing. The corollary implication is that the industrial network model should be a relevant framework for analysis of current supply issues. The main features of such an analysis are then brought up. Finally, the strategic issues in the supply network are identified.

The Company in the New Economy

Purchasing as a company function began a century ago. During this period some quite remarkable changes have taken place, both in terms of what companies do and in their environments. The changes can be observed in the names of the companies. A century ago the names of companies were dominated by personal or geographical connections like Krupp GmBH and Standard Oil of New Jersey. Today, most names have lost their roots in families or regions and are related more to brands and technologies, for example Nike and International Business Machines. If we investigate the content of the companies the changes are even more profound. Companies have certainly gone through a remarkable change process during the 20th century and so have their purchasing operations.

There are two different types of changes to consider. Companies have changed in themselves—in terms of operations, strategies, behaviour, etc. The concept of a company has also changed—possibly even more radically. One hundred years ago the general picture was quite clear, with two main types of companies. A company was either a production unit or a sales unit. Production units included factories and workers manufacturing physical products. This type of company could be illustrated in a picture with a drawing of a factory with smoke coming out of the chimney. Alternatively, the company was a selling unit—a store, or an outlet, with lots of goods brought together for various customers. Organizations like banks, hospitals, power suppliers, and insurance organizations were not generally perceived as companies; they were considered institutions or authorities.

Today, the concept of a company is something entirely different. Firstly, it now includes a large number of service oriented entities such as the ones mentioned above. This has clearly reduced the close connection to physical production. Secondly, even the impact of the human content is reduced. For example, the dot.com world is associated with virtual companies. A virtual (or hollow) company represents a business unit with very few employees and only minor investments in physical plants. Although virtual companies are still extreme, the whole concept of what a company is needs reinterpretation. The role of the company in the society, which used to be fairly clear, has become much more diffuse. At the same time, companies have become more important. Owing to privatization, companies are now affecting almost all sectors of our lives. The physical appearance of companies has also changed considerably, especially in terms of the reduced importance of manufacturing operations. Instead, other dimensions have become more focused.

The new roles of companies are reflected in several ways. In particular, it is possible to observe an enhanced focus on knowledge and knowledge generation. Of course, knowledge has always been vital to companies, for example in terms of the content of products and production processes. The enhanced attention to knowledge issues was initiated by the development of 'knowledge-intensive' companies, but later it became a crucial aspect for all types of firms. It is argued that 'knowledge today occupies a much more central and pervasive place than it has ever enjoyed' (Miles *et al.* 1998, p. 281). In the production unit knowledge utilization is related primarily to the development of new products and processes. Over time, knowledge became a matter for exchange in itself—subject to supply and acquisition. Increasingly, company activities and operations are dependent on knowledge. Furthermore, companies strive to be used as sources of knowledge by their counterparts in the networks in which they are involved. Therefore, the first of the complementary perspectives of the company is to view it as a knowledge

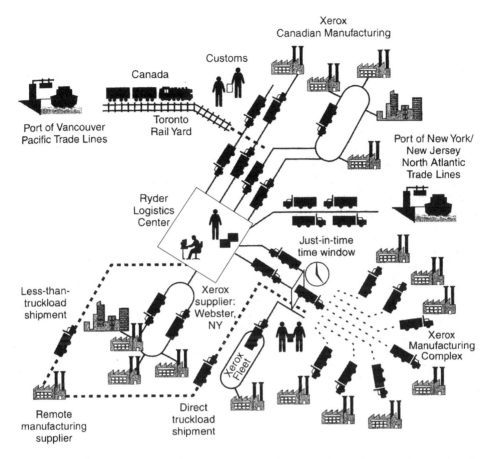

FIGURE 3.1   The company as a production unit—Xerox Corporation's manufacturing plants and supply.
Source: Minahan 1996a, p. 91. Reproduced by permission of Purchasing Magazine (www.purchasing.com).
All rights reserved. © Purchasing..

unit. The relevance of this approach is further explained by Brown and Duguid
(1998), who argue that 'all firms are in essence knowledge organizations' (ibid.,
p. 91).

The recent management interest in knowledge is assumed to be derived from
the development and deployment of information technology (Cole 1998, p. 19). In
particular, the expectations related to the Internet emphasize the company as part
of a large communication network. In these networks information may be
exchanged fast and reliably. Probably, the view of the company as a hub in a
(virtual) network is the most recognized perception of the new economy.
Therefore, it is most relevant to take information exchange and communication
as the point of departure for the second complementary picture of the company—
i.e. viewing the firm as a communicative unit. However, the Internet is only a minor
part of the substantial infrastructure for communication. For any company —either
buyer or seller—communication is a much more complicated issue.

The development of a new economy is always a transformation of the 'old'
economy. It is also a combined effect of several intertwined processes based on

different driving forces. Two of them have been discussed—knowledge expansion and communication. For our discussion, a third complementary perspective of the company is required. It has been evolving for some time and is now of crucial importance to the behaviour of firms. Any company must now consider its role in terms of investment opportunities. Acquiring capital resources from the stock market requires a capital-earning capacity, as has been increasingly stressed over the last few decades. Therefore, viewing the firm as a capital earning unit is the third complementary perspective.

Our discussion identified three perspectives of the company to complement the established view of the firm as a production unit: namely the knowledge unit, the communicative unit and the capital-earning unit. The reason to consider the way the company is perceived, particularly in relation to what is called the 'new' economy, is that the choice of perspective to a large extent determines the view of the supply side. When analysing the supply side one particular issue is 'what' should be supplied. The 'what' question is mainly a function of what the company is perceived as being. If we regard the company as a production unit, its input in terms of raw materials, components and other products is focused. However, if we see the company as a knowledge unit, a communicative unit or a capital-earning unit 'what' is supplied will change. These three perspectives are discussed below.

Purchasing in the Production Unit

As already pointed out, the perception of the company as a production unit has determined the view of purchasing. When the production unit perspective is emphasized the most important issue is about the relationship between what is supplied and its impact on the manufacturing activities of the firm. To analyse this interface it is important to categorize the different inputs. Therefore, almost all texts about procurement include classifications of the different types of products/ services bought. In such classifications one basic dimension has always been the role of the product in the buying company's production activities. Consider, for example, the following classification from van Weele (2000).

Raw materials include iron ore, oil, coal, grains, coffee, etc. These materials are used as a base from which more refined products are manufactured. There are some special problems associated with procurement of raw materials. Usually, there are major price fluctuations for economic-political reasons or because of natural conditions. Therefore, the time dimension is crucial when contracts are formulated. Other problems are related to logistics—transportation and handling are important cost drivers because of their large volumes.

Supplementary materials are used or consumed during the production process, and include lubricating oil, welding electrodes, industrial gases, etc. These products are closely related to the production process, and their utilization is very much determined by the technology and the design of the products and processes in the operations in which they are used.

Semi-manufactured products have been processed at least once and will be further processed. This group includes, for example, steel plates, rolled wire and plastic foils. One crucial issue related to these purchases is finding the right balance between the activities conducted by supplier and customer in terms of processing, and, furthermore, how planning and logistic systems can be linked. Another related factor is the relationship between different steps in the refinement process in technical terms. There are important connections between how the supplier has dealt with the material and the potential of the buyer to affect its own production process.

Components are of two types—specific and standard. These items are incorporated into the end product without any further change and include electronic parts, batteries, rolling bearings, etc. Critical issues regard the function and design of the components in relation to the final product/system. Standard components are often manufactured by large companies—working globally—for instance suppliers to the automotive industry. Specific—or adapted—components are products which are not very sophisticated from a technical point of view, but which require some kind of adaptation to the buyer's situation. Typical examples include plastic components.

Finished products encompass all products purchased to be sold, after negligible added value, either together with other finished products and/or manufactured products. Examples include automobile accessories, such as striping, car radios and ornamental wheel rims.

Investment goods or capital equipment are all those machines and equipment to be used as facilities over a long time period, for which estimates of life-cycle costs are important. Consequently, negotiations that precede acquisition are both extensive and complex, and include discussion of design and functioning of both the machinery and what is going to be produced in it. Major equipment is generally purchased through special projects where teamwork between technicians and purchasers is an essential aspect. One particular characteristic of this type of purchase is that the choice of equipment may restrict the freedom of the buying firm in the future.

MRO-items are used for Maintenance, Repair and Operation supply. These products, for example fastenings, hand tools, glue and sealant, and small grinding equipment, are often complex from the administrative and handling point of view. MRO-supplies typically consist of thousands of different items, the demand for which is difficult to estimate and plan. On the other hand, major inconveniences may occur if the purchasing company runs out of these items. In this case, the most significant issue is to find effective routines for dealing with the purchasing tasks.

Services, finally, are highly heterogeneous. Some of these purchases are fairly sophisticated, for example travel, transportation, management consulting, advertising services, and insurance. In addition, there are a number of less sophisticated services, similar to product purchasing, such as cleaning and some office services. The main problem with service procurement is that the value of the service can only be determined in retrospect.

FIGURE 3.2   Scheme for classification of purchasing situations. Source: Kraljic 1982, p. 112.

The classification indicates that there are different purchasing problems in relation to these various product groups. Some of them demand considerable technical expertise as they have major consequences from a production or development point of view. Others may be difficult to handle in terms of administration, as they include large numbers of items and frequent purchase orders. Some have substantial logistical consequences, and particular attention must be devoted to finding efficient transportation systems and sophisticated warehousing facilities.

Van Weele's classification is based on the characteristics of the products acquired as are most efforts to distinguish between different types of purchasing situations. The best known classification was developed by Kraljic (1982)—see Figure 3.2. In this classification the products are grouped according to two dimensions. The first is the economic impact, which depends on the way the product is used. The second dimension considers the risk on the supply market, which is contingent on the availability of suppliers. This scheme thus relates the supply of the product to the use of it. The four situations identified have different characteristics and purchasing behaviour is supposed to be adapted to these specific circumstances.

This product focus explains some of the basic characteristics of purchasing behaviour presented in the two first chapters. The focus on products puts the emphasis on price, and this, in turn, favours standardized solutions. When the company is considered a production unit the supply issues are centred on the interface between input products and the production process. The organization is most often designed accordingly. It became logical to establish a separate purchasing department with different groups of purchasers made responsible for specific products. Purchasing staff then became specialized in these different products especially in terms of how, and by whom, they were produced, while the knowledge about their use in various applications was limited.

Purchasing in the Knowledge Unit

The knowledge dimension has become increasingly focused in business over the last 20 years. For example, Teece (1998) concludes that 'the essence of the firm is its ability to create, transfer, assemble, integrate, and exploit knowledge assets'

(p. 75). This characteristic of firms in the new economy makes it reasonable to argue for a knowledge-based view of the firm (Nonaka and Takeuchi 1995) as knowledge is easier to transfer than it used to be, mainly because it is more codified (Teece 1998). This, in turn, enhances the opportunities to learn more quickly and more extensively. Furthermore, knowledge is to a large extent built into products and processes, which makes it easier to acquire and to use. These two factors in combination make it much more difficult to keep a competitive advantage based on knowledge, and so learning is now of crucial importance to companies. Knowledge thus becomes more focused, partly because it has become more problematic to keep it within an organization, partly because of the increased opportunities for utilization of the knowledge of others.

The increasing availability of knowledge increases the creation of knowledge. New knowledge is often developed in the interface between existing knowledge bodies. Thus, the more and the larger knowledge bodies there are, the more interfaces will be created and the greater the opportunities to develop new knowledge. For the individual firm this means that 'knowledge facilitates the acquisition of more knowledge' (Powell 1998, p. 236). The improving conditions for transfer of knowledge identified above are partly counteracted by problems related to the increasing amount of knowledge. The problem is not that some knowledge is hidden—the problem is to select what knowledge is relevant.

Knowledge is thus increasingly important to companies. Furthermore, the total body of knowledge is rapidly expanding. Consequently, firms need to 'manage' information in one way or another. For this reason 'knowledge management' has emerged as a term covering the activities of a firm to 'adding or creating value by more actively leveraging the know-how, experience, and judgment residing within and outside an organization' (Ruggles 1998, p. 80). The same author presents the results from a survey of more than four hundred US and European managers and their activities to manage knowledge. More than 50% of the executives in the sample felt it was valuable for their organizations to have a formal CKO (Chief Knowledge Officer). Other knowledge roles identified in the organizations with various responsibilities were, for example: knowledge editors, knowledge engineers, knowledge navigators, knowledge brokers and knowledge stewards.

The recent focus on knowledge has changed the strategic attention of companies as well. From a strategic point of view, there have been two key concepts: 'core competence' and 'capabilities'. Both affect the supply side considerably. These two concepts are directly related to which type of knowledge the company develops internally and what is made available from other firms. Another issue is related more to the transfer of knowledge. In particular, it is argued that there is increased attention paid to using knowledge more quickly than before—this has been formulated as the need to reduce time to markets—or time to technology. Certainly, the need to shorten time in product and technical development has influenced the way companies relate to their suppliers. We return to these strategic issues in Chapter 8.

Given this interest in knowledge: what are the implications for purchasing? When the production unit perspective is applied the product and its content are at the top of the agenda. Even in the knowledge unit the products delivered by suppliers are crucial knowledge sources. But purchasing now also has to consider the need to relate to the basic providers of knowledge—i.e. to the companies and organizations that 'produce' and thereby supply knowledge as such. Therefore, suppliers of products have to be seen in new ways, and there might also be producers of knowledge, who are not selling any products. Consequently, purchasing has to analyse potential suppliers in a new, extended, way.

Three issues become important in this process. The first has to do with identification of the knowledge areas that are important for the single company. Some of these are quite easy to define because they have been recognized and used for a long time, although they may need to be delimited in an appropriate way. However, it is much more difficult to be aware of emerging areas and/or how already available technology may be applied in new contexts. Purchasing can clearly contribute to these processes through its broad contact network with different knowledge sources—primarily the suppliers.

The second issue concerns the learning process in relation to individual suppliers or combinations of suppliers. This process involves learning in relation to new products and/or production methods and represents what is known as learning *from* collaboration (Powell 1998, p. 238). Powell also stresses the importance of learning *how* to collaborate. An organization must know how its counterparts learn, for example what kind of development processes the counterparts are involved in and what kind of counterparts they, in turn, have. In other words, it relates to learning how to develop bodies and networks of knowledge. The main effort from a purchasing point of view must be to use the existing and developing knowledge in the supply network as extensively as possible. The demand for shorter lead times in technical development has made it increasingly important to consider Powell's second question: how to collaborate. Takeuchi and Nonaka (1986) make a distinction between collaboration according to the relay principle and the rugby principle. The relay principle is a serial approach, where each phase of the development process is clearly separated and the relay baton is passed from one group to another (type A in Figure 3.3). The rugby principle, in turn, builds on what is usually called concurrent engineering, where the activities in the

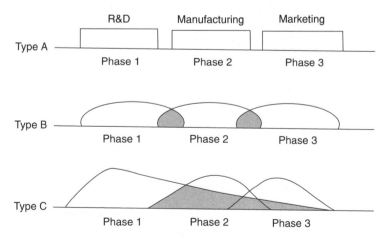

FIGURE 3.3   The rugby and relay principles illustrated. Source: Takeuchi and Nonaka 1986, p. 139. Copyright © 1986 by the Harvard Business school Publishing Corporation, all rights reserved.

development process do not only overlap. According to the authors, everyone should run most of the way from start to finish (type C). As in rugby, the team workers should 'run together, pass the ball left and right, and reach the goal as a united body' (ibid., p. 78).

Working according to the rugby principle requires extensive co-ordination because one activity must begin before the previous one has been finished. What is not evident from the figure is, as many studies have shown, that the total development time may be reduced when the rugby principle is applied (see, e.g. Sobek *et al.* 1998).

The third issue relates to the learning process going in the other direction. In order to influence the knowledge processes of suppliers it is important to make them learn the internal capabilities of the buying firm. The suppliers must be informed about the buying firm's own activities, knowledge and capabilities. The advantages gained from this type of learning in Fuji Xerox are illustrated in the following Box. This example shows that in order to use suppliers for developing the buying company's total knowledge base they must be given the opportunity to become educated. The internal resources of the customer firm must be used in an active effort to accomplish this. They must be used also to challenge the way suppliers look at and define problems and solutions.

Benefits From Making Suppliers Learn

We ask our suppliers to come to our factory and start working together with us as early in the development process as possible. The suppliers also don't mind our visiting their plants. This kind of mutual exchange and openness about information works to enhance flexibility. Early participation on the part of the supplier enables them to understand where they are positioned within the entire process. Furthermore, by working with us on a regular basis, they learn how to bring in precisely what we are looking for, even if we only show them a rough sketch. When we reach this point our designers can simply concentrate on work requiring creative thinking.

Source: Imai, Nonaka and Takeuchi 1995, p. 351.

In order to handle these three issues effectively suppliers must be perceived as knowledge reservoirs rather than as suppliers of products, as is the situation in the producing unit. Learning processes require both stability and variety (Håkansson 1993). More developed relationships create a stability that can be used from a learning point of view. Variety among knowledge sources improves learning conditions. Variation can partly be created from having some parallel suppliers but mainly through combining the resources of different suppliers. Powell (1998) expresses this by saying that 'heterogeneity and interdependence are greater spurs to collaborative action than homogeneity and discipline (ibid., p. 231). The conclusion is that it is important to move the focus from the products of the suppliers to the suppliers themselves. The crucial issue is not to select the 'best' supplier in terms of current offering (product/price ratio) but to select the right supplier in terms of potential contribution from a knowledge point of view.

Of course, products and services are still important, but only as components in the total knowledge package. Buying a product from someone is quite different from learning from someone.

All companies benefit from knowledgeable suppliers. However, only a small minority of companies systematically make use of their suppliers from a knowledge point of view. Interesting examples are found in procurement of electronic components, where the design of the products builds on methods that change quickly, at the same time as it must build on solving the buying company's problem. In such situations, the buying company needs assistance from suppliers. However, as stated above, most companies have a lot to gain from considering the view of the company as knowledge unit more deeply.

Purchasing in the Communicative Unit

The development and deployment of information technology has been an important prerequisite for knowledge management. In the study by Ruggles (1998), the four most practised types of projects in knowledge management were all related to IT. They concerned: creating an Intranet, establishing data warehousing, implementing computerized decision support tools, and implementing group-ware for supplier collaboration (ibid., p. 83). However, the role of a knowledge promoter is only one factor that makes it relevant to consider the company as a communicative unit. Information and exchange of information fulfil other roles in the company as well, as is illustrated in the following quote (Teece 1998, p. 60).

> Linked information and communication systems in production, distribution, logistics, accounting, marketing and new product development have the potential to bring together previously fragmented flows of data, thereby permitting the real time monitoring of markets, products, and competitors. The requisite data can then be fed to multifunctional teams working on new product development. Networked computers using rapid communication systems thus enable major advances in corporate and inter-corporate monitoring and control systems. Within organizations, computer networks can strengthen links between strategic and operations management, while also assisting linkages externally to discrete and geographically dispersed providers of complementary services.

Regarding the company as a communicative unit should thus increase our understanding of the new economy. From an information management point of view two main issues may be seen:

- What information is processed and used in the communicative unit?
- What is the purpose with the communication activities?

Gadde and Håkansson (1993) discuss these two issues from a purchasing point of view. For that purpose, an analytical framework is developed for the analysis of information exchange and communication. The two main dimensions of this framework are, accordingly, type of information and role of communication (Figure 3.4).

Type of information	The roles of communication		
	Co-ordination	Influencing	Learning
Technical information			
Commercial information			
Administrative information			

FIGURE 3.4 Roles of communication and type of information. Source: Gadde and Håkansson 1993, p. 148.

Three types of information are identified in the matrix. First, there is a need for exchange of technical information. A buying firm might need information to solve a problem in a specific buying situation, for example choosing among the alternative items in the standardized product range of a supplier. Another type of technical information requires more extensive exchange and is concerned with buyer–supplier exchange of information in joint product development work. Secondly, commercial information relates to the buying firm's need of information prior to entering into a business agreement. This includes identification of potential suppliers and evaluation of what they have to offer. From the point of view of the seller, exchange of commercial information is necessary to promote the goods and services sold. Thirdly, administrative information is coupled to the exchange of information associated with a specific transaction. Any business agreement involves many kinds of information from inquiries and offerings via delivery schedules to invoicing.

The second dimension of the communication matrix deals with the aim and role of the communication activities. This case, too, is subdivided into three different types. The first is the co-ordinating role, as was apparent in the quote from Teece (1998). It is about linking production, distribution, logistics and other activities together, both within the company and in relation to suppliers. The second role has to do with influencing other firms and organizations. For example, a customer may have an interest in persuading a supplier to adapt its activities and resources. The influencing role is important in any attempt to mobilize other actors and/or to convince them to change. The third role is related to learning and knowledge management. It has to do with transfer of knowledge between buyer and seller. Communicating the attributes of various resources is fundamental to efficiency in their joint utilization.

Communication and exchange of information are thus very significant issues for companies and for purchasing. Therefore, we should not be surprised that the evolving information technology is expected to revolutionize both companies and purchasing. However, further examination of the matrix in Figure 3.4 makes clear that IT already plays a significant role in some aspects of this complex communication structure. In other applications it will probably have an impact in the future. It is also clear that in some cases existing means of communication cannot be replaced by IT, such as most applications related to the influencing and learning roles. It is in co-ordination that IT is most significant and has made substantial contributions to rationalization of information flows. These developments are discussed in Chapter 4.

Reconsidering the expectations on information technology and its potential impact on business exchange, it is clear that actual developments have not lived up to expectations. One reason is that most attention has been focused on what types of solutions are technically feasible. Companies have made large investments in developing new communication systems. Most efforts have been devoted to developing technical solutions and related investments. In many cases the basic issues were forgotten: the content of the information and how to make use of it did not receive the attention it deserved. We need to elaborate on these two issues and how they relate to purchasing.

Handling information is certainly not a new question—only the technology is new. The importance of information, how it should be stored and handled, and how it is related to communication are issues that have long been discussed. In relation to purchasing there has always been the question of how to keep information updated, for example in terms of catalogues and files. For a long time, it was up to the individual purchaser or the single department, but since the advent of computers there has been more general interest in these issues. It has become part of the total management information system.

One very basic question is about the information content in terms of its breadth and depth. Most new technologies are very much focused on making it easier to collect and exchange more information. Many examples from the new IT-world illustrate how easy it is to collect information from any part of the world and then also to use it for managing in a boundary-less business world. There are at least two problems associated with this perspective. Firstly, this view of the information issues more or less automatically considers efficient purchasing as choosing the right supplier for a given product. The most significant task is then

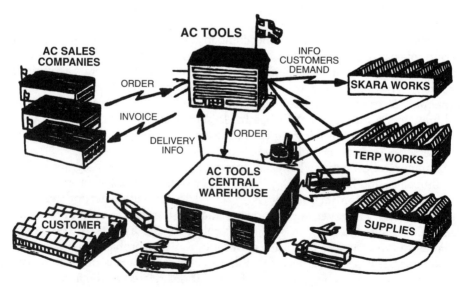

FIGURE 3.5   The company as a communicative unit. The information flow in Atlas Copco Tools.

to find alternative suppliers. Secondly, too much information can be a problem in itself. Information overload is of no use to the single decision-maker. It has been demonstrated in psychological tests that the quality of decisions decreases when the amount of information increases beyond a certain level. Still, even with these remarks in mind, it is clear that the new technology enhances the opportunities to be informed about products, suppliers and sales conditions all over the world. In this way IT facilitates international business, but only in terms of information exchange.

Other kinds of information technologies are more directed at developing the quality of information, for example the development of virtual multidimensional models for presentation and visualization of technically advanced and complicated products. Drawings can be exchanged and simultaneously worked on by several business units. Similarly, systems are being developed to track the position of single items in the logistic system in a much more detailed way than has previously been possible. Technical development in this way gives opportunities for design of information channels between organizations, with much larger capacities for information exchange.

It is interesting to combine the two types of information technologies with the purchasing approaches discussed in this chapter, one focused on products and the other on viewing suppliers as knowledge sources. The first type of IT-development based on a more extensive and broader information collection goes hand in hand with a product focus in purchasing. The new technologies then provide opportunities to find alternative suppliers all over the world. If the product is standardized the different alternatives can be easily compared and evaluated. This is a picture that has flourished when the advantages of the Internet have been discussed. Using this perspective the purchasing department may be perceived as an Internet portal where every purchase is handled as a single transaction independent of all others. This is certainly an option in situations when the production and transfer costs are close to zero—such as for computer software or music items. However, in most situations there are substantial costs for production and logistics. In these cases there are reasons to rely on other types of IT-solutions. Considering this aspect is important for the production unit as well, particularly in cases where suppliers are involved in technical development.

This second development is much more in accordance with the way purchasing is seen in the knowledge unit. In order to be able to use one another in better ways from a knowledge point of view, it is of central importance for companies to become involved in deeper interaction. All technical systems that may facilitate more extensive interaction are important, including systems for multidimensional visualizations, for increasing the speed or accuracy in the information flow and for facilitating personal or group communications.

Purchasing in the Capital-earning Unit

More and more interest is devoted to companies as investments; to capital earning, to investor friendly policies, to stock earnings. All the ups and downs of the stock exchange are followed in the media and it would be difficult for any general manager to disregard this fact. For the purchasing manager it is certainly important because purchasing impacts considerably on the financial performance of the company. Furthermore, purchasing is affected by the overall financial considerations of the firm.

Our discussion of the relationship between purchasing and increasing financial pressures begins in Figure 3.6.

This chart illustrates how a change in costs of purchased materials and services would affect the return on net assets (RONA) in Philips. If purchasing costs are reduced from 30,096 to 29,494 (i.e. 2%) RONA would increase from 12.08% to 13.55% (i.e. 12.1%). These calculations rely on a 'ceteris paribus' assumption, meaning that nothing else is changed except the costs of purchased materials. In many cases this is an unrealistic assumption, as illustrated in the discussion of direct and indirect costs in Chapter 1, but it is still clear that purchasing substantially impacts on financial outcome.

As van Weele illustrates, purchasing contributes to improving RONA in two ways. Firstly, the company's sales margin is improved through the reduction of direct material costs. Suggested means of achieving these effects are, among others, looking for substitute materials and making use of competitive tendering. Secondly, purchasing may reduce the net capital employed by the company, which in turn has a positive impact on the capital turnover ratio. Measures recommended for reducing the capital employed include lengthened payment terms, reduction of inventories and leasing instead of buying equipment.

There is no doubt that the requirements from the capital-earning unit have been an important determinant of purchasing behaviour and strategy in recent

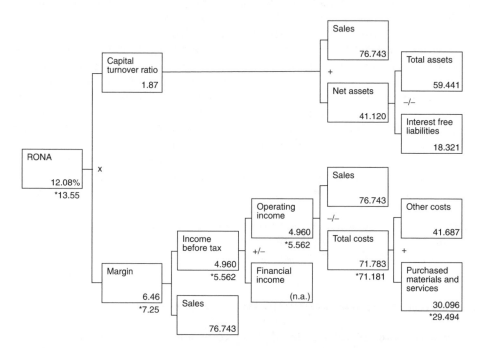

FIGURE 3.6 DuPont analysis Philips (1997): a 2% savings on purchased materials and services leads to a 12.1% RONA improvement. Source: van Weele 2000, p. 19. Reproduced from Purchasing and Supply Management by permission of the ITPS Ltd.

decades. Reducing the tied-up capital was one of the basic reasons for car manu-facturers in the western world to introduce JIT-deliveries. The effects of these changes proved to be highly significant (see, e.g. Minahan 1997 and Reese and Geisel 1997). However, even less sophisticated efforts may reduce tied-up capital. According to van Weele, purchasing may contribute by imposing solid discipline on suppliers (which, in turn, provides opportunities for reduced buffering), careful scheduling of deliveries, and special stocking arrangements with suppliers. Thus, reducing the balance sheet has become a prime objective for most companies. In fact it has almost turned into a goal in itself.

The recent interest in outsourcing is also contingent on the same objective. Divesting by outsourcing reduces the financial burden of a heavy balance sheet. However, the knowledge unit also contributes to these changes by promoting concentration on core activities. In both cases the importance of procurement is enhanced, while the significance of production is reduced. Purchasing thus becomes central when defining the efficient boundary of the company, and always remains a crucial means to influence the financial results.

In the two examples above, purchasing has an important function in making use of capital more efficiently. However, purchasing can also be involved in financing, for example, in investment projects. When there is more of a total solution, when the supplier has to invest in new technology development for the buying company, then there are reasons to consider financial aspects. In such cases purchasing people must be able to make more detailed financial analyses of the consequences of supplier relationships. This certainly gives the relationships still another dimension, and drives the developments in the direction of per-ceiving suppliers as sources of resources—including production, knowledge and financial resources.

There is another trend as well. In Chapter 2 we discussed the increasing consolidation of the supply base. Consolidation was a driving force in the re-orientation of IBM purchasing and one of the 'critical six' strategies as identified by Monczka and Morgan (2000). Achieving economies of scale through a com-bined effort of all business units in the same firm is a strategy adopted by many companies today. This development can primarily be traced to enhanced negotia-tion power and reduction of the supplier base which, on a group level, increased considerably during the decentralization era in the 1980s.

Implications for the Framework of the Book

The picture of the company has changed and will continue to change. Purchasing has changed and will also have to continue to change. The four pictures we have painted are all partial, and each of them only gives a fraction of a view of what purchasing is about. However, taken together, these pictures can be used both to indicate and explain the variety in purchasing when we compare different com-panies, and the development potential related to purchasing. There are reasons for all companies to develop the purchasing side. Over the years, purchasing has not at all received as much attention as sales, despite the fact that for many companies it may represent a key factor to business success. In order to function as an important factor, the people responsible for purchasing have to develop the content, for example in the dimensions described in this chapter.

The main development in purchasing has been formulated as a change from product based acting toward supplier based acting. This shift in attention also includes another change: a shift from a focus on structures toward a focus on processes. When purchasing is analysed in terms of procurement of products, it is a short step to analysis of market structures and from there to supplier structures. Issues like the number of potential and existing suppliers, their geographical locations, sizes and capabilities become important. On the other hand, when suppliers are considered resources the focus shifts and the interesting issues deal with learning, communication, and development, with a focus on processes where the company is successively becoming a very active node in a supply network. Creativity, relating and connecting are key words. It is a never-ending process where resources and activities are combined and recombined in co-operation with important counterparts. Nothing is certain and nothing should be taken for granted. There is no balance and there are no right prices or right qualities. Neither supply nor demand are givens. Buying and selling companies in interaction create supply and demand.

One ambition underlying this book is to contribute to such a process by offering a discussion of principal purchasing problems. There are already several books focused on the tactical and operative purchasing decisions and activities. Our analysis in Chapter 2 concluded that grasping the complexities of purchasing dynamics and challenges requires a holistic approach. The theoretical approach serving as the framework for this book is the industrial network approach.

The network approach has been developed on the basis of a large number of empirical studies. In the beginning these were focused on descriptions and analyses of business relationships both from the buying and the selling side (Håkansson (ed.) 1982, Turnbull and Valla 1986). Later, the studies developed, viewing these relationships as parts of networks. (Håkansson and Snehota 1995, Ford et al. 1998, Ford 1997). During these developments the purchasing side and its way of functioning has been a crucial issue (Håkansson and Wootz 1975, Axelsson and Håkansson 1984, Gadde and Håkansson 1993).

The basic point of departure for the network model is that business relationships are outcomes of interaction processes where both sides try to influence one another. These interaction processes develop over time in a stepwise manner and include technical, social and financial elements. Products, operations, and other technical attributes are successively adapted in these processes. The people involved develop relationships, in which the presence or absence of trust is of crucial importance to the nature and development of the relationship. Finally, the parties constantly strive to develop joint working methods and operations that improve economic efficiency. In doing this, the companies are successively bound together in three dimensions (Håkansson and Snehota 1995). Firstly, their activities can be more or less integrated. Secondly, their resources are more or less extensively combined. Thirdly, the people in the organizations interact more or less which, in turn, tends to 'glue' them together. This means that any relationship consists of a combination of activity links, resource ties and actor bonds. The characteristics of these relationships and their consequences are the basis of the industrial network model.

On a holistic network level, the existence of links, ties and bonds help to distinguish among three different network structures. Industrial networks can be analysed either in terms of their activity structure, resource structure or actor structure. Of course, these structures are interdependent: conducting activities requires resources, actors control these resources and undertake the activities. However, from an analytical point of view the distinction of the network structure in these three layers is advantageous. Each of these three perspectives makes different aspects of the network visible through the focus on only one of the dimensions. Therefore, combining these 'partial' pictures enriches the total understanding of the network.

The analysis of the company in the new economy enhances the relevance of the industrial network model. When the view of the company as a production unit is applied it is the activity structure of the network that is of most significance. However, as shown in this chapter, the company as a knowledge unit puts the emphasis on the resource dimension of the network. The actor level, in turn, is represented not only by individuals (as suggested above), but there is an organizational dimension as well. The impact of the capital-earning unit has to do with this level. Therefore, the understanding of the role and impact of purchasing in the companies of the new economy should be enhanced by adopting the industrial network model.

So far we have identified the first dimension of our framework—i.e. to view the supply issues in the three layers of an industrial network, using the content—or substance—of a relationship. The second dimension of the framework is associated with the strategies of the individual firm used to handle the issues on the supply side. Again, we rely on Håkansson and Snehota (1995) and their distinction between different functions of a relationship. They argue that what is going on between two companies both affects the relationship between them and each company internally as well. Furthermore, a relationship is embedded in other

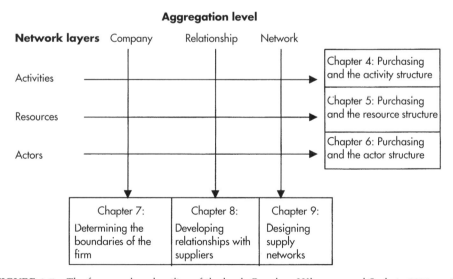

FIGURE 3.7 The framework and outline of the book. Based on Håkansson and Snehota 1995, p. 45.

relationships. Therefore, what takes place between two companies affects their relationships with other firms—i.e. has an impact on the whole network.

For the strategies of the individual firm the implication is that there are three dimensions to consider when developing a supply strategy. The analysis needs to consider the individual firm, the individual relationships with other firms and the whole network. Returning to the first two chapters, the industrial network model provides a most relevant approach for analysing and developing supply strategies. Firstly, outsourcing and make-or-buy decisions are strategic issues related to the decisions regarding what should be internal in the buying company. We define this as the strategy for determining the boundaries of the firm. Secondly, the discussion in Chapter 2 clarified that the nature of relationships with suppliers is a highly significant issue for companies today. Therefore, developing appropriate relationships with suppliers is the second strategic issue. Thirdly, consolidation and 'network management' as discussed in Chapter 2 are also high on the strategic agenda in purchasing. The third strategic issue is thus about designing supply networks.

This makes our framework complete. We have identified three layers in the network structure and three strategic issues on the supply side. In Figure 3.7 we have related the dimensions of the framework to the industrial network model. Figure 3.7 illustrates the structure of the book in relation to the framework.

Part II

NETWORK ANALYSIS

Chapter 4

PURCHASING AND THE ACTIVITY STRUCTURE

The first chapter of the network analysis deals with the overall pattern of activities in which a company is involved. In this perspective the company is seen as a bundle of activities. Such a view is taken, for example, by Porter (1985) who sees the firm as 'a collection of activities that are performed to design, produce, market, deliver and support its product' (p. 36). However, although Porter recognizes the interdependence to activities undertaken by other firms, he mainly emphasizes the value chain of the individual firm. In contrast, in a network approach, the main concern is to understand the role of the single company in terms of the overall structure, how its activities affect other firms' activities and how the company, in turn, is affected by these other activities. The activities of any company connect to those of other firms, such as suppliers, distributors, end-users and even competitors.

At a specific point in time the activities in the network are characterized by a certain division of labour among the firms involved. The activities of each company are directed towards fulfilling some specific function in the network structure as a whole. This division of labour among firms changes over time. For example, a company may start buying what it used to produce in-house or it may develop internal capabilities for producing what it has bought from suppliers. The network structure is affected in other ways as well. A first typical situation is when new technology makes it possible to perform a desired function in new ways. A significant example is when developments in electronics made a new 'infrastructure' available, thus offering opportunities to replace the mechanical devices used earlier. In such cases the network structure in terms of which activities are performed may change substantially. A second example is when technical development provides opportunities for conducting a specific activity in a more efficient way than before. One illustration is when orders can be processed faster and more reliably using sophisticated IT-systems than by mail or phone. This may change the sequence of activities and sometimes make specific activities obsolete. A third type of change is when the co-ordination mechanism between two activities is modified. One typical example is just-in-time deliveries. Before they were introduced, buffers in terms of inventories made the production activities of supplier and customer quite independent of each other. JIT-deliveries changed these conditions and introduced a strong interdependence among the activities of customer and supplier. At the same times inventories were reduced substantially, implying changes in other activities as well. All three examples of changes in the activity structure affect the conditions for the division of labour among the actors in the network.

In this chapter we analyse the company and its role in the network structure of activities. In the first section we discuss how single activities are combined to form activity chains and what impacts on the division of labour in these chains. The second section presents two concepts that can be used for analysing inter-dependencies among activities—similarity and complementarity. The two fol-lowing sections illustrate how efficiency in activity chains can be affected by changing the interdependence among activities. The third section deals with changes through increasing similarities, while the fourth section brings up the role of complementarity among activities and how these complementarities can be affected. Activities connected in a chain need to be co-ordinated. For this process to be effective, exchange of information is a key issue. In the fifth section we discuss the role of information in activity co-ordination. It is of particular interest in this respect to consider the opportunities provided by IT-systems of various kinds—such as the Internet. The sixth section focuses on these issues. In the seventh section we combine the various insights from the chapter in a dis-cussion of efficiency in activity chains. Finally, we summarize the main issues in an activity analysis.

Chains of Activities and Division of Labour

The perspective of a network as an aggregation of activities causes some analy-tical problems (Håkansson and Snehota 1995). For our purpose, no deeply prob-ing exploration of the activity concept is needed. However, one important characteristic is that any single activity builds on prior activities and is followed by others. Activities thus appear in sequences or in chains (Porter 1985, Håkansson and Snehota 1995). Defining a chain of activities is a way to reveal a specific type of connection among activities. This connection has its roots in a certain logic which can be either technical or timely (Håkansson and Snehota, 1995, p. 399). Examples include the activity chain for the manufacturing of a computer, or the activity chain for research and development in a strategic alliance in the pharmaceutical industry, or the activity chain underlying a service provider's offerings. An activity chain is thus directed towards a specific outcome and is identified from that perspective.

The activities that constitute a chain are interdependent because they are directed towards a common end. For example, a value chain is 'a collection of interdependent activities' (Porter 1985, p. 48). The activities in a chain are related by links, which can be more or less tight (Håkansson and Snehota 1995, p. 54). The tighter the link, the stronger the interdependence. One kind of tight link arises when activities are specifically adjusted to each other. Such adjustments can take various forms, for example mutual adaptations of information systems, transportation and physical handling, or payment routines. But they may also be one-sided supplier adaptations of product characteristics and delivery schedules to apply to the specific needs of individual customers. Adaptations among activities are made to improve performance in some respect. They are also always costly. Efficiency in activity chains is thus contingent on a mixture of tight and loose linkages among the activities. By minimizing linking in terms of adaptations, activities can be highly standardized. In other cases, however, unique activity configurations implying tight linking may be preferable.

To illustrate the conceptual discussion we provide an empirical example. Historically, a relevant distinction between the firms in a network structure of activities has been 'producers' who mainly dealt with activities related to 'manufacturing' and 'intermediaries' of various kinds, primarily involved in 'distribution'. Over time this classification has become increasingly obsolete, illustrated in Figure 4.1 showing the production-distribution network in the PC

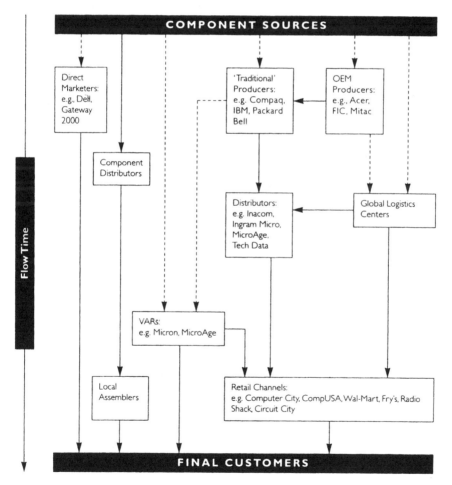

FIGURE 4.1 The distribution network in the PC-industry. Source: Curry and Kenney 1999, p. 21. Copyright © 1999, by The Regents of the University of California.

industry. Curry and Kenney (1999) show that the 'traditional' production-distri-bution channel (illustrated by IBM and Compaq) co-exists with new emerging structures represented by 'local assemblers' and 'direct marketers' like Dell.

According to Curry and Kenny the PC industry of today is characterized by the fact that there is a large variety of interchangeable components readily available. Therefore, they argue that 'there are many possible ways to organize the value chain' (ibid., p. 16). In our framework we say that there is an infrastructure available for production and distribution. This activity structure can be used in different ways and companies can take various positions in the overall structure. This leads to different activity chains. One extreme is represented by the 'traditional channel' where 'manufacturers' assemble standardized PCs which are then pushed through the channel to resellers who make an assortment available to customers. The other extreme exemplifies a just-in-time approach. 'Direct marketers' like Dell rely on customization. In this case, no assembly operations are undertaken until an end-user has ordered a specified PC. Components are then supplied just in time from a consignment inventory close to the assembly line. After assembly, the PC is shipped directly to the end-user. A third type of activity chain runs through 'local assemblers'. These firms integrate pre-assembled modules with supple-mentary hardware components and software. The local assembler may be a firm specializing in assembly or a so-called VAR (value-added reseller).

The network of the PC industry illustrates the huge number of options that are available from the variety in the total activity network. Companies take different positions in this structure. Sometimes, this is because of strategic considerations, sometimes other developments in the network may have driven them into a certain position. In the PC case, firms in the 'traditional channel' mainly rely on standardization of operations to bring costs down. This means that the choices of customers are restricted. The 'direct marketers' make it possible for end-users to get involved in the specification of the PC they buy. This means less stan-dardization and possible losses of economies of scale. It also imposes a strong interdependence among the activities in the production-distribution chain. In this case, no inventories serve as buffers.

The developments in the PC industry are typical of many activity structures in production and distribution. The outcome of these changes is an increasing differentiation. For buying firms these developments enhance the choice of oppor-tunities available. Variation increases the likelihood of finding solutions that adequately solve the problems of the buying firm. However, efficient pur-chasing is not only about evaluating the pros and cons of different suppliers' offerings. The buying firm may affect what alternatives are available through its own purchasing strategy and buying behaviour. By favouring the offerings of certain suppliers, a buying firm supports some of the potential activity chains. Furthermore, a customer may be able to have an impact on which activity chains never develop. In this respect purchasing plays a significant role.

The example from the PC industry and the positions firms have taken illus-trates two factors of importance for the allocation of single activities among actors. The first is related to the opportunities to reap economies of scale through standardization and specialization. The second is about the prerequisites for and the consequences of interdependence in chains of activities. The following section provides two concepts useful for the analysis of these issues.

Similarity and Complementarity Among Activities

An activity based framework for analysing division of labour and industry governance is provided by Richardson (1972). In this framework activities are defined in broad terms, including research, development and design, execution and coordination of processes of physical transformation, marketing, etc. Richardson brings up two characteristics of activities that are important for understanding division of labour: similarity and complementarity.

An important distinction is made between similar and dissimilar activities. Activities are similar when they require the same capabilities and resources for their undertaking. For example, manufacturing operations for two different products may use the same machining equipment or require the same skilled work force. Marketing activities are similar when one and the same salesperson is used for a whole range of products. Increasing similarity of activities follows from standardization and is a breeding ground for specialization. Ambitions to improve on economies of scale thus require enhanced similarity among activities. Mass production as developed in the Ford factory in the 1920s is an outcome of exploiting similarities. In Figure 4.1 the activities in the 'traditional channel' are more similar than those of the direct marketers. The similarity of the activities of the local assembler is somewhere between the two extremes. By relying on prefabricated modules this firm benefits from standardization to some extent while at the same time being provided with some opportunities for differentiation.

It is important to observe that increasing similarity not only leads to cost reductions in manufacturing and distribution. Similarity can be taken advantage of in design and development activities as well. In this case the most important outcome of enhanced similarity is that a company, by relying on specialized suppliers, may gain access to a variety of technologies. Owing to the pace of technical development, it has become increasingly difficult for a company to stay at the cutting edge in all the different technologies that impact on its operations. We return to this issue in Chapter 5 on the resource structure.

The second concept in Richardson's framework is complementarity. Activities are complementary when they represent different phases of a process of production. Complementarity is thus related to the sequential interdependence among the activities in a chain, as was also discussed in the example from the PC industry. In Figure 4.1 all the 'vertically' oriented activities are complementary: they have to be undertaken in a certain order. According to Richardson, some activities might be closely complementary. This is the case when it is necessary 'to match not the aggregate output of a general-purpose input with the aggregate output for which it is needed, but with particular activities' (ibid., p. 891). Sequential activities thus become closely complementary at the point where the object of the refinement process is made specific to a particular user. When activities are closely complementary it is necessary that 'two or more independent organizations agree to match their related plans in advance' (ibid., p. 890). This matching may concern both quantitative and qualitative aspects, i.e. it deals with how much, as well as what, is produced and exchanged. In Figure 4.1 the activities become closely complementary at different stages. For the direct marketers it happens when a customer order is received and assembly begins. For local assemblers close complementarity is introduced when the prefabricated modules are assembled according to customer specification. Finally, in the traditional channel there are no closely complementary activities until delivery to end-user. Increasing complementarity therefore increases interdependence among activities. The inventories in the 'traditional' channel serve as buffers. When these buffers are eliminated the need for co-ordination is enhanced.

The efficiency of various activity chains in terms of input and output differs depending on the similarity and complementarity among activities. The three types of activity chains in the PC industry provide end-users with variety in terms of costs, service levels and delivery times. This fact has considerable implications for the static efficiency of activity chains, and even more for the dynamics. A company may affect the efficiency of the activity chain in which it is involved by changing similarity and complementarity among activities. Such changes affect resource input and service output, as well as the division of labour among the actors. In the next two sections we provide some examples illustrating such changes and their implications. In particular, we discuss how a buying company may affect these conditions.

Changing the Similarity Among Activities

For the analysis of the prerequisites for and the implications of changing similarity we use an interesting case study presented in Dubois (1998). The case study describes SweFork and its attempts to reorganize one of the activity chains in which this company is involved. SweFork is a small firm manufacturing electric forklift trucks for loading, unloading and short distance transportation. One important sub-system of these vehicles is the machine body, which consists of 16 different parts. Some of those can be considered raw materials (steel plates); others are standardized components; while some are customer-designed components. The activities involved in transforming the plates to a complete machine body are the following:

- Machining (cutting, drilling and bending)
- Welding
- Painting
- Assembly, where the machine body is combined with other components

Dubois illustrates how the division of labour concerning these activities changed over time by changing similarities and complementarities. She identifies three phases where the activity chain was organized in entirely different ways.

Phase 1

At the end of the 1980s the activities were allocated to different actors in accordance with Figure 4.2.

SweFork procured six different types of pre-machined plates from a machining firm. Ten other components were delivered from different suppliers. SweFork's internal operations began when those 16 parts were taken from stock (the store)

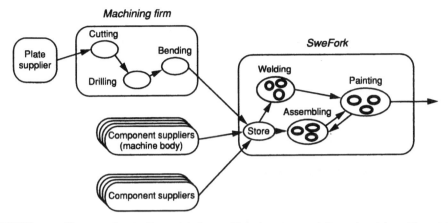

FIGURE 4.2   Phase 1—the starting point. Source: Dubois 1998, p. 76. Reproduced from 'Organizing Activities across Firm Boundaries. By permission of Routledge.

and welded together, after which the machine bodies were painted with primer and then assembled together with other components. The final operation was topcoat painting. This process was costly and two particular problems were identified. Firstly, the manual welding operations were a constant source of trouble. Secondly, the two-stage painting operation was inefficient: among other problems it required masking of some parts of the machine body. The quality of these operations was negatively affected when paint got stuck in cavities, causing various defects. Different ways of solving these problems were considered. Welding operations did not necessarily need to be manual and using equipment for two-component paint would make it possible to eliminate one painting operation. SweFork analysed these opportunities to reorganize the activity chain.

Phase 2

SweFork decided not to invest in robot welding or two-component painting. Instead, they looked for outsourcing opportunities. Outsourcing welding and painting activities implied that some kind of system supply was being sought. There seemed to be two types of system suppliers available. The machining firm that was used represented one type. The main advantages of these suppliers were flexibility and low prices. On the other hand, to keep costs down they relied on rather unsophisticated equipment. In general, they could not offer more advanced facilities than SweFork. Another type of suppliers had invested in new technology for welding or painting (or both). One of these companies was Systech, which offered two-component painting and was able to reduce painting to one operation. Furthermore, Systech had installed a flexible manufacturing system (FMS), primarily to serve companies like Volvo, Saab, Ericsson and ABB. Once this investment had been made Systech actively tried to use the full capacity of this equipment, thus offering machining to SweFork as well.

SweFork decided to move the machining activities from the present supplier to Systech. In spite of the fact that the machining firm was a low cost producer

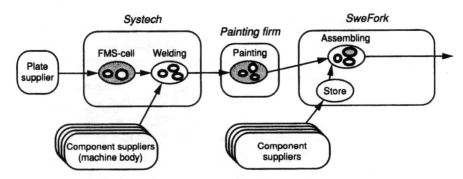

FIGURE 4.3   Phase 2—outsourcing. Source: Dubois 1998, p. 77. Reproduced from 'Organizing Activities across Firm Boundaries. By permission of Routledge.

Systech could undertake these operations more efficiently. Systech's painting and machining activities were characterized by larger scale than those of both SweFork (painting) and the machining firm. Moving these activities to Systech allowed SweFork to benefit from increasing similarity. Accordingly, Systech was appointed the system supplier of the machine body. The activity chain in Phase 2 is illustrated by Figure 4.3, which deserves some additional comments. Systech was made responsible for painting the machine bodies. However, due to their limited capacity, Systech in turn outsourced these activities to a painting firm also offering two-component painting. Furthermore, Systech was a much larger buyer of plates and most of the components. Therefore, outsourcing of these purchasing activities also made sense. For a few components SweFork offered similarities in purchasing. These components were used in a number of vehicle models implying better business terms for SweFork than for Systech.

Using Systech as a system supplier thus offered economies of scale through increasing similarity in the activities related to painting, machining and purchasing. Figure 4.3 shows that welding was outsourced as well. However, in this case Systech offered no increases in similarity. In fact, SweFork's welding equipment was moved to Systech and the operations were undertaken in exactly the same way as before. The main reason for outsourcing welding had to do with the complementarity among the activities. Welding had to be undertaken after machining, but before painting. Once Systech was made responsible for both machining and painting the complementarity among activities made it logical that welding should be located there as well.

When Systech delivered a complete system SweFork's store operations related to plates and most of the components could be eliminated. The complete bodies were delivered directly to the assembly line where they were combined with the remaining components to form the larger system. Inventory reductions decreased costs and increased complementarity.

Phase 3

Five years later, the activity structure was substantially reorganized. The outcome of these changes is illustrated in Figure 4.4.

The main change is that welding and painting have now become in-house operations. SweFork has insourced these activities. Painting was insourced when

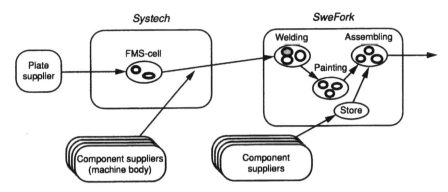

FIGURE 4.4   Phase 3—insourcing. Source: Dubois 1998, p. 79. Reproduced from 'Organizing Activities across Firm Boundaries. By permission of Routledge.

SweFork invested in new two-component painting equipment—primarily for other purposes. By bringing home painting of the machine bodies SweFork could improve utilization of the capacity of the new equipment and thus benefit from increasing similarity among its own operations. Concerning welding, we know that Systech offered no advantages in terms of efficiency. However, by insourcing welding SweFork could improve the efficiency of the logistic arrangements. Transporting knocked down components and machinery parts could be done at lower cost than transport of the welded machine bodies. But the main reason for insourcing was that SweFork had invested in robot welding. Manual welding offered few opportunities for economies of scale irrespective of where it was located. When the new investment had been made it became important for SweFork to increase the similarity of all the welding operations of the company.

In Phase 3 Systech's role had been substantially delimited. They were now responsible only for machining and purchasing. Insourcing machining was never a strategic alternative for SweFork. These operations were not undertaken for other vehicle models and had always been outsourced to suppliers.

Comments

The SweFork example shows how the efficiency of industrial activities may be affected by taking the interdependence among the activities into consideration. Changing similarity and complementarity impacts on the division of labour and thus on the way the resources in the network are used. Increasing similarity improves economies of scale, as was illustrated by outsourcing of purchasing, machining and painting in Phase 2, while interdependence in terms of complementarity was the reason for outsourcing welding. Once SweFork had invested in robot equipment the conditions changed. The investments in new equipment were primarily made for other vehicle models, but once they had been undertaken it was possible for SweFork to reap the benefits of increasing similarity within the boundaries of the firm. Machining remained with Systech, which offered economies of scale in these operations. Furthermore, staying with Systech provided opportunities for SweFork to gain indirect access to the capabilities developed by Systech through its interaction with large demanding end-customers in other industries.

The case clearly illustrates how purchasing, by combining insourcing and outsourcing, may contribute to efficiency improvements in the buying company. It also shows the importance of continuously monitoring the activity structure in terms of which activities are performed and how they are allocated to different firms. However, in many situations the changes needed might be difficult to accomplish because they require that other firms change as well. We return to these problems later.

Changing the Complementarity Among Activities

The direct marketers in the PC industry changed the complementarities of the down-stream activities which, in turn, provided opportunities for differentiation and customization of the end product and its delivery. Because this book is about the supply side of companies we are more concerned with cases where buying firms are involved in changing the interdependencies in the part of the activity chain directed towards suppliers. The 1990s were characterized by huge efforts in changing the extent of complementarity in these terms. The increasing attention to 'supply chain management' issues is the most significant sign of these efforts (see, e.g. Davis 1993).

The attention to supply chain issues stems to a large extent from experiences related to the reorganization of the supply networks of car manufacturers in the western world after the Japanese challenge around 1980. One of the most obvious differences between eastern and western assemblers at that time was the organization of the flow of incoming materials and components. Two American researchers visiting a factory in Japan expressed it as follows (Abernathy and Clark 1982, p. 8):

> It only takes ten minutes inside an assembly plant in Japan to realize that relationships with suppliers are very different. The visitor accustomed to the loading docks, the large storage areas and the large incoming area typical of US-plants, is likely taken aback by the stocking of Japanese assembly lines. Trucks from suppliers back up through large bay doors right to the assembly line; supplier personnel unload a few hours of parts, clean up the area and depart. There is no incoming inspection, no staging area, no expediting of material, just a seemingly continuous flow of material.

The experiences from the Japanese manufacturing systems were analysed in a huge number of articles and books (see, e.g. Womack et al. 1990, Lamming 1993). Concepts like 'lean production', 'lean supply' and just-in-time manufacturing and deliveries spread like wildfire, first to car assemblers in the western world and then to other industries. Introducing just-in-time deliveries did, in fact, make activities closely complementary. The main philosophy in JIT is to secure the availability of 'required items at the right quality, and in exact quantities, precisely as they are needed' (Minahan 1997, p. 42). JIT is thus not basically an instrument to reduce inventories, although these effects may be the most visible ones. JIT is a technique to co-ordinate and synchronize manufacturing activities.

Activity co-ordination has always been a prerequisite for efficiency in manufacturing operations. In fact, synchronization of production activities has been more important a determinant of manufacturing efficiency than the economies of scale provided by mass production. Chandler (1977) discusses the development of the modern business enterprise (MBE) that reshaped the American industry in the early 1900s. Typical representatives of the MBE were Ford, General Motors and General Electric. The MBE 'resulted from the integration of the processes of mass production with those of mass distribution within a single firm' (ibid., p. 285). However, the most significant efficiency improvements from the MBE were related neither to the size of the factory nor to greater specialization and sub-division of work. According to Chandler, the main determinant of performance enhancements was 'the ability to integrate and co-ordinate the flow of materials through the plant'. This means that the development of closely complementary activities within the organizational boundary was an important strategy behind the MBE. On the other hand, the links to the activities undertaken by other firms were not very tight—they were complementary, although not closely comple-mentary. Handling the synchronization of internal activities required the MBE to rely on substantial inventories on the supply side to compensate for long lead times in production and distribution. These inventories functioned as buffers of the technical core, in the terms of Thompson (1967), and guaranteed the efficient flow of materials *through* the plant.

Recent developments on the supply side emphasize the efficient flow of materials *between* plants. Today, most companies focus on a more and more limited part of the total activity chains in which they are involved. Increasingly, they have come to rely on suppliers for important input to their operations. Against this background, it becomes obvious that increasing comple-mentarity among activities crossing company borders should be an efficient means of improving performance in activity chains. However, implementing these changes required lead times in manufacturing and distribution to be shor-tened. Developments of information technology and transportation systems have substantially reduced lead times in distribution (Gadde 2000). At the same time, manufacturing technologies have been developed in such ways that production has been brought '... full circle from the days of Frederick Taylor: speed and flexibility have replaced cost and hierarchy' (Hayes and Pisano 1994, p. 42). In both cases it is a new 'infrastructure' for production and distribution that has made it possible to reorganize activities. When JIT-deliveries were introduced capital costs could be substantially reduced at the same time as delivery services were improved. The economic benefits received by buying companies through JIT-deliveries are illustrated, for example, in Gilbert (1990) and Dion *et al.* (1990). More recent experience is reported by Minahan (1997) and Reese and Geisel (1997).

Over time, the complementarity of activities in material flows has been even further enhanced. In the US new acronyms have been introduced, illustrating this increasing interdependence. For example, JIT II means that the supplier locates its own personnel in the factory of the customer. These people are responsible for securing the supply of the components and systems at the assembly line. For example, Honeywell Inc. has placed more than one hundred representatives at different customer plants around the world. For one customer purchasing costs were reduced by 10% the first year this system was used. The number of invoices decreased from 2,300 a year to 12. Delivery reliability was substantially improved and the number of orders that could not be delivered as requested was reduced by 90% (Minahan 1996b).

Finally, in JIT III the supplier establishes its own factory close to the customer's plant, which further enhances the opportunities for sequential deliveries. Supply of components and systems in sequence is a prerequisite for the buying firm's opportunities to customize its own offerings. This also calls for geographical proximity to suppliers. The Toyota system in Japan was established from scratch when the car industry was restructured after World War II and the bulk of suppliers set up close to the assembly operations. It has been more difficult for firms in the western world to apply this principle because these considerations were not taken into account when suppliers started their businesses. However, over time, successive changes have been undertaken. For example, in Toyota's Georgetown plant the majority of suppliers are located within 150 miles of the plant, some much closer. Volvo Car Corporation has established a 'supplier village' only two miles from the assembly line where ten main suppliers are located. When Nokia (the world's largest supplier of mobile phones) recently established an East European factory some of the suppliers were located door-to-door to the Nokia factory.

The substantial benefits that can be gained when the JIT-principle is adopted are described in a recent state-of-the-art review (Milligan 1999). For example, IBM plants reduced some of their inventory by as much as 70%, Tectronix cut total lead times from 45 to four days, while General Electric reduced them even further—from 13 weeks to nine hours. On the whole, however, Milligan is of the opinion that progress in the US could be better. One of the reasons given is the American tendency 'to look for quick-fix responses', which makes it somewhat problematic to launch solutions that pay off only in the long run. Furthermore, many pieces are required to make the 'JIT-puzzle' work: transportation systems that allow for quick delivery, efficient systems for information exchange, including the ability to track shipments. The conclusion of the article is that most of the pieces required to solve the puzzle have now fallen in place.

For purchasing, the main implication is that the basic principle of JIT—to eliminate as much waste as possible—should be adopted by all companies. However, this doesn't mean that all companies should ask their suppliers for just-in-time deliveries. As shown by Millen-Porter (1997a), some buying firms that adopted JIT are dissatisfied with the outcome. One purchasing director is of the opinion that it creates too much dependence on one supplier. Another found that 'JIT is reducing inventories too far'. JIT deliveries increase the complementarity among activities. In some situations, the benefits of this change outweigh the costs—in others the opposite is true. Hence, careful consideration must precede changes in the extent of complementarity among activities. Companies taking this route should be aware of the need to communicate with suppliers before the step is taken. Milligan (1999) reports on an attempt to implement JIT that was not successful. The main reason was that the buying firm did not adequately prepare the supplier for the new situation (ibid., p. 41).

> They came to us and said: 'We are implementing JIT and we want our components in JIT'. All of a sudden the rules had changed and we didn't know how to deliver just-in-time based on our system. They had not worked with us to do otherwise.

The Role of Information in Activity Co-ordination

An activity chain consists of a huge number of activities conducted by a large number of actors, involved in a highly complex division of labour. For this complex structure to function efficiently co-ordination is required. The activities within the boundaries of the individual firm have to be co-ordinated, for example the different stages in a manufacturing process. In the same way these 'internal' activities have to be co-ordinated with those undertaken by other firms, for example in logistics. There are also a number of indirect connections that may require joint considerations. Efficient co-ordination relies on exchange of information. Performing an activity in an efficient way calls for information concerning the activities undertaken before, as well as the ones coming after. The sequential interdependence in terms of complementarities must be handled. However, as was shown in the SweFork case, there is also a 'parallel' interdependence among activities. Exploiting potential similarities calls for knowledge about which other actors perform—or have the potential to perform—a certain activity. This section is mainly concerned with information exchange for co-ordination of sequential relatedness. Our analysis of activity chain reorganization through increasing complementarity identified JIT-deliveries as the most significant example.

JIT-deliveries enhance the interdependence among the activities conducted by customer and supplier and call for more co-ordination than is needed when inventories serve as buffers. We have mentioned the importance of new manufacturing techniques in making alternative activity chains available. In this section we bring up the shortened lead times in the distribution and transportation activities. These changes are discussed in relation to Figure 4.5, which illustrates the Odette system—a joint information system developed by European car assemblers.

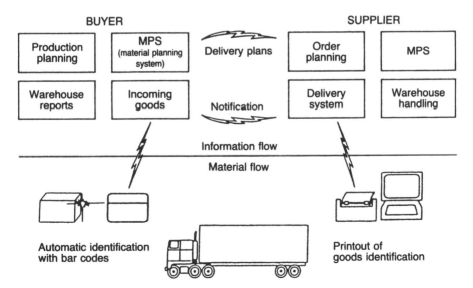

FIGURE 4.5 The principle of the Odette system. Source: Gadde and Håkansson 1993, p. 162.

This system was introduced in the 1980s when European car manufacturers began to require JIT-deliveries from their suppliers. Buyers' demand for efficient deliveries increased substantially, both regarding quality levels and time reliability. This enhanced the need for efficient information exchange through EDI (electronic data interchange) and speed and reliability in the material flow. The individual car manufacturer was dependent on supply from a large number of vendors. The flows of material from the various suppliers had to be synchronized into an integrated flow at the assembly line. Therefore, it is rational for the buying firm if both deliveries and exchange of information are standardized as much as possible so that all deliveries and all suppliers can be handled in the same way: increasing the similarity of these activities would be beneficial. Such standardization would benefit suppliers as well. Many suppliers have a number of car manufacturers as customers. If every manufacturer promotes a standard of its own, suppliers run into major problems. Against this background, it is understandable that car assemblers were able to solve the tricky problem of deciding on a common standard for information exchange and delivery conditions. Once the customers had defined the solution, suppliers could begin to perform the necessary implementations. Owing to the strong bargaining power of buyers the suppliers had no choice but to adapt to the new conditions which, on the other hand, provided them with long-term benefits.

Similar attempts have been made in other industries, where the effects, so far, have been less significant. The successful establishment of the Odette system relied on the fact that a few powerful buyers could agree on a common standard. This was further facilitated by fairly similar systems for product design and manufacturing outlays of the different car assemblers. 'Best practice' and 'benchmarking' originated in the automotive industry. Most other industries differ in this respect. In situations where the actors work in more diversified environments and conditions, standardization is not a suitable approach. In these cases, a common solution would require considerable compromises from each actor. One extreme outcome could be a system that is unsatisfactory to all parties. In these situations, the systems must be made more flexible, allowing for the variation in conditions. One example is a Swedish supplier of office stationery. This company has a multitude of customers with substantial differentiation with respect to the sophistication of information systems. Therefore, this supplier has developed four different types of IT-connections among which the customer can choose. Some customers have on-line access to the supplier's internal systems. Others use an EDI-connection implying that the systems of the supplier and the customer can communicate. Some customers rely on a Memo-system and transmit electronic order forms via electronic mail, while a fourth type of companies use hand terminals from which they can connect to the supplier's ordering system. This supplier has made it possible for different types of customers to get access to the ordering system. However, the number of solutions means that the similarity of the ordering processes of this supplier is somewhat limited. If all customers used the same type of IT-system, economies of scale in these operations would increase. At present, this supplier is adapting its ordering system to the Internet. E-commerce and in particular the opportunities provided by the Internet is a hot issue in most industries and for most companies. The next section is devoted to a discussion on this topic.

Co-ordination Through the Internet and other IT-systems

The potential impact of the Internet attracts a lot of interest these days—in society in general and in business in particular. A recent survey indicates that both access to and the use of IT in purchasing are increasing considerably (Fitzgerald 1999). In 1995, one quarter of purchasing managers had access to the Internet. In 1999, this figure had increased to 90%. In 1997, 45% of respondents reported that they used the Internet (mainly for other things than doing business), while the corresponding figure in 1999 was 81%. However, when it comes to e-business applications the situation is somewhat different (Brunelli 1999). For example, 'only a handful of chemical Web sites currently offer e-commerce capabilities'. In metal sales e-commerce accounts for 2% of nation-wide sales and in electronics one pur-chasing manager reports that about 1 or 2% of his purchases involve the Internet.

Most analysts expect these figures to grow dramatically in a short time. The present low figures are explained by implementation problems and the general consensus that e-business faces a glorious future are reflected in this quote: 'It is no longer a question of *if*, but *when*' (Fitzgerald 1999). When considering the future of e-business in purchasing it might be of value to reflect a little on what are the real opportunities provided by the Internet. An analysis in this respect reveals that the Internet is a means for exchange of information—and nothing more. It has certain advantages compared with other means of information exchange, in particular in terms of speed, user friendliness and accessibility. Therefore, in situations where exchange of information is the primary business aspect, the Internet may revolutionize business conditions. In some cases this has already happened. In other areas of business-to-business marketing and purchasing the situation is quite different, as illustrated in Chapter 3. Sometimes, information exchange is one of a number of important issues—in many cases increasing the speed of the information flow is of marginal value only. In these situations it would be surprising if the Internet leads to a revolution.

One of the purchasing managers in a study argued that the Internet has provided him with 'one more tool in his procurement belt' (Vigoroso 1999). But it was obvious that this additional equipment wouldn't radically affect his behaviour—'phones and faxes are not going anywhere, anytime soon'. Based on the reviews that have been undertaken it seems as if generally held beliefs about short-term Internet penetration in business purchasing have to be reconsidered. If the quotes in the box on page 74 are representative it seems likely that prevailing expectations overestimate future conditions.

The conclusion to be drawn is that it is not only the role of information exchange in the total business set-up that will determine the future of the Internet. The existing information systems and the investments that already have been made will also be decisive.

There are areas where we can expect a rapid penetration of the Internet. In particular, this is likely to occur in activity chains where firms today do not use EDI-applications. EDI is a complex and expensive solution for information exchange. Therefore, many firms in need of activity co-ordination were not able to invest in EDI to the extent that they would have liked. In comparison, the Internet requires less investment and is more user friendly. In such applica-tions the Internet may be very useful for co-ordination of activity chains. It might

---

Some Comments on the Potential Use of the Internet

- The real challenge for Internet marketers is to deliver products in the $700 million/year US Steel market, for example that are processed to specific end-customer requirements and ready to use in a just-in-time manufacturing environment.
- Many companies have invested millions in electronic data interchange (EDI) solutions and likely will not abandon EDI in the near future.
- People who have spent a lot of money on EDI are not going to get rid of the Vans and all the things they have set up.

Source: Brunelli 1999, pp. S6-S31.

---

contribute to increasing similarities as well, because order entries and order processing can be streamlined.

There has also been a debate concerning the structural effects of increasing utilization of the Internet. It has been argued that the main benefit is the increasing availability of supply alternatives. To analyse this issue it might be useful to look back to the middle of the 1980s when IT-solutions were launched. At that time, the opportunities of IT were supposed to reside in the establishment of electronic markets. IT was expected to remove the negative effects of existing business conditions related to insufficient capability to handle information. Porter and Millar (1985) argued that IT increases the power of buyers in two ways. First, IT would provide opportunities to identify 'all' the potential suppliers. Secondly, through increasing availability of information about the suppliers, it would be possible to better evaluate them. Customers would thus be able to make their purchases more efficiently—which, at the time, was the same as finding the most appropriate supplier for each transaction.

Once the view of purchasing efficiency changed so did the view of the benefits associated with IT. Over time, efficient purchasing turned more and more towards making the best use of existing suppliers. Therefore, instead of using IT to choose among suppliers the main applications were devoted to improving the performance in existing relationships. Much the same development seems to be going on today, as can be witnessed in the notion of electronic commerce rather than electronic markets. For example, Brunelli (1999) found that buyers already purchasing on the Web 'overwhelmingly indicate that they prefer supplier-hosted Web sites to third party sites'. This means that buyers find more interest in access to the information from one specific supplier than looking for potential 'better' solutions in a database run by some kind of information broker. In the same manner Extranets have increasingly come into use, particularly in the electronics industry. They are expected to become even more important in the future as OEMs reduce the number of distributors they do business with. According to Brunelli (1999), Extranets will handle the flow of information between OEMs, contract manufacturers and distributors who work together in joint constellations. In our terms, this means that Extranets are becoming important means of co-ordination of these activity chains.

The main implication of IT development is that we can foresee a continuous transition towards more rapid and reliable media for 'impersonal' communication

—from mail and fax to communication via computers. When routine transactions (such as inquiries, offers, orders, invoices, etc.) are transmitted by electronic channels purchasers gain more time to deal with strategic issues. This time can be devoted to monitoring supplier performance and initiating and participating in joint projects with suppliers.

Efficient Activity Structures

The analysis of efficiency improvements related to reorganization of the activity structure is illustrated below in a simplified example (see Figure 4.6).

This network includes one buying company, three suppliers to this company, one sub-supplier to each of these suppliers, one customer of the buying company and another buying firm. There are thus nine business units involved, each undertaking a huge number of activities among which different kinds of inter-dependencies prevail. We describe some of them and discuss their implications below. The purpose of this analysis is to illustrate the dependencies between a buyer and a supplier. However, to a large extent those interdependencies stem from other connections in the network. Therefore, we begin with these indirect interdependencies.

Between Two Suppliers (a)

There are interesting interdependencies among different suppliers, concerning similarity and complementarity. The fact that the two supply the same customer gives rise to both effects. For example, co-ordination of incoming goods from different suppliers can benefit the buying company. System sourcing, as illustrated in the SweFork case, is another example. The Odette system showed the benefits of increasing similarity in administrative routines through a joint information system exploiting similarities among activities. Through this standardization

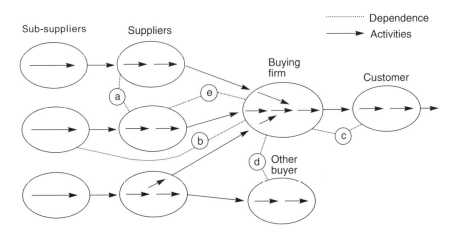

FIGURE 4.6   Illustration of activity interdependencies among different actors.

the buying firm may rationalize its internal administration without adaptations to individual suppliers. The same goes for technological systems (concerning standardization) and social systems (shared values among people). Thus, there are a number of reasons for a customer to support the development of similarities in the operations of suppliers.

Between Buyer and Sub-suppliers (b)

There are also interdependencies among firms belonging to the same chain of activities that are only indirectly connected. Those indirect partners govern some important conditions for what benefits the direct partners can achieve. Sometimes, the intermediate firm (the supplier) handles these dependencies. However, when conditions are complex, for example in technical development, direct exchange of information between buyer and sub-supplier might be required. Sometimes, the buying firm may have to intervene to ensure that the end-user perspective is taken into account. These interventions can help to increase similarities, for example by giving a supplier the opportunity to deliver to other vendors of the buying company. Increasing complementarity in the chain of activities may require specific adaptations in the sub-suppliers' outbound logistics.

Between Buyer and Customer (c)

In the same way as the sub-supplier sets some of the conditions for the supplier, the customer of the buying firm provides opportunities and restrictions for the behaviour of the buyer. The customer may require specific functionality or specific deliveries or product documentation that impose restrictions of various kinds. Changing something in relation to a supplier may thus require that customers first must be convinced about the benefits of a change. This illustrates the complementarity of the activities. Similarity is important in this context as well. By influencing customers so they choose certain components, applications and technical specifications substantial rationalization benefits can be attained through economies of scale. This was illustrated by the IBM example in Chapter 1. The buyer's dependency on the customer corresponds to the seller's dependency on sub-suppliers. In both cases these indirect connections require careful consideration.

Between Buyer and Other Buyers (d)

Two buyers may attain great benefits by co-ordinating their activities. The combined actions of buying firms set the conditions for the supplier's technical development and efficiency in manufacturing operations. Again, both similarity and complementarity apply. The common behaviour of a group of buyers significantly impacts on the economies of scale in the operations of the supplier. Similarities increase if buyers ask for the same type of solutions, while customization and adapted solutions lead to reduced similarities. Each buyer also must consider how different types of solutions impact on other activities. For example, adaptations may make other substantial opportunities available.

Between Buyer and Supplier (e)

Above, we have briefly summarized some of the dependencies to other actors that impact—directly or indirectly—on the interdependence between a buyer and a supplier. The relationship between the two parties reflects to a large extent the network of which the two companies are parts. However, the most important thing about the relationship is that it has a life of its own. The most obvious effects in terms of similarity and complementarity are captured in the relationship. With the most important suppliers (whoever they are) the buyer stands to gain by continuously reconsidering and changing the nature of the interdependence among activities. Audits need to be jointly undertaken with suppliers, and can concern any type of activities: R&D, manufacturing, logistics, administrative operations, etc. Increasing similarity is about more efficient resource utilization. This might concern how the resources of the supplier are used, or how one's own resources are used. By adapting to the behaviour of other buyers a customer can gain through similarities. This can always be done—the main question is to which types of behaviour the buying firm should adapt. There are no absolute limits to which similarity and complementarity can be increased. There are always opportunities to extend them. However, it must be remembered that a buying firm always has to compare the potential advantages of similarities and complementarities with its disadvantages. Increasing similarity means reduced opportunities for differentiation, while increasing complementarity increases sequential interdependencies.

Analysing Activity Structures

This chapter presents a framework for analysing the network structure in terms of the activities conducted. One profound characteristic of today's network structures is an increasing interdependence among the various activities. The analysis of this interdependence in terms of similarity and complementarity reveals some guidelines for improving performance.

From a purchasing point of view, it can be seen how a mixture of insourcing and outsourcing of activities may contribute to enhanced efficiency. The most effective mixture in this respect is contingent on the resources available and how these may be combined. Interdependent activities require co-ordination. In this process, exchange of information plays a significant role. Therefore, information sharing and joint information systems are prerequisites for efficiency in activity structures. In certain situations the Internet may be an important mechanism for co-ordination. In other cases it may prove to be only a marginal complement to other means of co-ordination.

Securing long-term efficiency and effectiveness requires changes in the similarity and the complementarity among activities. Therefore, the conditions governing efficient activity structures must be continuously monitored. Analysing the opportunities for reorganization of the activity structure makes it necessary to extend the scope beyond the individual buyer–seller relationship. A supply chain perspective is also an insufficient framework for this analysis. As shown in the previous section a network perspective is required to grasp the complexity of activity interdependence.

We conclude by pointing out some of the most important questions to be included in an analysis of the activity structure:

- What does a complete activity chain from the supplier's supplier to the customer's customer look like?
- Can any activity be eliminated or moved to another actor's sphere?
- In which ways can co-ordination of activities in a chain be improved?
- In which ways can co-ordination among activity chains be improved?
- Can any activity be made more effective by adapting it better to other activities?
- Can any given activity chain be replaced by any other?

Chapter 5

PURCHASING AND THE RESOURCE STRUCTURE

The efficiency of the activity structure is contingent on the way the resources in the network are utilized. In a short-term perspective, when the resource structure is perceived as more or less given, increasing similarity in resource utilization enhances efficiency. In the long run, however, the resource structure may be changed. The resources available can be combined in new ways, which introduces dynamics and innovation. And as demonstrated in Chapter 4, the resources used by a company are not only those residing inside the boundary of the firm. Outsourcing and supplier involvement have made access to the resources of other firms as important as the resources acquired and handled inside the company.

In the first section of this chapter we discuss the ways in which a company combines its internal resources with those of other actors. We go on to take a closer look at two different, contrary ways of relating resources to each other. The first situation, discussed in the second section, deals with combining resources in order to use them in the best way. In the third section we discuss potential gains from systematically confronting different resource elements with one another. Purchasing is involved in both these tasks. In the following sections we analyse the role of purchasing in two cases of development of buyer supplier relationships. Suppliers may be critical in the development of both products and production processes, as is illustrated in the fourth and fifth sections. One example deals with a US–Japanese co-operation project, while the other involves European companies. In these development processes the role of information exchange proves to be highly significant to the outcome. Exchange of information to promote resource development is discussed in the sixth section. We conclude the discussion by relating to the dynamic dimension of resource structures and its connection to systematic organizing. The final section summarizes the main issues to be dealt with in a resource analysis of the network structure.

Combining Internal and External Resources

It is common to perceive a firm as a resource entity—see examples from micro-economics in Penrose (1959) and Alchian and Demsetz (1972). This view is also shared by scholars representing the industrial organization approach (e.g. Scherer 1970). More recent advocates represent the resource based view of the firm (Wernerfelt 1984, Barney 1991). Every company is unique in terms of its resource base, which in most cases has been built up over many years. In many manufacturing companies some of these resources are plainly visible. They consist of plants with large buildings full of equipment and machines. For process companies, investment in terms of a new production line or new machinery and processes represents enormous economic value. These resources can be extremely impressive both in size and in function. The investments required to develop a new car or a new mobile phone system are huge. There are different ways of classifying resources. Some of them are tangible, such as people, products, production facilities, etc. Other resources are intangible, including know-how, skills, goodwill, trust, brands, image (see, e.g. Itami 1987). As was illustrated in Chapter 3, knowledge has now become a crucial resource for most companies. The company's resources are often illustrated in terms of descriptions and pictures in annual reports, and tangible ones are made visible to visitors. These are the internal resources supposed to be subject to the control of the company since they reside within the ownership boundaries.

However, an important part of a company's total resource base is located beyond these boundaries. Here, we think of all the resources the company has been involved in shaping through its business relationships. Internal resources are thus not at all independent—they are not an isolated island—but are part of a larger resource constellation (Håkansson and Snehota 1995). External resources can be very substantial—in many situations they are more important than the internal resources. The external resources are spread over a number of suppliers and customers. In Figure 5.1 we illustrate the fact that every company relies on both internal and external resources. The picture clearly indicates that one key issue on the supply side is how to combine these two types of resources.

Many studies point out the important role an advanced customer can play in the selling company's technical development. The products supplied are to be used by the customers and their facilities and knowledge are important factors influencing their resource utilisation. This characteristic is nicely captured by the concept 'lead-user' (see, e.g. von Hippel et al. 1999). Close and demanding customer relationships are prerequisites for any company's development. Similarly, relationships with private or public research units might be very important in this respect. The pharmaceutical industry is one obvious example but in many cases producers of advanced materials or equipment are in the corresponding situation. The interest shown in science parks situated close to large universities is a pertinent example. What is important in relation to customers and research units is equally true concerning suppliers. Handling the interface between internal and external resources is certainly a key problem for purchasing. How this can be done is the main issue of this chapter.

Combining external and internal resources involves a number of tasks. The first relates to the utilization of internal resources. It is a responsibility of purchasing to

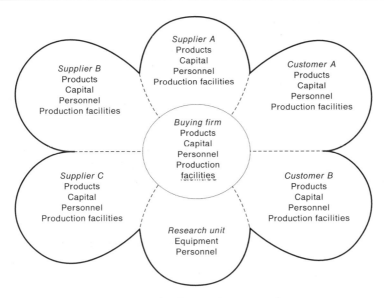

FIGURE 5.1   Internal and external resources of a company.

continuously evaluate the internal resources by making comparisons with what might be gained from using external resources. In this way purchasing can be used to challenge the internal resources, as illustrated by the external sourcing at IBM discussed in Chapter 2. A second responsibility is the handling of external resources—which, of course, is the same as handling the suppliers. It also includes a number of sub-issues, one of which has to do with the initiation of co-operation projects with suppliers controlling important resources, and another involves the monitoring of the ongoing work. The third main responsibility of purchasing is related to developing relationships in order to make better use of the available resources. The fourth is to reduce involvement in certain relationships in order to free the company of some of the existing resource ties to make new relationships possible. Furthermore, there are specific issues related to how to utilize technical versus human resources.

Thus, a large number of important supply issues are closely related to the resource dimension and how resources may be combined. The next sections illustrate two important aspects of resource combining.

The Co-operative Dimension of Resource Handling

One important building block for the analysis of the resource structure is the notion that resources are always used in combinations. The products/services delivered from one supplier are generally used in combination with deliveries from other suppliers. Therefore every component must fit with other components. Raw materials and processed materials have to work together—and also work in relation to the production operations in the buying company. All kinds of equipment must function in relation to other equipment and to input products. The supplier is another resource that has to fit in with other suppliers and with the buying firm. For example, matching is required in terms of precise deliveries or in terms of competence and knowledge. Always, when resources are used in combination there are a number of interfaces with other resources that have to be taken into account. This is a complex task for those being responsible for the supply side of a company. In this section, we try to give a first overview of this issue but we return to the same problem elsewhere as well.

The basic question is how to get the most out of any single resource element: be it a person, product, facility, business unit or business relationship. We argued above that every resource element is used in combination with other resources, there are interfaces between them. In Figure 5.2 we provide one example of the complexity that may prevail in these interfaces. The figure illustrates the components constituting and relating to the instrument panel of a car. The development and the manufacturing of such a system require a number of interfaces to function. Firstly, all components and systems have to fit together from a physical point of view. Some need to be located in close proximity to each other, and at some stage in the production process the components and systems are assembled into a complete car. Together, the components of the instrument panel constitute an important part of the visible car—from the driver's point of view. Secondly, they have to fit together from a functional point of view. For example, a number of these components and systems together form the electric system of the car. Thirdly, they have to fit together from a technical point of view. Different parts of the total system have to be connected to other parts of the car and each part has to function without disturbing the function of the others. Fourthly, each part must be designed so that it can be efficiently manufactured. Fifthly, the components and systems have to be designed so they are easy to assemble and transport. And there is more to add regarding deliveries, packaging, spare parts, service, and so on.

Thus far, we have mainly discussed the technical side of this complex issue. It is also necessary that the business units producing the different components and sub-systems fit together, that the people involved function together, and that the competence and knowledge of the companies engaged in designing and producing all these products fit together. There are so many interfaces involved that we can conclude even at this stage that they can never be designed in an optimal way. There will always be reasons to develop some of them in new directions. Furthermore, as soon as some interfaces are changed there will be effects on the others. Thus, one first important conclusion is that purchasing always has a large number of such interfaces to handle. These interfaces can be developed and the development potential is huge. We return to this issue and to the example in Chapter 10.

Handling this complexity has become increasingly important owing to the ongoing changes of activity structures in industry. As illustrated in Chapter 4, increasing reliance on outsourcing causes substantial interdependencies among activities conducted by different firms. Companies have tried to solve this problem by relying on modular design and product platforms (Baldwin and Clark 1997, Robertson and Ulrich 1998). Von Hippel (1990) discusses different forms of task partitioning for subdivision of a whole into its parts (the modules). The main

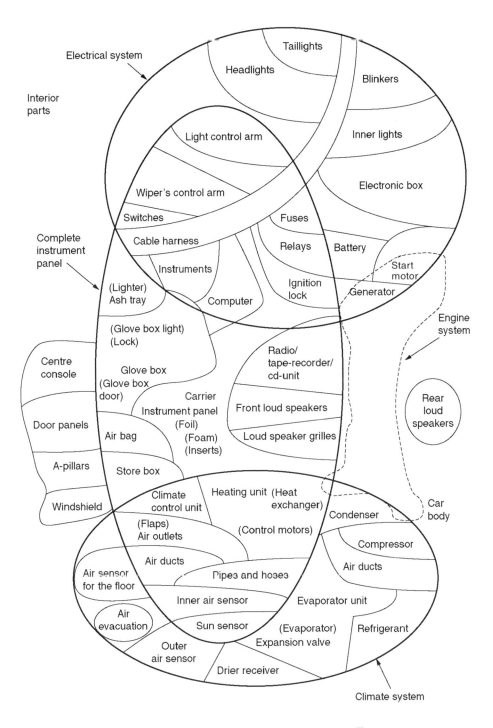

FIGURE 5.2   The interfaces of an instrument panel. Source: Jellbo 1998, p. 55.

problem identified in this process is that the most appropriate partitioning for efficient manufacturing differs from the most effective partitioning for innovation.

Given this extremely complex picture of the totality, we need to focus our analysis. We do so by regarding suppliers as resource elements in the total supply structure of the buying company. The first issue that has to be addressed is how the suppliers as resource elements fit with the company's internal resources. There are two aspects of this issue. One has to do with the composition of the internal resources and how it should develop. The other is about what kind of external resources exist. Suppliers have to be selected and approached in relation to both these aspects. They have to be chosen in relation to all the external resources, but they also have to fit with what the company wants to have internally for the future. A number of dimensions are required both to describe what resources are needed by the company and what is available in terms of external resources. This issue is clearly a highly strategic one and has to be discussed in all parts of the buying company. Furthermore, the relevant dimensions change over time and it is necessary for them to be continuously evaluated and developed.

The second issue relates to the division of labour among the parties and the design of the production facilities within the company in relation to the complementary facilities of the suppliers. It is important for the supply side to map and characterize the most important streams of input from suppliers and the ways in which this input is used within the company. The facilities have to be mapped in terms of investments, scale effects and technical design. Closely related to this mapping are descriptions of the flows between the facilities. These flows, in turn, are contingent on the way facilities function. For example, just-in-time deliveries may be difficult to establish without flexible manufacturing equipment. The design of the facilities is clearly an issue where the production department is responsible internally but the importance of the external connections make it necessary that also those responsible for suppliers should be deeply involved. We return to this problem when discussing the development cases in the next two sections.

The third main issue has to do with products and services. In the same way as with production processes, it is necessary to have a complete mapping of all products and services used and produced within the company. This task has to be handled in co-operation with R&D and marketing staff. The most important interfaces must be identified and assessed in terms of potential development opportunities. The matching of products and services will also be illustrated in the two cases.

The fourth issue for the purchasing function is concerned with relationships with other firms. Different relationships have to be matched and fitted together. Purchasing is in a good position to handle single supplier relationships—and, to some extent, constellations of suppliers. However, when it comes to matching suppliers with customers—or relationships to competitors and other horizontal counterparts—other departments of the buying company need to be involved.

All four types of resources discussed can always be changed in order to make them fit better together. This is done through adapting the respective resource elements to each other. Adaptations can be made between resource elements of the same type such as among production facilities. They can also take the form of adaptations between resource elements of different types, for example between a

	Products	Production facilities	Business units	Business relationships
Products	New product development			
Production facilities	Design for manufacturability	Process development		
Business units	Developing brands	Specialization of facilities	Identity development	
Business relationships	Customized products	Supply chain arrangements	Connecting relationships	Networking

FIGURE 5.3 Adaptations among resource elements.

production facility and products. Some examples of adaptations are illustrated in Figure 5.3.

Confrontation of Resource Elements

Resources are always combined and the question of how they are combined is of utmost importance for what can be accomplished. Resources are heterogeneous, i.e. the value of a specific resource element depends on the other resources with which it is combined (Alchian and Demsetz 1972). This is a similar situation to that of individual players on a soccer team. Different types of players are required to make a team, and in the same way there is a need for different resources to create something useful from a commercial point of view. There is also another similarity. A soccer team consists of 11 players but if they are 11 individualists it will not be a good team. A large part of the training is directed towards creating team-effects, i.e. that the aggregation of the 11 should be more than the sum of the individual players. Through training it is possible to help them to get more out of each other. It is the same with the resources of firms. For example, Lundvall (1988) points to the substantial gains for innovation when 'team-effects' can be created. Above, we have discussed one of the reasons—the co-operative element. Training corresponds to co-operative efforts to increase the fit between resource elements. This matching improves conditions for resource utilization. However, there is an important restriction to consider. The training should not deprive each player of his specific and unique features. It is the same with all types of resources. If the resources are adapted too much they may lose value. They can become so integrated that they are regarded as more or less one single resource element. The co-operative short-term effect of this integration is normally very high. However, there is also a negative long-term effect—the development dimension may suffer.

The development of individual resource elements is determined by the total development efforts. If some resource elements are too strongly integrated, the development efforts will be directed to only a few dimensions. All other dimensions will be more or less neglected, despite the fact that the main potential for development may be in one of these dimensions. Keeping some of the uniqueness of individual resource elements enhances the opportunities for development. Our conclusion is that it is important to stimulate confrontation among resource elements. In the absence of confrontation it is likely that the buying company will lose its ability and capacity to innovate.

Thus, it is crucial to start from the assumption that suppliers and relationships with suppliers and with others will always have an important ingredient of conflict. The existing resource structure must constantly be challenged and questioned from several directions. The buying company must challenge its suppliers. In the same way, suppliers should be challenging the buying company and so should customers and horizontal units. The need for this confrontation is attributable to the existence of heterogeneity among resources. By combining resources in new ways it is always possible to create new effects. This explains why so much technical development takes place on the borderline between different disciplines. Encouraging confrontation is one way to promote these effects. However, there is also an important restriction on this confrontation. It is vital that it remains constructive. This means that it must be formulated in ambitions to reach targets that might be mutually contradictory. It also means that some of these confrontations will have to be faced within the organization. One way of accomplishing this is to run projects that compete for resource utilization.

Developments in Buyer–seller Relationships—a US-Japanese Case Study

We now present two cases to illustrate the importance of suppliers in technical development and the way co-operation among companies may be organized. The first case is taken from a study by one of our colleagues—Laage-Hellman (1997). In his book dealing with business networks in Japan, he makes a thorough analysis of two cases of joint supplier-customer product development. The first is the co-operation between Nippon Steel and Toyota for development of a two-layered Zn-Fe electroplated steel sheet. The second, which we examine here—is about the development and commercialization of structural fine ceramics. In this case, there is close co-operation between Toshiba, the Japanese producer of the ceramics and Cummins, the American manufacturer of diesel engines.

Cummins' Early Interest in a Ceramic Diesel Engine

Between 1974 and 1984, Cummins' basic idea was to use the excellent insulating and high-temperature strength properties of ceramics to make a diesel engine without a cooling system. The project was driven by one enthusiastic researcher—Dr Kamo—who managed to get external funding for the project. One crucial problem was to develop a ceramic material that was of good enough quality. During this period there were high expectations concerning future applications of ceramics—almost a ceramic fever. Dr Kamo contacted all potential producers, including those in Japan. One Japanese supplier—Kyocera—had established a branch in San Diego and this company showed a keen interest. The initial contacts were followed by deliveries of some test pieces. However, the relationship between Cummins and Kyocera did not develop further. The material showed some weaknesses and at the same time Kyocera started its own project with the aim of developing a diesel engine. Cummins redirected their attention to Toshiba. Dr Kamo was impressed by Toshiba's competence and concluded that this was the most progressive company and that it seemed to have the best material in its hot-pressed silicon nitride. From 1977, Toshiba became a supplier of several engine components that were tested by Cummins. Thus, during this period Cummins, and especially Dr Kamo, managed to build up a huge international contact network focused on the combination of ceramics and engines.

In the early 1980s, some major changes took place. One was that it became clear to Cummins that substantial gains in energy efficiency could be made by improving the design of the conventional engine. The same was true for the cooling system. However, at the same time, it was discovered that fine ceramics could be used in other applications than insulation. One important characteristic of the material is its wear resistance, which was considered worth exploring. In this process, Cummins realized that they did not have the competence they needed to develop the solution. At the same time Dr Kamo left Cummins and started his own business.

Development Programme for Wear-resistant Components and the Search for a Partner

In the light of these changes Cummins initiated three different R&D programmes. Our case is one of them. A first step in the process was to make a thorough survey of all the potential materials and suppliers. The survey involved studies of the literature, patent research, and a large number of interviews. All potential suppliers in the world, several government laboratories, and other experts were visited and interviewed. The result of these efforts was that silicon nitride was selected as the most promising material, and the patent search showed that Toshiba had by far the best patent position in regard to this material. But there were certainly other choices on the list of potential partners: five Japanese, three European and several American. The next step was to contact the firms on the list to see whether they were interested in co-operation and how well they would fit with Cummins. Cummins had at this point not decided what type of relationship they wanted. All sorts of responses were received from the suppliers. Some were willing to supply components but were not at all interested in becoming involved in development work. Others had specific requirements in terms of volumes and capacities, etc. After sorting out those who were lacking capabilities and those who were not interested in close co-operation five companies remained—three from Japan and two from the US.

The selected companies were revisited and discussions held, mainly at senior management level. These meetings indicated a good fit between Cummins and Toshiba. The companies seemed to have people with the same type of personalities, similar ways of working with people and commonality in business objectives. After a number of meetings in the autumn of 1984 Cummins decided on Toshiba as partner for this programme. Kyocera was one of the alternative suppliers but the Cummins management had problems in reaching an understanding with this company at that time.

The Co-operation Between Toshiba and Cummins

The negotiations between the companies were extensive and perceived as difficult by both sides. There were language problems as well as other difficulties. One problem was to decide to what extent the agreement should be exclusive. When the agreement was signed in November 1984 it was non-exclusive, which made it possible for both Toshiba and Cummins to work with other partners as well. However, both parties clearly declared that the intention was to focus on the joint relationship. The first agreement was for three years, mainly owing to the fact that Cummins was working with a three-year planning horizon. In the discussions, both parties had indicated that they believed that five–six years was a more realistic time period for this type of combined effort.

A joint project team was put together. The core group consisted of three to four full-time people from Cummins and eight to nine part-time people from Toshiba. Their work had already began before the formal agreement. The procedure was to jointly decide which components to develop. The wear resistance of the components was tested on both sides and the joint project team evaluated the results. The selection of components was based on several considerations. One important factor in this analysis was the development costs in relation to expected revenues. This led the project team to decide to go for the simplest components in order to minimize the technical problems. Choosing simple components made both the design of the components and the manufacturing process easier. Cummins concentrated on the design aspects and Toshiba on the manufacturing. The two companies felt that they were breaking new ground together. There was a lot of uncertainty about what would happen in the engine. For example, how would the interaction between ceramic-on-metal or ceramic-on-ceramic work out? How could ceramic and metal be attached? There was a whole series of questions that had to be answered. If there were no answers to these questions there would be no business!

Adequate responses to the questions above required a great deal of testing. One problem for the team was that they were unable to test the components in working engines. The Material Engineering Department on Cummins side participated in the project as a service function. When they approached the Engine Development Group of Cummins this function was not at all interested. Therefore, the Material Department had to acquire its own test cell and some engines. From late 1986, these engines were equipped with ceramic components and they worked surprisingly well. The most crucial issue was then to develop an appropriate engine design.

In 1987, the team had achieved favourable performance data but still had no customer. At this time, Cummins experienced some serious engine component wear problems, which required redesign of several components. One component with particular wear problems were the 'long links' in the mechanical fuel injector. These links are critical to the function of the engine. The problems with the long links created a window of opportunity. Cummins decided to make a first test on

50–60 engines. The end-users of the engines were all informed about the test and given some extra support. However, Cummins quickly lost track of which engines had been equipped with ceramic links but, fortunately, none of them failed. Two more field studies were carried out with the same good results and now some customers became aware of this solution and started to demand it. Now the Engine Development Group could no longer go on resisting ceramics, and in 1989 the ceramic links were launched on the market. This was done gradually and it took about one year until all engines with mechanical fuel injection were equipped with ceramic links.

In 1989, the joint development effort was perceived as so successful that a decision was made to form Engineering Ceramic Technologies Inc. (Enceratec). This is a joint venture between Toshiba and Cummins located in the US, and its main task is to market ceramic components domestically. There were two reasons underlying the establishment of Enceratec. Firstly, both Toshiba and Cummins felt that they had developed a unique competence together. Secondly, Toshiba had idle capacity in its production plant and thus an interest in bringing in new customers. Cummins was also interested in this because it might reduce the production costs of the components they purchased. The potential customers were, among others, Cummins' main competitors.

Comments From a Purchasing Point of View

Below, we summarize some of the most important findings indicated by the case study, which are also representative of many similar situations.

The case study demonstrates how important a single person can be for the development of a relationship, thus indicating the significance of what every single person can do in relation to establishing external relationships. Furthermore, this person—like Dr Kamo—is often not a purchaser by profession. Still, he or she must be incorporated in the discussions concerning potential partners and how relationships to key suppliers should be developed.

The Toshiba-Cummins case study illustrates very well the complex relationship between evaluation and selection. Many aspects have to be considered in an evaluation process and these aspects also change over time. Close relationships often evolve gradually, as is also apparent in this case. It is important to evaluate the different options and alternatives existing or appearing in this development process. In general, it seems to be more important to evaluate than to select. Real opportunities to select are quite rare while there is a more or less continuous need for evaluation. In this particular case, there was only one period when there was a real selection—and the decision was certainly important. However, after this selection there is a continuous need for further evaluation despite the fact that there is no active selection being made. The fact that the companies continue their co-operation is a sign of a decision that it is worthwhile to continue the process, and in this sense there is a 'selection'.

The importance of continuous evaluation is closely connected to the need for redirection of the process, as is clearly illustrated in the case study. All development processes involve learning and only seldom can a project follow the precise path that was planned from the start. The same is true of the choice of a co-operation partner. There may be good reasons to exclude certain potential partners at the beginning of a project. However, later the same partner may be a most appropriate candidate for co-operation.

The case study also illustrates the importance of being systematic and careful in negotiations. As stated earlier, the reason is not to solve all problems, which is always impossible, but to learn the way the counterpart thinks and works. Negotiation should not stop when two parties reach an agreement, as unforeseen events may occur after the agreement is reached. All close relationships include a continuous negotiation and evaluation process even if it may be concealed as part of the problem-solving process.

The co-operation project of Toshiba and Cummins exemplifies the importance of organizing the relationship. There are several important aspects associated with organizing relationships. One is about organizing the activities performed within the relationship. In this respect the case study seems to have worked very efficiently. What is going on between two units in two different companies must take other units and their relationships into consideration. This appeared more problematic—especially on the Cummins side. Several problems were associated with involving the internal user of the developed components. Probably, this was due to limited experience of systematically working together with others and the need to anchor the process in a broader internal environment.

Finally, the case study shows that a well functioning buyer–supplier relationship can lead to the establishment of a new business. Relationships provide possibilities to find new business opportunities in the interface between what the company and its counterparts are doing. The interface provides opportunities to find new technical solutions while the network connections (relationships to other companies) provide the business opportunities.

Developments in Buyer–seller Relationships—a European Case Study

This case study deals with IKEA—the world's largest furniture retailer. By the end of the 1980s, IKEA was becoming interested in environmental issues, owing to its major consumption of paper. Every year, IKEA prints 100 million copies of its catalogue, which makes the company a very large paper consumer. One issue of particular concern was whether a more environment friendly paper quality could be developed. The paper used was an LWC (light white coated) quality based on primary fibre and chlorate bleached pulp. Both the use of primary fibre and the chlorate bleaching were perceived as problematic from an environmental point of view. The case is described in detail in Håkansson and Waluszewski (1997).

The Problem

IKEA was eager to find a satisfactory solution before the environmental issues escalated to an image problem for the company. Therefore, IKEA formulated a goal of having the catalogue printed on paper free from any chlorate and with at least 10% recycled fibres. In spite of these changes, the catalogue should still have an attractive appearance. IKEA turned to its suppliers with this request. The existing suppliers could not comply with this demand. The main supplier—the German company Haindl—replied that it was not possible to deliver such paper in the quantities IKEA required.

However, IKEA had not made these requirements without good reasons—on the contrary, they were based on qualified knowledge. IKEA had been in contact with a number of companies and organizations—among them Greenpeace. Greenpeace was at the same time highly involved in its 'Paper and pulp campaign' where more than 15 persons world-wide tried to map the ongoing technical development in the forestry industry. Through these contacts IKEA gained an extensive knowledge of all the existing possibilities. For example, Greenpeace printed 'Das Plagiat', which was an exact copy of Der Spiegel, on a totally chlorate-free paper based on pulp from the Swedish producer Aspa.

The lack of interest and negative attitudes shown by the existing suppliers made IKEA's management angry. They considered the paper industry conservative and too narrow in its view of customers. According to IKEA, the paper suppliers perceived the printing companies as their customers. These companies were also regarded as the most important users. Therefore, quality aspects like runability, printability and brightness were assumed to be the most important properties of the paper. IKEA, on the other hand, perceived the readers of the catalogue as the users of the paper and the important issue was thus their quality requirements. IKEA doubted that the readers shared the quality preferences of the printers—instead, they were probably concerned with quite different features, for example that the production and use of the paper should be associated with minimum negative environmental consequences. IKEA perceived the reactions and responses from existing suppliers to be inadequate and chose to break their relationships with the established vendors. Then followed more than six months of complex negotiations before the company managed to find some suppliers who were prepared to try satisfying the new demands. One Italian supplier—Burgo—and three Finnish producers, were most open to trying. The most important actors in the network involved in this development process are shown in Figure 5.4.

The Development of the New Paper Quality

Without the broad contact network and the knowledge and experience gained in earlier studies of the forestry industry IKEA would have had severe problems in reaching their objectives. One of these contacts was with the German equipment producer Sulcher Escher Wyss. This company is one of the leaders in the area of removing colours from secondary fibres. Another important relationship was with Eka Nobel, one of the major players in bleaching chemicals. A third contact was with Södra Cell—one of the pioneers in producing totally chlorate-free pulp that was bright enough to be used for top quality printing.

These three contacts served as an important basis for the discussions with the paper producers because they provided IKEA with technical arguments supporting their claims. IKEA also tried to make use of their close contacts with five of the six

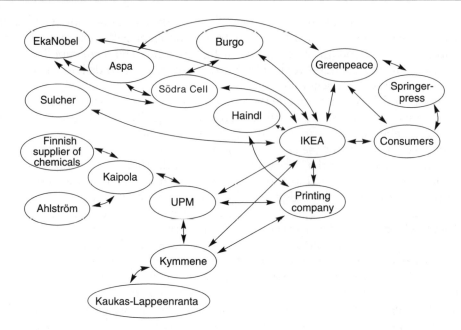

FIGURE 5.4   Important actors in the IKEA case.

largest offset-printing companies in Europe. IKEA argued that if one producer succeeded in developing a 'green' LWC-paper—defined as totally chlorate-free and with at least 10% recycled fibres—IKEA would be of help in launching this quality of paper because all the largest printing companies would become involved to some extent.

Two Finnish producers, UPM and Kymmene, realized the opportunities created by the new requirements. IKEA's demands were in line with a development towards more high-quality papers that these companies had been involved in since the late 1970s. The Finnish companies had been IKEA suppliers, i.e. to the printers of the catalogue in the late 1980s. Finnpap—the jointly owned marketing organization of the Finnish companies—was also positive. Their attitude was that 'if IKEA needed LWC-paper with this content they would also get it'. Of course, the fact that the companies had already made technical attempts in the same direction strongly contributed to their favourable attitudes. For example, Kaipola—one of the UPM mills—had invested in equipment for washing of secondary fibres in 1989. The main difficulties with using secondary fibres in the production of LWC-paper are that the remaining elements of 'impurities' might cause production problems, especially in relation to the surface of the paper. Another negative effect is low brightness.

In order to be able to use secondary fibres the problems with discolouring had to be solved and all 'sticks' in the pulp had to be eliminated. The sticks could both create holes in the paper and cause breakdowns in the production process. For these reasons, the secondary fibre to be used had to go through a cleaning procedure that was so extensive that the yield was only 75–80% compared with 90% when the same pulp is used for normal newspaper. Despite these exertions and cleaning efforts, Kaipola had considerable problems to solve in the manufacturing of the paper. However, in the end the new quality showed no differences in comparison with the paper that had been produced from primary fibres. The problems thus resided in the production process.

When it came to the other quality dimension—the requirement for chlorate-free paper—Kaipola could benefit from the technical development their supplier of kraft-pulp had been through. This supplier had satisfied the requirement of chlorate-free pulp early because it supplied producers of hygiene paper. The company was also highly aware of the demands for 'green' products—especially in Germany. In 1990, they started a development project together with their Finnish supplier of bleaching materials to develop a chlorate-free pulp. In September 1991, they invested in a new plant where oxygen, peroxide and enzymes were used in the bleaching stage. The pulp did not reach full brightness but was bright enough for producers of paper to be used in printing of magazines. The strength of the paper was similar to that of chlorate-bleached paper but there was a tendency for the pulp to yellow over time. During 1992, another step was taken, when the company introduced ozone bleaching together with the equipment producer Ahlstrom and some research organizations, both in Finland and abroad. In November 1993, the company was able to deliver pulp that reached full brightness and that was totally chlorate-free. For the pulp-customer, Kaipola, the first years with the new pulp were not without problems. However, by adapting the paper machine and successively training their personnel the company finally managed to reach the same quality as the chlorate-bleached alternatives.

Even the other Finnish supplier—Kymmene—was able to benefit from opportunities residing in the existing resource structure. In its Kaukas-Lappeenranta mill the company had already produced chlorate-free pulp, but the secondary fibre based pulp had to be bought from an external source. Chlorate-free production had been established in 1991 and was based on the use of oxygen. Thus, for Kymmene, IKEA was not the first customer since some German magazine producers had already bought this type of pulp. However, it was far from an established product at that time.

Comments From a Purchasing Point of View

There are a number of conclusions to be drawn from this case study. The buying company, IKEA, is a very important change agent in this development process. The company decided to try to comply with the new demands being made by some customers and environmental groups. In this way, IKEA both directed the development in a specific way and speeded up the process. One reason IKEA could play this main role is that it is a major buyer of paper. Companies that were not yet IKEA suppliers realized the opportunities in exploiting the new situation. But IKEA would not have been able to make its claims without the broad contacts and knowledge they had developed through previous networking. These processes provided IKEA with both the motivation and the arguments needed. Major change processes are normally met with resistance and are often counteracted. In many cases there are fairly good reasons to try to resist change. Recombining resources is a cumbersome process, disturbing efficiency in day-to-day operations. Therefore, a strong and powerful agent for change is required.

Another conclusion is that even within such a mature area as the paper industry there are important differences between the experiences of suppliers and their potential capacities and capabilities. This variation is explained by the various learning processes the companies have been through. During the development process IKEA realized that the resources of some suppliers fit better with IKEA's than those of other suppliers. It is also obvious that the development patterns in some supplier companies were more in line with the pattern of IKEA than others.

Furthermore, the differences between the suppliers' capabilities are closely related to their sub-suppliers. In this case, it is the ability and competence of suppliers of bleaching chemicals and equipment that was most significant. Thus, when investigating and evaluating potential suppliers it is crucial also to include their relationships and how these are, or could be, used. From the buying company's point of view the case illustrates how much there is to know both about individual suppliers, and about the whole supplier structure in a certain sector.

Finally, the development process described indicates that it is always a question of both co-operation and confrontation among resource elements. Companies have to co-operate to be able to take advantage of the potential complementarities. They also have to handle the conflicts arising from the confrontation of the various resource dimensions. Resources may be recombined in many different dimensions—some of which are not easily compatible.

The Role of Information Exchange in Resource Handling

The two cases illuminate the crucial role of information exchange in combining and recombining of resources, thus changing the configuration of resource structures. Combining external and internal resources in novel ways as well as stimulating co-operation and confrontation among resource elements requires knowledge about the resources. The outcome of recombining, in turn, increases the available body of knowledge.

Looking back at the two cases it is clear how important the exchange of detailed technical information can be for the development processes. In the Toshiba-Cummins case study this exchange primarily concerned the buyer and the seller. In the IKEA case study the communication between the suppliers and their sub-suppliers was a prerequisite for the successful outcome. It is the same with other types of information, for example estimations of costs. Buyer and supplier need to jointly consider the life cycle costs of the solutions that are developed in co-operation. Such estimates require considerable amounts of information to be exchanged. The more such data can be made available the easier it will be for a buying and a selling firm to find better ways to allocate investments in production facilities.

This is clearly an area where developments in information technology have an impact. One major breakthrough has already appeared in terms of new ways to design, present and assess technical specifications through the use of multi-dimensional electronic and virtual tools. These new tools improve the conditions for exchange of detailed technical information. In this way, a great deal of data and information regarding resources can be exchanged more effectively now than in the past. The technical opportunities for exchange of information will increase even further so the main limitation will probably be concerned with making use of this information. The main question is when and how more detailed information can and should be used.

However, as discussed in Chapter 3, the main advantages related to electronic exchange of information are related to 'standardized' communication, which explains why the main role of IT to date has been to improve co-ordination in activity structures. When it comes to information exchange for recombining the resource structure, the situation is different. For example, Nonaka (1991) emphasizes the need for redundant information as a means to increase creativity in innovation. Although IT can contribute to redundancy through its capacity as mass information provider, transmitting information also requires structuring which, to some extent, destroys redundancy. Therefore, the creative dimensions of resource handling have mainly to be based on person-to-person exchange of information.

One tendency which is expected to be further re-enforced is that large buyers demand more transparency concerning technical details and cost estimates for production operations and handling of different products. This is particularly true for components and processed materials. By getting a more detailed picture in this respect the buying companies may increase their ability to identify important cost and revenue drivers and also to find economically efficient solutions. These changes provide purchasing with new opportunities. More information of this type increases the potential for sophisticated analysis of outsourcing and in-sourcing decisions, as well as for developing more efficient supplier relationships.

In Chapter 4 we showed how the development of information technology makes it possible to link the manufacturing, planning, and logistics activities of different actors. These linkages tend to be accompanied by long-term and close relationships. However, the major potential of close relationships probably resides in technical development. In particular substantial gains may be made when it is possible to involve suppliers' suppliers and suppliers of other products in the development projects. In these situations, information technology will be of help in designing development networks where resources can be systematically combined in a much more extensive way than is possible today.

This systematic combining of information covers internal and external resources and it involves co-operation and confrontation. Purchasing has an important role to play both in short-term combining efforts and in long-term recombining.

Dynamic Resource Structures

This chapter deals with the importance of the resources controlled by the suppliers in relation to the buying company's total resource base. Our message is simple: everything that can be done should be done to take advantage of these external resources. We dare to claim that even if the company has already done a lot—and this is true for few companies—there are always a large number of opportunities for further developing the utilization of these resources. As our case studies demonstrated, a supplier can be an important resource for a buying company in many different ways.

Firstly, a supplier may have important production resources that are complementary to the buying company's own production facilities. There are always ample opportunities to develop this complementarity further through internal adaptations or through influencing suppliers to change.

Secondly, the supplier may have knowledge and/or competence of vital importance for the buying company. In this chapter, we illustrate how this knowledge can be activated. Again, buying firms are only beginning to take advantage of this potential.

Finally, the supplier may have relationships to counterparts who can also be important resource providers for the buying company. Every business unit has relationships that might be useful for others. Thus, there are good reasons for purchasing to be aware of the possibility of making use of these indirect relationships and resources that can be accessed via a supplier.

In this way, a supplier can be seen as a complex resource collection where several of the resources may be of interest to the buying company. If we take all the suppliers together the purchasing function is responsible for a very large resource constellation. This is also a very complex resource constellation. In particular, two factors cause this complexity. The first is that the resources often are scattered over a large geographical area. Most companies have suppliers in a number of different countries. The second factor is the large variety of resources that can be of interest to one buyer. Both these dimensions must be considered in relation to the total resource structure. There are good reasons to find ways to systematically exploit this variety both in relation to geography and resource type. Some companies have established purchasing offices in different countries to make use of the geographical dimension. When it comes to the resource type dimension, various strategies may be applied. The resources can be categorized in many ways, for example in terms of technology or in terms of provider. It is useful to try some form of classification because it serves as a basis for specialization and organizing of the resource handling activities. There is huge variation in how companies deal with this issue. One popular way to specialize was presented in Chapter 3: to make use of key account managers. Such persons—or units—are made responsible for a specific supplier. This means that they can develop considerable knowledge regarding this co-operative unit and they can learn to take extensive advantage of the supplier's resources. Another form of specialization is based on type of product. In this case individual purchasers focus on raw materials, different components, and so on. The variation in behaviour indicates that there is not one single dimension that is more appropriate than others for covering and exploiting the total resource constellation.

In the heading of this section we used the word 'dynamic'. This is clearly a key factor that has followed us through the chapter in several ways. Dynamics is about changes and change certainly is a key word for purchasing. Purchasing represents an interface between the internal and external resources that are used by a company. Therefore, purchasing must closely follow and affect what is going on inside the buying company and also monitor and evaluate the resources developed and controlled by individual suppliers. Furthermore, purchasing has to be observant with regard to the main development patterns within the total supplier resource constellation in which these companies are directly involved, and to trace changes in related areas or in areas that may become important in the future. But, most importantly, following and evaluating change is highly relevant to the way resources are handled. It is possible for an individual company to influence the development of the total resource constellation. Actions can be directed to affecting the resources and capabilities of specific counterparts. The most important dimension is probably combining the resources with those of other firms. In this process, the buying companies are vital also to the development of the whole resource constellation. The more companies try to affect the surrounding network the more they will be able to impact on the total resource constellation. These issues are dealt with in Chapters 7–9 where we analyse supply network strategies.

Analysing Resource Structures

The starting point of this chapter is that resources have to be inter-related. We began by pointing out that resources can be combined in a number of ways and that it is crucial to find better means of combining them. There are always reasons to confront resources with each other. This is by no means simple, either at the level of suppliers or at the level of single products or services. It is difficult to get top management involved in these issues. They who must be prepared to invest enough to make use of these resources. This problem is related to the lack of strategic orientation of the purchasing function in most companies. There are seldom long-range ambitions to develop the external resource base or to increase its utilization. The objectives on the supply side tend to be formulated in terms of cost reduction. This is seldom the right way to approach the problem, although lower costs might be an important effect.

One of the major advantages of formulating the supply issues in resource terms is that they immediately become strategic. There are clear reasons for any company to be active in planning its future external resource structure. What should characterize this structure in ten years and what is the most important aspect to begin working on? With such a question as a starting point it is easier to get the involvement from top management, as the issue is so obviously a strategic one.

Finally, the most important questions to involve in an analysis of the resource structure are the following:

- What are the critical resource elements in the various resource dimensions?
- How are these critical resources distributed among the actors and how are they inter-related?
- Should the company insource some of the resources controlled by other firms?
- What co-operative projects are ongoing with suppliers who control critical resources?
- How can the relationships with the most important suppliers be developed in terms of mutual adaptations in technical development?

Chapter 6

PURCHASING AND THE ACTOR STRUCTURE

Chapters 4 and 5 dealt with the activity and the resource dimensions of the network. The ways in which activities are co-ordinated and resources are combined have a profound impact on network efficiency and effectiveness. We have illustrated the types of improvements that may be obtained from increasing co-ordinating and combining efforts. However, activities and resources are not co-ordinated and combined spontaneously. The benefits obtained required major modifications in the actor structure. The most significant change is the development of closer buyer–seller relationships, as illustrated in the first chapters of the book.

In the foregoing chapters we reported on actual changes of resource combinations and activity co-ordination and mainly focused on the outcome of successful interventions. However, as was evident from some of the illustrations these changes required a number of other actors to change as well. Neither SweFork nor IKEA would have been able to succeed without their suppliers. Any change in the co-ordination of activities and combining of resources calls for mobilization of other companies. Therefore, in re-organization of the network structure it is necessary for the change agent to be able to persuade other actors. In many cases a buying company must influence other firms than the direct supplier to attain desired objectives. As discussed in Chapter 4, the indirect interdependencies in relation to sub-suppliers, customers, customers' customers, etc., can represent either obstacles or opportunities for the buying firm. Furthermore, any change in the activity and resource dimensions affects the relationships among the actors. Therefore, activity co-ordination and resource combining rely on interaction among the actors involved. The closer the complementarity among activities, the more interaction is required. Furthermore, substantial interaction is needed to identify opportunities for enhancing similarities, and thus the potential for economies of scale. In the same way access to, and efficient utilization of, the resources of other firms, call for extensive interaction.

Interaction involves individuals. However, an individual is a representative not only of him/herself. The individual also represents the company in a specific function. Therefore, it is relevant to consider interaction among company functions in the buying firm, for example between purchasing and manufacturing. To a certain extent this interaction is conditioned by the people occupying the positions in the department. But if these individuals leave the companies they are to be replaced and new representatives continue the inter-departmental interaction. This means that some elements of the interaction are determined by the positions of the individuals. Similarly, it becomes meaningful to consider interactions between functions in different firms, such as between purchasing in one company and marketing or design in another. In some situations it is even relevant to analyse interaction on the corporate level.

Intervention Through Interaction

Traditionally, purchasing tended to be reactive rather than proactive. Adversarial types of relationships made it difficult to affect suppliers in other ways than playing them off against each other in terms of price. The main concern of purchasing was to identify and analyse the strengths and weaknesses of different suppliers. No particular efforts were devoted to affecting suppliers so they developed in a certain direction. On the contrary, such adaptations would introduce interdependencies, which, in turn, were considered signs of inefficiencies because they restricted the freedom to act. However, over the last few decades this type of behaviour has been increasingly questioned and reconsidered. On the selling side companies have always made enormous efforts to encourage customers to develop in desired directions. Today, this is increasingly taking place in purchasing as well. We have shown how a buying company can improve its operations by combining resources with others and co-ordinating activities. These efforts may take the form of unidirectional adaptations to suppliers but in many cases even greater benefits may be obtained if the buyer can persuade the vendor to adapt to the customer's specific situation—or through mutual adaptations. The SweFork case showed that even a small company may be able to influence its situation considerably.

Interventions require lots of interaction because mobilizing other actors is a cumbersome task. One reason is that the supplier must be convinced to direct the attention to the specific needs of the buyer. The supplier must find it worthwhile to invest the time, money and resources necessary for more thorough interaction. But this is only one side of the coin. The supplier must also redirect some attention away from other customers, because the supplier's resources for interaction are limited. Again, the supplier can be expected to have an interest in doing so if the benefits from increasing interaction with a certain counterpart are more substantial than the sacrifices. In both cases it is not only the attractiveness of the customer that counts. In many cases the customer's connections to other firms can be important for a supplier when deciding to which customers to give priority. The opportunities for mobilization of suppliers are thus affected by the customer's position in the surrounding network. We use 'identity' as a label of this position. In a similar way, we can argue that a customer will evaluate suppliers in terms of the identity they occupy in the network. In the next section we analyse how the identity of a company affects its opportunities to intervene.

A proper match between the identities of the two parties is a first prerequisite for interaction aiming at resource combining and activity co-ordination. However, an 'ideal' match between identities is a necessary, but not a sufficient, precondition. The outcome of the attempts at interaction is largely determined by the atmosphere in which the interaction takes place. Critical aspects in this respect are the trust developed between the parties, how committed they feel to each other, etc. In the third section, we bring up some of the important ingredients in the atmosphere that impacts on the conditions for interaction.

The attempts on the part of purchasing to influence require interaction with people in other functions in the company and people in other companies. Therefore, interaction can be facilitated, or hindered, by the organizational arrangements adopted. The organizational structure of a company will affect the interaction among people in the buying company. For example, interaction between a purchaser and a designer is to a certain extent, contingent on the way the company is organized. This issue is discussed in the fourth section. In the same way the organizational structure sets the conditions for interaction with suppliers, as described in the fifth section. Two final sections conclude the chapter. The first deals with central issues in organizing networks, while the second summarizes the main steps in an actor analysis of the network.

In Figure 6.1 we have summarized the most important factors impacting on the opportunities for intervention through interaction. What actually can be achieved in a buyer–seller relationship depends to a large extent on the extent of involvement between the two parties. Chapter 8 on the development of supplier relationships is devoted to this discussion.

The Role of Identity in the Actor Structure

The identity of a company has a profound impact on its opportunities to act in the network (Håkansson and Snehota 1995). Any firm's identity is multifaceted and involves a huge number of dimensions. Some of the attributes forming the identity are internal, while others stem from the relationships to other actors. For example: 'being seen as a "close friend" to a company known as advanced or powerful helps in other relationships' (ibid., p. 32). The identity of a company is affected by the surrounding network. The identity of a company reflects two things of importance for interaction with other actors. Firstly, as suggested above, the identity of a company is partly determined by its belonging to a larger entity. It is a way to describe how an individual actor connects to other actors. Secondly, identity also reveals the specialities of an actor. In this respect, the internal capabilities are important, such as technical knowledge, how well established the company is, etc. The identity provides a picture of what the company is— and what it is not. Both aspects impact on the potential for action and by which actions the company will be affected.

To a large extent, the identity of a company is determined by its position in the activity and resource structures. The resources a company controls and the resource ties that provide access to the resources of others are always important

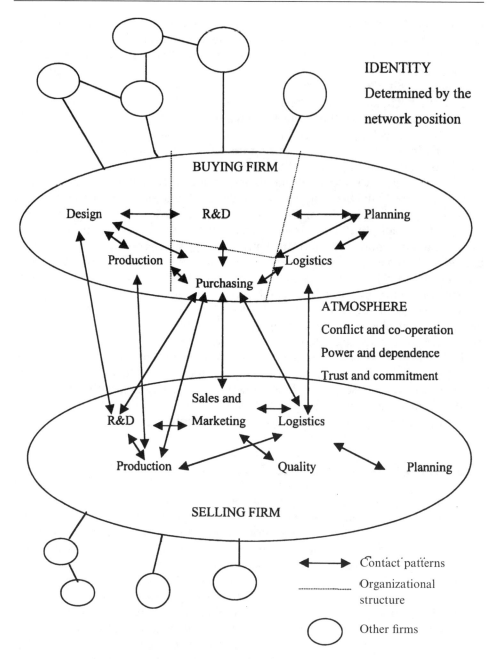

FIGURE 6.1 Determinants of purchasing's influencing opportunities.

factors in shaping identity. In the same way, the company's position in the activity structure affects its identity. However, 'there are actions that cannot be explained from the resource and activity dimensions alone' (Håkansson and Snehota, p. 192). It is a fact that customer and supplier structures of quite similar companies operating in the same industry differ greatly. The relationships companies develop to suppliers, customers and others are always company specific. One might wonder, for instance, why a certain German customer prefers a certain Italian supplier when closely located domestic suppliers have analogous resources and technology. Furthermore, what makes two companies develop a close relationship and co-operate in technical development while attempts to co-operate with others fail, despite the fact they have the same type of resources and activity structures? In other cases, it has been shown that being a supplier to demanding customers may open many purchasing department doors even when the vendor's actual capabilities may be lower than those of its competitors. These situations illustrate that the identity of a company is also determined by the third of the network dimensions—the actor structure.

We argued above that the actor dimension is multifaceted. Actors can be identified on the individual level, the business unit level, the company level, etc. The identity of the company is an important dimension in the actor structure. This identity is determined by the way people perceive the companies in which they are involved as well as how they perceive other companies. This means that the identity of an actor is 'in the eye of the beholder'—there will never be common agreement on the identity of an actor. Therefore, the perceived identity of a company depends on actual conditions in the network, such as structures and changes of various kinds, as well as on perceptual issues that may be affected by interaction among the actors. The identity of a company stems to some extent from the direct experience of past interaction, but also from what is known, or believed to be known, about the counterpart (Håkansson and Snehota, p. 32). This means that identity is shaped in the direct business exchange but also through other actions—or their absence. It is of the utmost importance to any company to develop a favourable identity in relation to other actors crucial to its future. Otherwise, it will be impossible to generate the resources and capabilities that are needed.

The identity of a company is important for several reasons. Firstly, the underlying identity of an actor impacts on the interpretation of its actions. Identity, thus, will affect how other actors perceive and react to various actions undertaken. For example, it is likely that the reactions of other actors will be different if a specific action is carried out by someone identified as a central actor (like IKEA) than someone perceived as an 'outsider'. Depending on the perceived identity of the change agent the counterparts can be expected to put more or less effort into interpreting the actions undertaken. In the same way, it is likely that the counterparts make a more thorough analysis of the potential reactions from another company, the more positively attributed the identity of that company is. Secondly, the identity of a company impacts on prioritization not only in terms of interpretations of actions. Both in the day-to-day operations and the long-term strategic analysis, giving priority and being given priority are central issues in business exchange. Especially when supplier bases are reduced, it is important both for suppliers and customers that priority is given to the most appropriate potential partner. The decisions taken in this respect are always conditioned by the identity of the actors.

Identity is important to interaction. It sets the conditions for which actors are perceived valuable counterparts. It also impacts both on the interpretation of the behaviour of others and the principles for the company's own behaviour. In the same way, interaction impacts on attitudes. Purchasing, being an interface with suppliers, has an important role to play in these processes. On the one hand, purchasing has to develop and make use of the buying firm's identity in relation to the suppliers. In these efforts both the internal capabilities of the buying company and the collective participation in the surrounding network must be emphasized. The outcome of these efforts is an important determinant of the priority the buying company is given by suppliers. It is important also to consider how the suppliers used affect the identity of the buying company. It is most likely that the customers' perceptions of the supplier's identity are conditioned by the supply arrangements. For example, buying from vendors using child labour may not build up an identity with positive attributes. For these reasons many companies have developed a purchasing policy involving, for example, ethical and environmental issues. For the same reason, the way a company handles its purchasing operations is one of the main determinants of its identity as perceived by suppliers.

The Interaction Atmosphere

In the first IMP-study (Håkansson 1982) the 'atmosphere' of a relationship proved to be very central. The atmosphere affects and is affected by the interaction processes going on in a business relationship. The variables relating to the atmosphere were seen as intervening variables, functioning as mechanisms by which the interacting parties, the interaction processes and the interaction environment are inter-related. In this section we describe three aspects related to this atmosphere. The first is the simultaneous occurrence of conflict and co-operation prevailing in the interaction among firms. The second are the power-dependence conditions associated with interaction. The third is related to the impact of trust and commitment on the relationship. Before discussing these atmosphere elements we need to elaborate a little on the relevance of the atmosphere.

Business deals always contain uncertainty. Some uncertainty is about the future (for example, in terms of business cycle development) and is genuine, i.e. it can never be eliminated, but needs to be handled with more or less sophisticated assessments. Other aspects of uncertainty are directly related to the other party in the transaction. For example, there are time lags between transaction, delivery and payment. In addition, it is impossible to specify all the functions and details of a product or a delivery beforehand. Instead, they become visible gradually. Unexpected events may also mean that the content of the business deal must be adjusted, and the technology may be both complex and difficult to assess in advance. Thus, there are a number of factors, which are difficult to foresee at the point when the deal is made. These difficulties are so great that it is often point-less—or far too costly—to try to formulate agreements to cover all conceivable situations. Instead, the relationships with suppliers and customers have to provide the security. This is why the atmosphere of the interaction is crucial to its outcome.

Conflict and Co-operation

Business relationships are always characterized both by conflict and co-operation, because the parties have both contradictory and shared interests. There are several contradictory interests in relationships. In a short-term oriented and isolated perspective the price paid by the customer is the income of the supplier, which makes financial conditions a conflicting issue. When a longer-term view is applied the two parties may have differing opinions of what is the most appropriate direction for technical development and joint projects. To a large extent, these different perspectives are rooted in perceptions of what is important for the future identity of the two companies. Therefore, one should not be surprised that conflicts arise even in what seems to be well functioning co-operative relationships. On the contrary, the absence of conflicts is likely to reflect the fact that the two companies have not really 'clinched' with each other, and are not really trying to explore the potential for collaborative actions. However, particularly in the short run, conflicts tend to be a problem for the efficiency of the day-to-day operations, which require limited disturbances. Therefore, conflicts have to be handled. It is important to observe that handling conflict should not be confused with elimination of conflict. In this we agree with Gemunden (1985, p. 405) who argues that 'buyer and seller should neither smooth over existing conflicts nor let them escalate'. The conclusion is thus that effective relationships require both co-operation and conflict at the same time (see Figure 6.2).

The four cells in the matrix represent relationships with different combinations of co-operation and conflict. A relationship characterized by low co-operation and low conflict is considered a marginal one. It is not likely that it is especially important to any of the parties. If there is high conflict and low co-operation one would not expect the relationship to survive, unless it is for some reason important to at least one of the parties. The most significant relationships are, by definition, characterized by a high degree of co-operation in some dimension. A relationship scoring high on co-operation and low on conflict can tend to be somewhat too 'nice'. This atmosphere may imply that the parties place too few demands on one another. Provided that it can be handled well, an increasing conflict level might enable a better climate for innovation and development. As long as conflicts can be managed, they are a breeding ground for creativity and are therefore a necessary ingredient in a working relationship. It is important for both parties not to neglect their own aims and interests. The only possibility for establishing well-functioning relationships is for all the parties involved to have the courage to work on the basis of their own ambitions at the same time as they accept the fact that their collaborators have different motives and that these must also be taken in account. The purchasing function acts as a mediator between the buying company and its suppliers. In this position, they can affect both the extent of co-operative efforts and the level of conflict. Sometimes, purchasing staff tend to feel more obligated to suppliers than to their own companies.

	High	Nice	Creative
Extent of co-operation	low	Marginal	Hostile
		Low	High
		Level of conflict	

FIGURE 6.2 Relationship characteristics in terms of conflict and co-operation.

Power and Dependence

Power and dependence are important concepts in inter-organizational analysis. Emerson (1962) concludes that the power concept is based on the idea that social relations commonly entail mutual dependence between the parties. This mutual dependence arises because each party is likely to aspire to goals that are in some way conditional upon the actions of the other party. From this, Emerson asserts that the power to control or influence the other resides in control over the things he values, which means that power stems implicitly from the other's dependence. For example, as described in Chapter 4, the suppliers of the European car manufacturers had to adapt to the Odette system. For large firms the most important supplier relationships always involve large volumes of business and represent major values from a financial point of view. They also affect the customer in a number of indirect ways, which further increases their significance. Significance imposes dependence and the way in which power and dependence issues are handled thus becomes an important issue for purchasing. In the past, it was recommended that buying firms should try to behave in such a way that dependence would not arise, because avoiding dependence on individual suppliers was a key objective. Prevailing supply strategies of buying firms made suppliers dependent on powerful customers who shifted their purchases from one supplier to the other depending on the conditions offered. One supplier in the automotive industry characterized its main customers as follows (Helper 1986, p. 17):

> They are nasty, abusive and ugly. They would take a dime from a starving grandmother. They steal our innovations, they make uneconomic demands like 'follow us around the globe and build plants near ours. We need good suppliers like you—but if you can't do it we'll find somebody else'.

Recent changes in purchasing strategy and purchasing behaviour have affected this situation. Customers have deliberately entered situations where they become dependent on suppliers. We have shown a number of examples in the two first chapters and return to this issue when analysing supplier relationship strategies in Chapter 8. The present situation is thus characterized by more mutual dependence between customer and supplier and the focus of purchasing efforts has been shifted from avoiding dependence on suppliers to finding mechanisms to handle dependence. This does not mean that power is less important than before, but it is used in a more constructive way. Today, companies do not tend to exploit the power they have in relation to each other in the primitive way they used to. The reason is that the future well being of each firm is conditioned to a large extent by prosperous counterparts.

Trust and Commitment

We mentioned above that one important function of interaction is to reduce uncertainty. Security in a relationship cannot be created on a single occasion, but develops over time. The connection between two parties can only be built up through a process of interaction in which reciprocal trust can be successively deepened. In this process both sides gradually get a more accurate perception of the business conditions. Typically, the two parties first test one another through minor business deals and then move along to more complete deliveries. Interaction plays a crucial role for the outcome of this process. Firstly, it is important that the individuals involved get to know each other well on a personal basis. Secondly, it is important that they learn about the operations of both companies and how they can fit better together. Thus, it is necessary to create social situations to encourage contacts among individuals. The benefits of, and the need for, personal contacts in building up this confidence cannot be overemphasized. This approach is often recommended for marketing, but is certainly equally important for purchasing. Social interaction is necessary because it is the primary driving force for development of trust. The relationship between trust and social exchange has been explored by Blau (1964, p. 454):

> Since the recipient is the one who decides when and how to reciprocate for a favor, or whether to reciprocate at all, social exchange requires trusting others, whereas the immediate transfer of goods or the formal contract that can be enforced obviates such trust in economic exchange. Typically, however, social exchange relations evolve in a slow process, starting with minor transactions in which little trust is required because little risk is involved and in which both partners can prove their trustworthiness, enabling them to expand their relations and engage in major transactions.

Developing trust is important because trust is a prerequisite for commitment (Håkansson and Snehota, p. 198). Commitment is a tendency to persist with causes of action, often without an apparent causal motive, on the basis of vague expectations; it is always to some extent an 'act of faith' by which the actors handle uncertainty and complexity. Commitment is central to business relationships. Gaining benefits from relationships requires a long-term perspective. Now and then, the parties may identify short-term gains from giving priority to other relationships. In such situations, commitment to a certain counterpart may cause an actor to refrain from breaking a relationship for the sake of short-term benefits.

Building trust and commitment are time-consuming processes in which relationships between individuals are crucial. These personal contacts are important for interpretation of what is going on. Through this social exchange a relationship between two actors can withstand substantial strain occasionally, as long as the underlying policy is perceived to remain. On the other hand, even small changes may impact greatly on the relationship if they are interpreted as shifting the underlying philosophy. This means that trust can be dissolved fairly quickly, while it takes long time to develop.

Particularly when relationships have been adversarial, trust and commitment take time to develop. This is clearly illustrated in studies conducted in the automotive industry. In the early 1980s, car manufacturers began to reconsider their relationships with suppliers. For example, in 1982 a representative of one of the Big Three in the US argued that his company needed new types of relationships with suppliers (Berry 1982, p. 26):

> We need new relationships with what we have to think of as a family of suppliers. We need to throw off the old shackles of adversarial confrontation and work together in an enlightened era of mutual trust and confidence.

In spite of such statements and measures undertaken by the buying firms in the car industry suppliers tended to be sceptical. In a study conducted in the late 1980s the relationships were characterized by the fact that 'suppliers still felt a lack of commitment, since their level of trust in the customer did not increase' (Helper 1991, p. 19). Even more than ten years after the declaration of the revised policy the atmosphere seemed not to have changed much. In a study published as late as in 1995 it was shown that 'suppliers do not feel that their customers are more trustworthy than they were five years ago' (Helper and Sako 1995, p. 83). Trust building is obviously a cumbersome process, especially when it comes to changes from a 'negative' to a more 'positive' atmosphere. In many cases, a change of purchasing policy must be accompanied by a change of purchasing staff. It might be difficult to convince suppliers that a new procurement regime has been launched unless the individuals associated with the old policy are replaced.

The Organizational Structure and Internal Interaction

The opportunities for interaction among the actors in a network are conditioned by the way companies, business units and departments are organized. In this section, we analyse the impact of the organizational structure on the interaction within a company.

In Chapter 1, we discussed some of the pros and cons of centralized and decentralized organization of purchasing activities. This choice has a profound impact on the interaction that takes place between individuals within the buying company. When a centralized purchasing organization is applied purchasing becomes a specialised function and it may become difficult to integrate the operations with those of other functions. The main 'internal' reasons for centralization are that it promotes professionalism among buyers and that resources may be allocated efficiently. Advocates of the decentralized approach argue that purchasing should not be seen as a specialized function. On the contrary, it is part of the total operations of the company, implying that integration with those other activities is a main concern. In the decentralized purchasing organization buyers are located together with people from manufacturing and engineering rather than with other purchasers, simplifying inter-departmental interaction, but making purchasing per se less professional. Various organizational settings also create different values and cultures. A buyer sitting close to other buyers is likely to develop different values than a buyer located together with technicians.

Over time, it has become increasingly important to promote the internal interaction in buying companies—especially among purchasing and the technical functions. One reason for this need is that purchasing has become more complex. Components, materials and equipment are increasingly technically sophisticated, which puts new demands on technical competence in the procurement process. This development affects the general demands on the people dealing with purchasing, as well as calling for interaction with the technical side. Another reason for enhanced interaction is that purchasing staff have long argued that they can contribute to improved performance in design and product development if they are involved earlier in these processes. Similar arguments have been put forward by researchers, observing that purchasing staff may contribute substantially if involved in the design phase (Burt and Sukoup 1985).

An illustration from practice is the restructuring of product development activities undertaken by Harley Davidson some years ago (Fitzgerald 1999). Before the restructuring, engineering determined product design. In this process engineering received some input from marketing and some from styling but on the whole 'there wasn't much interaction between the engineering team and purchasing or manufacturing' (ibid., p. 51). In 1997, purchasing at Harley Davidson was divided into three different groups: corporate, development and operations. Development purchasing is staffed with about 30 purchasers who are totally dedicated to product development work. They work side by side with the engineers and supplier engineers in the new-product development centre that was established to accommodate a team approach to design. These teams are responsible for all design and development activities for a particular product platform. There are four lead members on each team, representing purchasing, engineering, manufacturing and marketing. In this new structure purchasing is on an equal footing with engineering and has an equal voice in terms of the future of the platform. The responsibilities associated with this new position go far beyond traditional purchasing.

Multi-functional Team in General Motors

GM's worldwide purchasing is leading the corporation in its globalization efforts. In this process 150 'creativity teams' play an important role. These teams combine people from different functions; purchasing, engineering, design, quality, marketing, and finance. The main task for these teams is 'to coordinate sourcing decisions for everything from door handles to anti-lock braking systems on a global basis'. The members of these teams reside in different countries and continents and have telephone meetings twice a week. According to the purchasing director these people together 'bring the skill levels up for our buyers' and often uncover new strategies and sourcing opportunities.

When developing parts and systems for future models GM relies on 'advanced purchasing teams' which pair buyers and engineers during the design stage for the new vehicle. Together they decide on the functional requirements and ask suppliers for proposals. Based on these proposals the advanced purchasing team makes a final recommendation to the sourcing committee.

Source: Minahan 1996c, pp. 44–45.

Increasing interaction between purchasing and engineering provides a number of benefits—see the Box above. However, these benefits are not attained without problems. Bonoma and Zaltman (1976) found that, in general, there are considerable differences in the 'cultures' of those functions. According to their study, engineers perceived purchasers to be too much focused on costs, while purchasers were of the opinion that the engineers overlooked costs to the benefit of technical performance. These attitudes from a study 25 years ago still appear to be valid. The main problem is that each function perceives the other as invading its specific area of competence. For example, purchasing people perceive their freedom of action as severely restricted if the components are specified in too great detail. This is clear in the following quote from the purchasing director of General Motors (Minahan 1996c, p. 45):

> We don't want the minutia specification or a brand name, just tell us what you want it to do.

In the same way, engineers resist too much involvement from purchasing in a process engineering traditionally ruled 'with an iron hand' (Fitzgerald 1999, p. 54). Fitzgerald's conclusion is that integrating purchasing and suppliers into design can be threatening to engineering, because they traditionally completely 'owned' product-design activities. In the same article, a representative of Pratt & Whitney argues that engineers want complete freedom to design and deal only with the technical issues of the engine—which are considerable. It is not always easy for them to accept the added complexity introduced by someone saying that 'this feature will drive cost up' (ibid., p. 54).

Handling these potential sources of conflict calls for management intervention. In this respect the first obvious requirement is that the actors involved are informed about the changes and the reasons underlying them. At Harley Davidson, management knew that communicating the reasons for the new structure clearly was vital to create an understanding that purchasing and suppliers are part of the product development team. In spite of their efforts one representative of the company admits that 'our communication could have been more solid to keep everyone aware' (ibid., p. 54).

One way to reduce friction and tension is to recruit purchasers with a technical background. Bergman and Johanson (1978) recommend that purchasers have a solid background in the technical core of the company. A more recent example is given in Fitzgerald (1999) where it is reported that Pratt & Whitney made a 'concerted effort to hire purchasing pros with backgrounds in engineering and other technical disciplines'. Furthermore, at the time when procurement was restructured at Harley, several development purchasing engineers were hired from product design and process engineering positions within the company to make the change smoother. However, according to Fitzgerald, it is not only the need to reduce cultural clashes that calls for purchasers with other capabilities. The main reason is that 'skills for purchasing are much more multifaceted and sophisticated as the game changes'. The changes in the game require more emphasis on the ability to discover, link and manage supplier resources with those of the buying firm, which, in turn, calls for leadership talent. Representatives of Harley Davidson report that the required skills have been redefined for all purchasing pros, in order to be consistent with the supply management strategy. In particular, stronger competence in engineering and product development is necessary. These changes define a new kind of purchasing professional (ibid., p. 54):

> The new design responsibilities required of purchasing create a natural need for a new breed of purchasing professional, one who is technically competent, has multifunctional skills, capable of working in a team atmosphere and is able to take control of design project and manage it through to completion.

Another type of management intervention is to enhance the status of purchasing in the organization. As shown in the historical overview, purchasing had a very low status in the past. The same conditions are reported much more recently, for example by Axelsson and Håkansson (1984). They describe purchasing as having developed out of the administrative and inventory operations of companies and claim that this explains the difficulty purchasing has had in generating its own status. Gadde and Håkansson (1993) report some studies illustrating this situation. Purchasing management in one large divisionalized Swedish company felt that they were held back in the organization owing to their being under the direction of the production manager. In another case, purchasing felt that there was a 'poor response both from the division and the corporate management', and in a third case purchasing was said to be 'unfortunately treated as a stepchild in our corporate group' (ibid., p. 132). Corporate management representatives also confirmed the low status of purchasing, expressing the opinion that this led to recruitment problems since purchasing was often considered a department to which people were demoted. As illustrated in Chapter 2, describing the developments at IBM procurement, these attitudes have continued to impact on the position of purchasing. However, with increasing insight in the strategic importance of purchasing, the position has been improved substantially. Today, most purchasing managers report directly to corporate management.

The Organizational Structure and External Interaction

The organizational design impacts considerably on the opportunities for, and the outcome of, interaction with external counterparts. The discussion in this section is focused on two aspects. Firstly, we discuss the benefits of supplier involvement in product development. Secondly, we analyse the way in which the choice between centralized and decentralized purchasing impacts on external interaction.

In the foregoing section, it was argued that purchasing involvement in design and development would improve performance in these activities, the main advantage being that purchasers are better able than technicians and engineers to bring in the supplier side aspects. It is clear that even more benefits would be obtained if suppliers become directly involved. In the late 1980s, a number of authors provided arguments for increasing co-operation with suppliers in technical development (Burt and Sukoup 1985, Takeuchi and Nonaka 1986, Clarke and Fujimoto 1991). The 1990s were characterized by considerable changes in the level of supplier involvement in design and development (Hartley *et al.* 1997, Ragatz *et al.* 1997, Wynstra 1998). A US survey revealed that about 50% of the respondents had made suppliers responsible for design activities (Purchasing 1997). To be able to contribute to design and development suppliers must be involved early in the product development process. Around 70% of the respondents reported that suppliers were involved considerably earlier than they had been five years ago. Primarily, two main reasons were given for these changes.

Firstly, the increased technical complexity made it necessary to make use of suppliers with advanced capability in their areas of specialization. Secondly, increasing demands for shortened R&D lead times and reduced costs required new arrangements. For example, early supplier involvement in design might have a major impact on cost control. A number of illustrations are provided by Fitzgerald (1999) where it is argued that engineers by nature tend to focus on the technological and performance aspects of a product. By integrating purchasing and suppliers deeply into the design process from the very outset, OEM manufacturers have avoided a lot of later expenses, especially manufacturing costs. One example is that Pratt & Whitney now brings suppliers into the design process very early, partly to ensure that designers take the cost of manufacturing into account. Furthermore, they want to get input from suppliers as to what would make a part more friendly to manufacture and ultimately more cost-effective—'cheaper to make, cheaper to inspect' (ibid., p. 54).

A huge number of studies report on the benefits that may be obtained from reduced lead times in product development. As early as 1991, Raia provided a number of examples of benefits associated with collaborating with suppliers. At that time, Xerox had been able to reduce time-to-market by more than 50%. An important determinant of these effects was that suppliers were encouraged to come up with suggestions for quality improvements and cost reductions. The outcome of the changes undertaken based on these suggestions was quite dramatic: product quality increased considerably at the same time as costs decreased substantially. Ingersoll-Rand involved an injection moulding supplier and some other suppliers in a development project when the new product was only 'a gleam in the eye of the marketing manager' (ibid., p. 39). This contrasted with the earlier strategy of Ingersoll-Rand and gave rise to unexpected benefits. Achieving these advantages requires that suppliers become involved in the design teams on the buying side, as discussed in the foregoing section. A representative of ITT Automotive expresses the benefits of joint teams in this respect as follows (Purchasing 1997, p. 32517):

> Every time you have a team approach with a common objective, then you're highly focused. When you get a supplier, an engineer, and a purchasing person together, you can co-ordinate the interfaces of the applications of parts. You can review the cost parameters versus a target. If you have the suppliers in up front they understand where you are starting from, and what the target is. By having them work as a team, by having all expectations set out with respect to quality, cost, timing for prototypes, etc., it's just a much faster process.

The same article reports that IBM works actively to make its own technology converge with the suppliers' technology. This is achieved through two-day seminars where technicians from suppliers and purchasers and design people from IBM meet to keep each other informed about ongoing development projects. In this way, IBM tries to keep its own development and the suppliers' activities 'on the same track' (ibid., p. 32S17).

There is a connection between external interaction and the size of the supply base. One of the ongoing developments reported in Chapter 2 is consolidation of the supply base. For example, the John Hancock Insurance Co. reduced the number of suppliers of contract labour from 109 to four primary suppliers. Each of these suppliers, in turn, manages a sub-tier of suppliers, because contract labour is a commodity for which diversity is paramount. The main reason for reducing the supply base was the substantial contact costs of the original supply base. It was difficult to develop top-quality relationships when 'we had 109 salespeople wandering around our building' (Avery 1999a, p. 56). Similar observations have been made in other studies. For example, one company reported the effects of the consolidation of the supply base to be that they now are dealing with fewer suppliers which, in turn, means that a lot less contract work has to be involved (Milligan 1999).

The choice between centralized and decentralized purchasing organizations impacts substantially on contact patterns with suppliers. With centralized purchasing the buying company relies on specialized purchasers with substantial bargaining power, in comparison with a decentralized organization. Purchasing staff are specialized and benefit from advanced knowledge in their areas of responsibility. Sometimes, they may be more qualified than the representatives of the selling companies. On the other hand, as mentioned above a centralized purchasing department meets problems in the buying company because it is somewhat 'outside' the actual operations. The decentralized purchasing organization, typical of project based businesses, has quite the opposite characteristics. In such cases, purchasing is strongly integrated with the operations. These buyers are responsible for a multitude of components and systems, which are bought in smaller quantities than in a centralized organization. This leads to reduced bargaining power and problems in achieving economies of scale. Furthermore, the wide scope of responsibility makes it difficult for the individual buyer to develop a deep knowledge along the whole spectrum of purchasing. It then becomes a problem for this buyer to meet the various specialists from the selling firms. For the selling company, a decentralized organization may lead to substantial contact costs because salespeople must deal with a large number of representatives of the buying company. This, in turn, increases costs which, in the end, have to be paid by the buyer.

The obvious response for a buying company to this dilemma is to apply a combined approach, i.e. to try to reap the benefits of one organizational form and then minimize its corresponding disadvantages. For example, General Motors has adopted a matrix organization for its procurement operations (Figure 6.3).

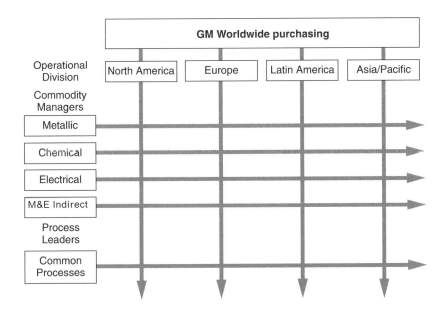

FIGURE 6.3   The purchasing organization of General Motors. Source: Minahan   Reproduced by permission of Purchasing Magazine (www.purchasing.com). All rights reserved. © Purchasing. 1996, p. 41.

The two dimensions of the matrix represent commodity groups and geo-graphical location. The commodity managers act on a centralized basis and are responsible for developing GM's world-wide strategy within the commodity groups they rule. Furthermore, 'process leaders' act on a global basis, responsible for processes that are supposed to be adopted world-wide, such as quality management, benchmarking, supplier development, etc. The other dimension covers the various assembly operations in the different parts of the world. These operational divisions are responsible for the implementation of the central policies. They also have some freedom in maintaining certain decentralized operations when this contributes to improved performance on the local level. The main objective underlying this change was to make better use of the scale of the operations than was possible when GM consisted of 27 reasonably autonomous and decentralized purchasing organizations. But it was of equal importance to develop a global competence for the entire organization and to improve communication with suppliers. The purchasing director expressed the underlying thinking as follows (Minahan 1996, p. 45):

> When we had 27 purchasing organizations we had the same supplier shipping the same parts to different locations at different prices. Not anymore. Today buyers know every single system we're buying around the world and have a process in place to easily communicate that information.

This example illustrates that a company that relies primarily on a decentralized organization may gain certain advantages by centralizing some of the operations. Similarly, a mainly centralized organization will benefit from decentralizing some activities to the local level. The combination of centralization and decentralization is sometimes recommended to be that strategic purchases are handled centrally while operational purchases may be handled locally. However, we argue that in some situations this is not the most appropriate approach. In many cases, stan-dardized components and MRO-supplies are suitable candidates for centralized purchasing, because of the economies of scale a large purchasing organization may be able to obtain. Strategic components and systems often require decentralization because purchasing activities need to involve technicians and engineers. There are thus no simple checklists available for decisions concerning the most appropriate purchasing organization. The choice is always context dependent, and reaping maximum benefits from one organizational form also means sacrificing the main benefits of the other. Because the context changes continuously the organizational form must be closely monitored and adapted accordingly to new conditions.

Organizing the Network

To this point, we have dealt mainly with the buying firm's relationships with single actors. In this section, we bring up some issues related to the whole net-work of suppliers. However, the main discussion of supply network is presented in Chapter 9, where network strategies are discussed.

Problems related to internal organizing have been important and relevant to purchasing since the function was established. During recent years, external issues have come into focus as well. The enhanced importance of suppliers has made it more and more important to be involved in the organizing of the entire supply network. The buying firm must be aware of and take advantage of opportunities for 'networking'. The company has access to a large resource base in terms of related suppliers and this resource must be adequately used—which can be done in many different ways. We give some examples below of how it can be used, and then we discuss what means the buying firm can use in this networking process.

One key issue we have stressed both in the activity chapter and in the resource chapter is to find ways to connect and relate several activities and/or several resources. Designing and developing activity patterns and resource con-stellations are important tasks in 'networking'. In both these cases, it is necessary to relate several companies to one another. This means that networking, which is basically working with or through others in relation to others, is crucial in supply networks. In order to manage this, the purchasing company needs knowledge about these actors and also a social capital in terms of its ability to influence. This capital is, to a large extent, established through the business relationships. If the company has been able to develop a strong identity and has managed to build up a certain number of well functioning relationships, it has something to network with. The ultimate aim of these efforts is to increase the efficiency in the activity pattern or to enhance innovation and resource utilization. As we have mentioned in previous chapters, there are financial reasons for the buying company to try to influence suppliers to use specific sub-suppliers, and there are also good reasons to try to influence them to develop certain customer relationships. In the same way, the buying company can try to use its suppliers in relation to its own customers. Suppliers can also be used to approach complementary producers, competitors or research institutes. There are a large number of opportunities to combine each of the key suppliers with other important external parties. These combining efforts can be directed towards the activity structure or the resource structure or to build positive actor bonds for later use. There is every reason to be highly aware of the external organizing at the network level, and companies need to have clear aims in this respect. It is important to observe that increasing attention to key account management leads to focusing on individual relationships. Consequently, there is a risk that network issues will be neglected.

Companies may use several different means of organizing and networking. The most significant one is the personal network. It is a key task for all the people involved in purchasing to develop an extensive and dense personal contact net-work in relation to suppliers and suppliers' suppliers. In the Cummins-Toshiba case study in Chapter 5, we noted how important one individual can be to the development of a new business relationship. The capacity of having and developing personal networks is crucial, and must be considered both when hiring new staff and when discussing and designing development plans for the purchas-ing personnel. Some companies use seminars with suppliers and joint training programmes to enhance these individual networks.

Another means of attaining the same objective is to work systematically with projects where suppliers and sub-suppliers are involved. These projects should always also include visits and meetings with other people within the companies in order to make it easier to develop such networks. These projects should, preferably, involve more than two parties. However, there are reasons to limit the number of participants, as those involved must always feel a personal responsibility for the project.

We emphasize the informal means of organizing above and they are undoubtedly the most significant ones. However, there are reasons to take advantage of some formal means as well. Alliances and other formal agreements with suppliers are ways to improve the conditions for networking. This is of particular interest in cases of extensive knowledge exchange, where two or more parties agree to make use of one another's technology.

Analysing Actor Structures

Chapter 6 provides a framework for understanding how the buying company can influence its business partners. Actor interaction is required for co-ordination of activities and combining of resources. The chapter shows that the impact of the interventions of actors is primarily determined by two factors: the identity of the actors and the interaction atmosphere. The identity of a single actor is formed by the characteristics of the actor, but also by the company's connections to other firms. The atmosphere in terms of trust and commitment, power and dependence, and the simultaneous occurrence of conflict and co-operation, is of crucial importance for the outcome of attempts to bring an influence to bear.

The organizational arrangements are also significant in this respect. The organizational design chosen affects the conditions for communication and influence. Our examples showed the relevance of the organizational structure for internal communication and information exchange with other companies as well as for the identity of firms and the interaction atmosphere.

The main questions in an analysis of the actor structure can be summarized as follows:

- What characterizes the central actors in the network—e.g in terms of size, competence, location, financial strength, and which are the main weaknesses in this structure?
- What is the identity of the buying company in the actor structure?
- Which changes in the interaction atmosphere with suppliers are needed?
- What is the relationship between the actor structure and the continuously changing resource and activity structures? What kinds of supplements are needed and are there partners who are unable to keep up with the pace of technology?
- How can the organizational structure be made more appropriate for internal and external interaction?
- In which ways can other firms be mobilized in attempts to influence suppliers?

Part III

SUPPLY STRATEGIES

Chapter 7

DETERMINING THE BOUNDARIES OF THE FIRM

Chapters 4–6 provide the analytical tools for network analysis. The next three chapters apply these tools for developing supply strategies. The first of the supply network strategies relates to the boundaries of the firm. The main issue is to decide which activities and resources to handle in-house and which to outsource to suppliers. As discussed in Chapter 3, this boundary takes different forms depending on which perspective we use when analysing the company: whether it is regarded as a unit of production, knowledge, communication or capital-earning will impact on the way the boundary is perceived. In the first part of this chapter we analyse the position of the firm in the production structure and how this position affects the possibilities of making use of the resources of other firms. The scope of the firm in its activity structure is traditionally analysed in terms of the extent of vertical integration, i.e. the number of successive stages of a production system (or value chain) in which the company is involved. Outsourcing of activities to suppliers affects the extent of vertical integration and thus the position of the firm in the activity structure. Outsourcing also impacts accordingly on the position of the company in the resource structure. Specialization and outsourcing imply that a company becomes increasingly dependent on the resources of other firms.

In the first section we discuss the efficiency improvements that can be attained through outsourcing and focusing on a limited part of the total activity structure in which the company is involved. The boundary of the firm is affected by changes in the extent of vertical integration. In purchasing terms, the extent of integration is determined by the make-or-buy decisions taken by the firm. In the second section we go on to discuss the pros and cons related to make versus buy. We point out that this decision has to be seen in a different light than has traditionally been the case. One of the main arguments for outsourcing is that firms should be able to focus on core competence. The third section is an analysis of the problems concerned with identifying the core competence of a company. In the fourth section we argue that the current reliance on outsourcing needs to be supplemented with corresponding considerations about insourcing. The resource requirements and internal capabilities of a firm change over time, and so do the resources that can be provided through suppliers. In the fifth section we present an alternative way of looking at boundaries, based mainly on the view of the firm as a knowledge unit, as discussed in Chapter 3. In this perspective, the boundary is not a dividing line between the firm and its environment, but more of a base for the signals given to the environment regarding the kind of knowledge the company represents. The chapter concludes with the managerial issues related to the determination of the boundaries and ways to approach the boundary issue.

Benefits of Specialization Through Outsourcing

In the purchasing review of the 20th century (Morgan 1999) the years around 1990 are characterized as the time of the re-engineering of purchasing. One of the main changes in the improvements of the supply operations was increasing attention to outsourcing. According to Morgan, outsourcing is about 'taking an operation or function traditionally performed in-house and jobbing it out to a contract manufacturer or third-party service provider'. The main arguments for this approach are the opportunities to conserve corporate resources for use where they are most effective. Most companies, it is argued, no longer have the resources to be best at all that they do, so they look for suppliers who are strong where they are weak.

The automotive industry in the western world was one of the forerunners in the outsourcing race. In relation to the Japanese challenge at the end of the 1970s, the characteristics of the supply side were perhaps the most remarkable phenomenon. The big three carmakers in the US favoured vertical integration while Japanese manufacturers relied more on outside suppliers. The American firms were main players in the development of the 'Modern Business Enterprise' (Chandler 1977), discussed in Chapter 4. According to Chandler, the growth and structure of the MBE was a prerequisite for the restructuring of the industry at that time. Without the ownership control in the hands of one actor it would not have been possible to make the investments required for efficiency improvements in scale and scope of the operations.

Over time, however, it became increasingly difficult to undertake all the various activities in the vertically integrated company in an efficient way. The capabilities and resources necessary were so different among all these operations that it became impossible to be an expert in all of them. The gigantic River Rouge Michigan plant established by Ford in the 1920s was an attempt to control the entire process of making and moving all the supplies and parts needed. Drucker (1990) has characterized this plant as an 'unwieldy monster' as a consequence of Henry Ford's ambitions to control much more than the manufacturing of components (ibid., p. 100):

> He built his own steel mill and glass plant. He founded plantations in Brazil to grow rubber for tires. He bought the railroad that brought supplies to River Rouge and carried away finished cars. He even toyed with the idea of building his own service centers nation-wide and staffing them with mechanics trained in Ford-owned schools.

According to Drucker, this unwieldy monster, over time, became increasingly 'expensive, unmanageable, and horrendously unprofitable' (ibid., p. 100). One of the main reasons underlying the development of the MBE was the ability to reap benefits from economies of scale. At this time, the main cost advantages arose from the standardization of the whole production process—i.e. the design of the activity structure. Over time, when this structure had taken the form of an organizational 'dominant design', the main cost advantages were instead obtained from improving efficiency in individual activities. When most manufacturers came to rely on the same dominant design, the main benefits in terms of costs could be gained from increasing the scale in the manufacturing of parts and components. One and the same supplier could be a vendor to many car manufacturers, with substantial financial savings through large production series.

An even more important determinant of outsourcing is the increased speed in product development. Today, most products are affected by a multitude of complex technologies, which makes companies dependent on a large number of technologies (Granstrand *et al.* 1992). The speed of the technological race has made it impossible for the individual company to remain at the cutting edge in all these different areas. Instead they have realized the benefits of utilizing the technical capability that can be attained by a company focusing on a narrow range of technologies. These benefits have been expressed as giving the buying company (Quinn and Hilmer 1994, p. 43):

> full utilization of external suppliers' investments, innovations and specialized professional capabilities that would be prohibitively expensive or even impossible to duplicate internally.

The outcome of the increasing level of outsourcing in the auto industry has been substantial vertical disintegration. As mentioned in Chapter 1, costs of purchased goods and services account for 70% of total costs at Volvo Car Corporation. Twenty years ago, Ford manufactured 70% of its assembly input in-house. Today, the corresponding figure is 30%, implying the same outsourcing level as Volvo (Quinn 1999). These changes have spread to other industries as well. In Chapter 2 we described the reorganization of the supply side of IBM. When IBM 'woke up' the portion of IBM's revenues spent with outside suppliers increased dramatically because they realized that they could not be experts at everything. They also realized that outside suppliers had technology IBM needed and that competitors were reducing their costs by outsourcing. It was not only IBM who could make the critical components for IBM computers. So could suppliers—often at lower cost.

Outsourcing is a characteristic not only in the areas of parts and components. Table 7.1 illustrates the proportion of firms in a US-survey stating that they outsourced activities in various service operations. The table clearly shows that today's activity structures are characterized by an increasing reliance on outside suppliers even when it comes to services such as warehousing, facilities management, telemarketing, sales training, market support and after-sales services. However, there seems to be an even greater unexploited potential offered by 'intellectually-based' services (Quinn 1999). The main reason is the development of large specialized service firms with sophisticated capabilities and expertise

TABLE 7.1 Outsourcing of services in US companies in 1996. Source: Quinn 1999, p. 14.

Finance and accounting	18%
General administration	78%
Human resources	77%
Information systems	63%
Marketing	51%
Transportation and distribution	66%

as compared to the scale and resources that may be attained in an integrated company.

The expanding service sector makes it possible for these specialists to develop greater knowledge depth and invest more in software and training systems. Therefore, they can be more innovative and efficient, which also means they can offer higher wages to attract highly trained people. Quinn illustrates his discussion with interesting examples. One of them is about Dell Computers, presented as a classic case about the way strategic outsourcing can revolutionize an industry. Dell has focused its operations on knowledge about customers and a downstream support system, as well as on a shared information system that deepens its relationships with suppliers. Outside suppliers not only provide manufactured components. They are also responsible for most component design and innovation and software for the computers. Royal Dutch Shell is reported to seek outside experts' different views and more specialized knowledge for the scenario building that is central to its strategic planning. Oil and mining companies hire professional real estate firms to develop and manage their surface land resources. Ford has used ABB to develop new plants at 70% of the previous in-house cost. Finally, Quinn reports the findings from a recent survey of outsourcing of human relations activities. In this sample, more than 75% of companies outsourced management of retirement plans, 40–50% outsourced reimbursement and payroll activities, while approximately one-third outsourced health and welfare management activities.

Make or Buy?—a Decision in a New Light

The decision of whether to produce in-house or buy externally has been a fundamental issue ever since the industrial revolution. However, it seems not to have been viewed as a strategic issue until recently. Culliton (1942), Jauch and Wilson (1979) and Leenders and Nollet (1984) are of the opinion that the decision generally was determined by short-term tactical and operational considerations. Jauch and Wilson (1979) argue that managers have tended to ignore the make-or-buy issue. In most cases, they have left decisions in the hands of the purchasing departments, where assessments have been made less in terms of strategic analysis than of retrospective cost data and estimations of future capacity utilization. Jauch and Wilson recommended that firms increase their strategic attention to this supply issue. There is no doubt that companies have come to rely on these suggestions. Today, most companies are very busy analysing which activities may be outsourced to suppliers. As illustrated in the previous section the result is that in some industries and for some companies a substantial portion of the total value of the offerings of selling companies is based on products and services procured from other firms. On the basis of these facts, it is interesting to discuss further the make-or-buy issue.

Culliton (1942) advocated increasing reliance on buy rather than make. His analysis highlights some severe disadvantages related to in-house manufacturing, primarily associated with opportunities to adapt to rapid changes in the environment. The advantages of external procurement he identified (writing in 1942) were related to the improvements of the capabilities of independent suppliers, and the developments of production techniques and transportation systems, which satisfied high demands for performance. In light of subsequent changes regarding manufacturing systems and logistic facilities, it is hardly surprising that 'buy' has taken the upper hand over 'make'.

This means that cost and capacity as primary determinants of the make-or-buy decision, over time, have been supplemented. Barreyre (1988) points out the importance of technological capability and product development resources. In general textbooks (e.g. Webster 1991), it is recommended that other factors be taken into account as well. The desire to protect technical solutions may lead the company to in-house manufacturing, while outsourcing makes it possible to assess the resources of capable suppliers. Furthermore, the need for co-ordination of activities is suggested as an argument for in-house making, while it is supposed that a greater flexibility could be achieved through buying. Ford et al. (1993) emphasize 'cost performance' and 'policy reasons' to be of equal importance, while Brandes (1993) identifies factors related to economy, strategy and power as most significant.

Over time, it is possible to trace an increasing awareness of the difficulties associated with comparing the costs in the two alternatives, make-or-buy. Webster (1991), for instance, points out the problems in making realistic estimations—even in retrospect—of the real costs of changing from buy to make. In the same way, it is problematic to analyse which costs would disappear if a change in the opposite direction were to take place. Venkatesan (1992) concludes that the accounting systems used by companies are of little help in these efforts. He perceived the principles used for distribution of costs as so arbitrary that the choice between make and buy was primarily determined by 'emotion and myth'.

The increasing significance of purchased goods and services directly affects the control structure in industry. Historically, ownership of resources has been considered the only opportunity to secure access of strategic resources. Furthermore, ownership control was assumed to be the most appropriate mechanism for managing different business units towards one and the same objective. Vertical integration was *the* mode of control in Chandler's MBE. Through ownership the big car manufacturers were provided with unlimited means of control. However, the options for this type of control are limited to the owned part of the structure. It is most likely that the integrated company will primarily devote its resources to running the operations they control as efficiently as possible, thus focusing on existing operations. This may cause problems regarding development and innovation. Furthermore, the flexibility of integrated firms is affected by the investments undertaken. A company may be well aware of needed changes, caused for example by a technical shift, but financial limitations may make it impossible to take the desired steps.

It is not surprising therefore that 'make' has lost out to 'buy'. One important explanation of this change in the automotive industry is that today's cars are entirely different machines than they were when Ford and GM established their integrated enterprises in the 1920s. A car is designed and manufactured in different ways than before. Also, its content in terms of materials and components has changed radically. Iron and steel have been replaced by plastics and aluminium. Electronics have come to play an increasingly important role (see Table 7.2). These new resources and capabilities were not available in the integrated companies, who obviously perceived them as too demanding to develop internally compared with accessing them from suppliers. To rely on buy rather than make also increases the flexibility of manufacturers. It is thus possible to observe a changed view of the value of ownership control as compared with the freedom provided by increased flexibility. Control, in terms of ownership, has been reduced considerably while flexibility has increased in terms of decreased lock-in-effects. There is thus a clear relationship between control and flexibility. We return to this in the section below on core competence.

The make-or-buy decision in today's industry is quite different than it used to be. The very question—make-or-buy—implies a choice on the part of the buying firm. In the 'old economy' this change could be made quite easily—even from one year to the other. As illustrated in Chapters 4 and 5, companies today are involved in complex activity and resource structures characterized by substantial interdependencies. Therefore, a decision either to make or to buy is less reversible today. Once a company has started to rely on outside suppliers it can be difficult to turn back to a make-strategy—at least in the short term. This means that the decisions companies take regarding outsourcing are indeed strategic. Monczka and Morgan (2000) argue that outsourcing has evolved from what used to be a tactical job to a strategic responsibility deeply embedded in revenue generation, owing to better product features or more efficient management of capital resources. This transition has increased complexity in decision-making

TABLE 7.2   Materials in a typical North American-made sedan (pounds). Source: Stundza 2000, p. 5.

Material	1998	1977
Iron	359	540
Regular steel sheet, tube, bar and rod	1,408	1,999
High- and medium-strength steel	319	25
Stainless steel	49	25
Plastic and plastic composites	243	168
Aluminium	219	97
Powder metal parts	32	15
Zinc die casting	13	38
Magnesium castings	6	1

considerably. According to Monczka and Morgan, outsourcing strategies have evolved from simple forms of contract manufacturing to strategies that encompass sizeable teams of key people on the technology, commercial and manufacturing sides of the business.

Core Competence—a Problematic Concept

One of the primary driving forces for companies to rely increasingly on outsourcing is gaining access to the resource collections of specialized actors. The corollary of this argument is that the buying firm can in this way concentrate its own resources on improving its capabilities within its own area of focus. According to Quinn and Hilmer (1994), such a focus provides the company with two strategic advantages. Firstly, a company may maximize return on internal resource investments by concentrating efforts in areas where they have already developed an advanced capability. Secondly, developing this capability (entitled 'core competence') functions as an entry barrier to competitors.

There are significant benefits to be gained from specialization, as illustrated in the first sections of this chapter. However, specialization has its drawbacks as well. A prerequisite for successful specialization is that the company is able to identify which are the 'core' and critical resources. The British subsidiary of IBM is one of the companies that has outsourced quite a number of activities to specialized suppliers. According to IBM management, it is a very difficult task to decide which activities are so critical that they need to be kept in-house. The company defined its strategic core in terms of activities that had the following characteristics (Gillett 1994, p. 46).

They provided management and direction.

They maintained competence and control.

They differentiated IBM from its competitors and

they established its uniqueness.

Company representatives admit this to be a critical task. They argue that there is a slight problem with today's general recommendations to promote outsourcing. In this atmosphere companies might take deliberate decisions to divest resources that could become important in the future.

Quinn and Hilmer (1994) identify three different problems that can arise from a concentration on the 'core competence'. From their point of view, the main underlying motivation for outsourcing is that by delimiting the internal resource base a company gets opportunities to deepen its knowledge and capabilities within a limited scope. However, it is never possible to know what will be 'core' in the long term—this changes over time. A company that has deliberately avoided maintaining its own competence base for a number of years may find it very problematic to redevelop it when it is needed again. We agree with Quinn and Hilmer regarding these consequences of outsourcing.

The second problem they discuss is that the buying company, through specialization, may lose what they identify as 'cross-functional skills'. These skills stem from the fact that in the daily contacts between various corporate functions new resource combinations are sometimes developed. When a company limits its own operations the number of internal connections is reduced, which is assumed to affect cross-functional skills negatively. However, in our view, this is only one side of the coin. Similar interaction can be developed with the functions in the supplier company. Therefore, outsourcing can lead to improved conditions for inter-functional interaction. To achieve these benefits the buying company has to develop relationships with suppliers that favour this type of interaction.

Thirdly, Quinn and Hilmer argue that outsourcing leads to loss of control. The discussion is based on Figure 7.1.

In this diagram, and in most cases, the relationship between flexibility and control is seen as a fairly simple trade-off—increasing one of the factors means reducing the other. The resource input needed by a company is then inserted in diagrams of this type with flexibility on one of the axes and control on the other. For some resources the buying firm is assumed to need total control, implying ownership, which in turn means low flexibility. Concerning other resources, the need for control is limited. The buying firm is then expected to prefer flexibility. However, in our view, it is important to question the relationship between flexibility and control indicated in Figure 7.1. Both concepts are multidimensional, with different types of relationships among them.

According to the diagram, ownership is associated with limited flexibility and substantial control. But in this respect control can only be attained over the limited part of the total resource constellation and activity structure within the

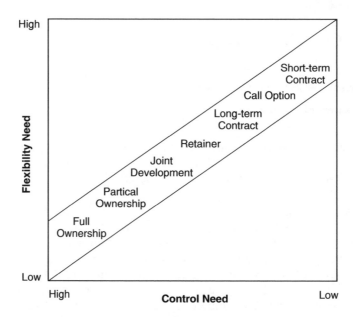

FIGURE 7.1   A perceived relationship between flexibility and control. Source: Quinn and Hilmer 1994, p. 50. Copyright © Sloane Management Review Association. All rights reserved.

boundaries of the firm. Reduced ownership leads to a situation where the 'area' that is fully controlled is reduced. However, a company may attain various forms of partial—or indirect—resource control from its co-operation with other companies as illustrated by the case studies in Chapter 5. Through its relationships, a company may establish indirect control of the resources within the ownership boundaries of other firms. This means that upward movement along the diagonal in the figure does not necessarily represent reduced control. The gains in indirect control might outweigh the loss in direct ownership control. In the top right-hand corner of the diagram the buying firm deals with short-term contracts and is supposed to have limited control only. This interpretation makes sense. However, we question the perception of flexibility, which in this case is assumed to be high. The buying firm is obviously in the position of switching easily from one supplier to the other, which represents one type of flexibility. On the other hand, this flexibility is conditioned by the fact that only standardized solutions can be used. In fact, this may be regarded as a low level of flexibility in terms of which technical solutions that can be used. Obviously, there are different dimensions related to both flexibility and control. Therefore, the strategic issue in this case is which type of flexibility is preferred rather than increases and decreases in general flexibility.

The most significant change related to control is that ownership control has been reduced through outsourcing. However, as discussed above, control can be attained by different means. Blois (1971) introduced the notion of 'quasi-integration', which means that a company connects its operations with those of suppliers —without establishing ownership ties. The basic concern in this strategy is to combine control and flexibility and maintain the advantages associated with vertical integration without the corresponding disadvantages. Managing supply networks by reliance on indirect resource control through relationships deals with issues that are focused on in Chapters 8 and 9.

We have tried to show that 'core' competence may be a somewhat dubious strategic concept to rely on. Firstly, it may be difficult to identify—in particular, what will be core in the long run. Secondly, the complex relationship between flexibility and control illuminates that the overall long-term consequences of outsourcing and focusing on core activities are unclear. Thirdly, the first of our three main supply strategies is about determining the boundary between the internal operations of a company and those of its suppliers. So far, the discussion has primarily focused on narrowing the scope of the firm through outsourcing activities to suppliers. However, it is also important to consider insourcing as a viable option.

Outsourcing and Insourcing

We argued in the second section that the make-or-buy decision has changed in character. The prevailing industry structure and behaviour make the decision much more irreversible than it used to be. There is another change as well. Companies have been moving between make and buy according to conditions at hand. Today, however, most recommendations are fairly one-sided: you should outsource non-core activities to other actors that are more efficient and effective.

We think these recommendations have to be supplemented with an argument for insourcing. On some occasions, it may be important for a company to insource activities that are conducted by suppliers. One reason might be that a company realizes that activities earlier perceived as non-core have become critical from a strategic point of view, making it necessary to incorporate them. It might also be the case that the buying company has relied on a supplier of a distinct 'customized' technology, critical to its success. For various reasons, this supplier may eventually find it more appropriate to turn to a generic technology. If so, the customer may be forced to insource this activity to ensure supply of an adapted solution.

Chapters 4 and 5 illustrated the need of combining outsourcing with insourcing. Efficient co-ordination of sequentially interdependent activities may sometimes require insourcing of complementary activities. Insourcing may also be a way to increase the similarity of the activities within a company, for example improving the capacity utilization of machinery and equipment. In the same way, the border between external and internal resources must continuously be reconsidered. Therefore, owing to changing conditions, a company needs to monitor and evaluate its position in the activity and resource structures. This position must be adapted to new requirements and new opportunities provided through insourcing and outsourcing (see Figure 7.2).

In many cases make-or-buy decisions have been taken on the basis of short-term considerations. Some companies have found that 'buy' decisions have meant that they are dependent on a particular product supplier that no longer regards the relevant technology as part of their own long-term strategy. Others have

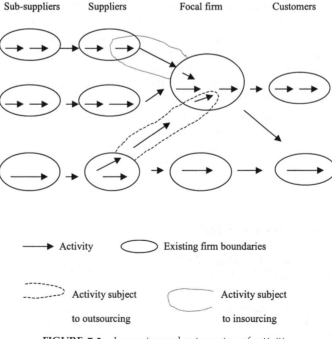

FIGURE 7.2   Insourcing and outsourcing of activities.

found that a 'make' decision might mean that the technology base of their product becomes inadequate. Such companies may also find that the costs and time needed to reverse their strategy are too great, and they may even have to withdraw from the market (Ford and Saren 1996).

Furthermore, companies may change their view of what resources need to be controlled through ownership. However, it must be emphasized that direct control does not automatically guarantee efficient utilization of resources. In many cases, the reverse is true. For example, a company may find that it maintains expensive test facilities solely for its own use. This problem is compounded in the case of speculative development work, where an overabundance of resources may well be necessary to provide the required flexibility when directing the development (Ford et al. 1998). It must also be remembered that direct control not only implies freedom of choice, but also risks of committing the company to choices that uncertain future developments could make costly.

Thus far, we have discussed the advantages and disadvantages of outsourcing/insourcing and specialization for individual companies. On a more aggregate level, other considerations become apparent. Piore (1992) analyses the impact of specialization on the structural development of industries. Sharing the common view of division-of-labour as the principal determinant of economic growth, he makes a couple of important contributions regarding the implications of specialization at the corporate level. The main argument is that specialization anywhere in an industrial system will require integration somewhere else. Therefore, the basic issue related to division of labour is not specialization per se—but the combined effects of specialization and integration. The concept used by Piore to analyse specialization is 'partitioning of activities'—i.e. how the tasks in the activity structure are allocated among the different actors.

According to Piore, different ways of partitioning have their particular consequences for integration. What must be achieved is that the 'total' production structure 'mirrors' the consumption structure. It is highly unlikely that a specific partitioning of activities advantageous for efficiency in the production structure would take a form automatically relevant to the consumption structure. Therefore, organizational changes need to go hand in hand with technological changes. Piore argues that the individual tasks subject to partitioning have to be re-assimilated 'into a cognitive form wherein they have economic meaning' (ibid., p. 442). The modern business enterprise was one form of reorganization relying on integration of resources directly controlled through ownership. The present developments towards specialized actors combining their resources require new organizational forms. Thus, the technological changes paving the way for outsourcing have been accompanied by organizational changes. For example, Lorenzoni and Baden-Fuller (1995) have identified 'strategic centres' fulfilling the integration role that is a prerequisite for outsourcing. We return to the strategic centres in Chapter 9, where we discuss the design of supply networks.

In the review of 'supply strategies for the 21st century' (Monczka and Morgan 2000) insourcing/outsourcing decisions are regarded most fundamental. Monczka and Morgan argue that history shows that attention to these issues tends to come in waves and is typically driven by financial problems or resources shortages. They say that the main thing for the new century is that organizations need to 'take much more ongoing and strategic views of insourcing/outsourcing decisions across business units' (ibid., p. 54). They claim that quite often the business units of big companies make their own decisions in these matters. Consequently, many decisions are subject to much company-wide oversight, without considerations regarding how such decisions may affect the strategic direction of the business. Therefore, according to Monczka and Morgan, it is necessary that big companies develop insourcing/outsourcing strategies from a company-wide perspective.

An Alternative View of Boundaries

In Chapter 3, we discussed different ways of looking at the company and at purchasing. We argued that the firm as a production unit used to be the dominant perspective, supplemented over time with an increasing interest in viewing companies as knowledge, communication and capital-earning units. The discussion of the boundaries of the firm presented in the previous sections fits nicely with the production view. The analysis of insourcing and outsourcing is very much a consequence of the production perspective. The main question is what the company should do in relation to what the company is good at. Alternatively, if we take as our starting point the view of the firm as a knowledge unit other important aspects are revealed. This section is devoted to that kind of analysis. Our aim is to provide an alternate way of looking at boundaries, which also gives some other insights. The discussion is focused on a comparison of the production view and the knowledge view. To a large extent, the perspective of the firm as a communicating unit coincides with the knowledge view, while the capital-earning perspective, in terms of boundary effects, corresponds to the production view.

If the company and its counterparts are regarded as knowledge units, the boundary cannot be seen as separating knowledge bodies—because the knowledge of the different parties always partly overlaps. Knowledge has no clear boundaries regarding content. The boundary can instead be perceived as the 'signals' going out from the company or its 'knowledge surface' as viewed by other actors. These signals or surfaces tell us something about the content of knowledge, and even more about how it is used and brought together.

If the company uses a certain technology in order to produce or design its product or service then it will be seen as representing that technology and if it uses a specific area of knowledge it will be seen as representing that area. In knowledge terms, every business unit represents a specific way of approaching a problem area. Therefore, one crucial issue for any firm is to be perceived as a representative of some specific knowledge. This is an important aspect of what we described as the identity of an actor in Chapter 6. If the company sends out very diffuse signals or has very unclear knowledge surfaces, the counterparts will have no clue about when—or why—to approach it. Furthermore, knowledge is always related, which means that the signals will also indicate a certain position in relation to other firms and their knowledge. For anyone to be interested in taking part in interaction with someone the other has to represent something—something that can not be found somewhere else.

The main issue is to consider what can be outsourced without leading to a reduction in interest from others. Keeping production capacity in-house is not always the most important thing, especially where the production technology is easily available on the market. But outsourcing is not just about getting rid of things—normally, it must be combined with strengthening something else. Instead of focusing on production capability the firm may have to increase its design capability.

What is critical from a knowledge point of view—and perhaps generally from a resource point of view—is that the company needs to be seen as important by the others. When the production view is applied, the focus is on working as cost efficiently as possible. It is important for a company how it is perceived by others. The company as a knowledge-unit-perspective highlights other aspects than does the company as a production-unit-perspective.

However, looking at boundaries in this way emphasizes not only what the company controls internally but also what it may access through its partners. The signals include what knowledge resides within the firm, but also what the firm is perceived as being able to mobilize. As explained in Chapter 6, the identity of the company reflects its close partners—i.e. its social capital. The firm is seen as a representative of the total knowledge that can be activated.

Managerial Tasks

The outsourcing approaches adopted in both manufacturing and services are not unproblematic. According to Greco (1997), a survey has shown that 51% of the respondents brought back an outsourced activity in-house. The main reason for the problems and pitfalls seems to be that decisions concerning this important issue are not given the strategic attention they deserve. For example, Ellram and Billington (2001) argue that US companies, in general, still continue to outsource primarily to save on short-term costs such as overheads. Other writers have found that outsourcing decisions are too often hasty decisions 'made in the face of looming deadlines or drastically reduced budgets' (Greco 1997, p. 52). The problems associated with this approach are of various types. Greco reports that one common problem is that the buyer fails to co-ordinate its in-house operations with those of the supplier. Furthermore, sometime the provider fails to properly explain what it can and cannot handle. Greco also states that in many cases an outsourced task is 'thrown over the wall' by the customer with a big sigh of relief and no intent to follow up the outcome. Therefore, Monczka and Morgan (2000) argue for the need to carefully manage outsourcing operations. They conclude that many companies have failed to understand that when in-house manufacturing is replaced with outsourcing, there is still a need to be involved in managing the supply.

Managing insourcing and outsourcing involves two important issues. The first is the decision concerning an appropriate division of labour. The second is about the implementation of this decision. When it comes to decisions as to how the various activities should be allocated among actors the examples above indicate that there is a need for more strategic thinking. In spite of the increasing attention to these issues a great deal seems to remain to be done in this area. The US airplane manufacturer Cessna has established a strategic make/buy process (Morgan 2000). It took about a year to come to a consensus on what the process ought to be and then to decide what, in a general sense, should be bought and what should be made. Factors involved in these decisions are economic capacity, core competence, supplier capability and corporate relations. When items that are not part of the core competence are still manufactured in-house, the make/buy committee asks itself why this is the case. A number of similar issues are raised to keep the discussion concerning insourcing/outsourcing ongoing (see following Box):

Make and Buy Issues in Cessna

- Is there a competitive advantage to keep this technology in-house?
- Do we make it because we do it cheaper than anybody else?
- Do we do it because there's nobody out there who can do it effectively?
- Do we do it just because we've always done it?
- Do we need to outsource it just because we don't have the capacity?
- Do we have the capacity, but are we better served by spending our capital on something else?

Source: Morgan 2000, p. 5.

The second managerial issue is about the implementation of the decision. Ellram and Billington (2001) report on two unsatisfactory outsourcing experiences. The first is about a company in the field of personal motivation services. The company specializes in public and in-company training and sells accompanying printed material and tapes. Initially, the company produced its own audiotapes, but soon discovered that this activity was not a core business and so it was outsourced. However, because the company wanted to continue to get favourable prices from suppliers they purchased all the parts, which were then drop-shipped from manufacturers to the contractor. The buying organization received and paid the invoices and kept track of the inventories. This division of labour created some accounting problems. If any of the inputs were unusable inventory counts had to be adjusted accordingly. Furthermore, there was a great danger of being out of stock of something owing to the physical distance and separation of accountability. Unexpected out of stock situations required rush orders, premium transportation and higher total supply costs. These problems were raising transaction costs, creating excess paper work and inefficiency and duplicating the efforts of the parties. Furthermore, discussions and negotiations with the contractor revealed that this firm was buying similar parts for other customers. By combining the volumes, the contractor was able to negotiate lower material costs than the outsourcing firm. Thus, all of the excess work and hassles were actually increasing the out-of-pocket material prices of the outsourcing firm, as well as transaction costs.

The second case was a leading firm in the manufacture and sales of farm, lawn and earth moving equipment. This company had been outsourcing an increasing number of its components, systems and operations, this, in particular, being the situation in the areas of machining, tooling and other metal working operations. One outcome of this outsourcing was that the buying firm witnessed a considerable downward shift in the tonnage of steel purchased and used in its internal operations. As a result, it was paying comparatively higher prices for steel after the outsourcing decision. In addition, most of the contractors were relatively small and were therefore also paying higher steel prices, even higher than the buying company was paying for its internal uses.

These examples show that there are some important managerial issues to consider in the outsourcing process. However, it is very important that 'managing' is conducted appropriately. For example, Quinn (1999) is of the opinion that the buying firm should avoid too detailed direction of suppliers because the provider has been chosen for its competence and, typically, has more knowledge depth than the buying firm. A common pitfall appears when the outsourcing company defines a broader area of responsibility for the supplier (for example, system supply) but continues to manage suppliers as component sources. One symptom of this problem is to try to retain control of second-tier sources while encouraging first-tier suppliers to take a wider role.

Quinn (1999), in fact, argues that the real question is not just whether to make or to buy. It is also about how to evaluate and achieve the desired balance between the incentives needed to stimulate the supplier, and the buying firm's ambition for control and security. For the customer, one crucial step in this process is to shift the buyer outlook to managing *what* result is desired, rather than managing *how* the result is going to be produced. If the buyer specifies how to do the job in too much detail 'it will kill innovation and vitiate the supplier's real advantage' (ibid., p. 19). We will return to this issue in the following chapter on developing relationships with suppliers.

Key Issues

Outsourcing of activities to suppliers is directly related to the specialization of the 'production unit'-company. Outsourcing and specialization provide benefits in relation to both the internal and the external resource structure. Internally, specialization promotes economies of scale in manufacturing and outsourcing makes increasing resources for product development available. Externally, benefits are reaped through the use of more specialized suppliers who can be combined in productive ways. However, there are some crucial issues buying firms must consider when following the outsourcing route:

- **The decision to rely on buy rather than make is more irreversible than before.** Owing to the rapid pace of technical development and the increasing interdependence among technologies it may be very difficult for a buying company to change back from buy to make.
- **Insourcing is as important as outsourcing.** Companies must regard insourcing as important as outsourcing. For a highly specialized company there might be good reasons to insource activities performed by suppliers. The division of labour between a producer and its suppliers is dependent on the developments on both sides. Thus, it is important to consider this issue in terms of a process where resources are created in interaction with suppliers rather than a process where the producer just is trying to 'outsource'.

- **Defining core competence is a difficult task.** Every company needs to specialize and at a particular point in time it is possible to identify what competence can be perceived as 'core'. However, the make-and-buy decisions taken today have far-reaching consequences. For any company, it is extremely difficult to know what will be core tomorrow. Thus, there are reasons to be careful in using this concept as a basis for outsourcing decisions.
- **The buying firm must consider several boundaries.** Insourcing and outsourcing, generally, are related to changes in the ownership boundary of the firm. For the firm as a knowledge unit this boundary is less important. Increasingly, companies rely on access to resources controlled by others, which to some extent overlap with internal resources. One important consequence is that the company can make use of mechanisms like alliances, technical co-operation, relationships, etc., in combination with in- and outsourcing. Thus, the key issue regards the degree of control or access to crucial resources.
- **Specialization affects the depth and scope of knowledge.** It is the capabilities of the company in relation to the capabilities of the business partners that determine how interesting the company will be perceived by others. Specialization promotes knowledge depth but narrows the scope. Therefore, the single company has to develop through interaction with its partners. Co-evolution is a key issue.

Chapter 8

DEVELOPING RELATIONSHIPS WITH SUPPLIERS

In Chapter 7, we analysed important principles underlying insourcing and out-sourcing decisions. The benefits a company may gain from outsourcing are to a large extent contingent on the nature of its supplier relationships. Therefore, the second supply network strategy deals with relationships to suppliers. Buying companies develop various types of relations to different vendors. In some relationships there are close interpersonal contacts, in others suppliers are kept at arm's length. Joint product development projects are conducted with some suppliers, while others are typical sub-contractors relying on customer specifica-tions. In some cases products are delivered just-in-time, while in other relationships buffers and inventories are at hand in the material flows.

On the whole, it appears to be justified to have different types of supplier relationships within one and the same company, since suppliers make different types of capabilities and resources available to the buying firm. This chapter analyses the implications of the different relationship strategies that can be used by a company. The classification of buyer–seller relationships we use is based on the level of involvement between customer and supplier (Gadde and Snehota 2000). We distinguish primarily between high- and low-involvement relationships. The classification of a relationship in one of these two categories is based on the occurrence of activity links, resource ties and actor bonds. Some supplier relationships score high on all three dimensions, while others score low on some or all of them. In the analysis, we refer to relationships characterized by either extensive activity links, resource ties or actor bonds as high-involvement relationships and those that score low on all three as low-involvement. We discuss the advantages and disadvantages of the two strategic options and come up with the conclusion that a company needs a variety of relationships in terms of involvement.

Analysing the pros and cons of different levels of involvement will require a framework for understanding the economic consequences of buyer–seller rela-tionships from the customer point of view. We discuss the costs and benefits of supplier relationships in the first section. In the next section we analyse the characteristics of high- and low-involvement relationships in terms of this frame-work. Buyer—seller relations on industrial markets tend to be long lasting. In the third section we discuss the reasons for this and the consequences thereof. The fourth and fifth sections are devoted to discussions of the need for variety in the supply base and how different relationships complement one another. Finally, we bring up three important implications related to the managing of supplier relationships, which concludes the chapter.

Economic Consequences of Supplier Relationships

No business can do without suppliers, and as a rule, there is a substantial continuity in the relationships with suppliers. Therefore, the relationships in the supply base of a company represent one of the most important assets of the company. As with all other assets, the value is not absolute but context dependent.

Some supplier relationships are important because of the volume of business they represent, others because they affect the future of the company in that they are important for the quality of the customer's own offering or the technical development of the company. The impact of a specific supplier relationship depends on how it fits into the operations and the strategy of the buying company and how other supplier and customer relationships are affected. Therefore, the role and value of a particular relationship cannot be evaluated from its product and service content only.

A number of technical, commercial and organizational solutions in a supplier relationship affect costs and benefits of both companies. Some of these conse-quences are quite easy to describe, measure and quantify, while others are less obvious, more indirect and difficult to measure. Sometimes, these economic con-sequences are of a much greater magnitude than those that are easily revealed. It is clear that the recent developments on the supply side of companies are outcomes of attempts to affect these important, but less immediate, economic consequences.

In order to develop effective supply strategies, buying companies need to understand the multiple economic consequences of supplier relationships. In par-ticular, it is important to be aware of the possible effects of changes in the level of involvement. The costs and benefits a supplier relationship can entail are analysed by Gadde and Snehota (2000)—see Table 8.1.

On the relationship cost side, the most obvious item is what shows up on the invoice from the supplier—'the direct procurement costs'. These costs are easy to

TABLE 8.1   Financial consequences of supplier relationships. Source: Gadde and Snehota 2000, p. 308.

Relationship costs	Relationship benefits
Direct procurement costs	Cost benefits
Direct transaction costs	Revenue benefits
Relationship handling costs	
Supply handling costs	

identify and measure. Reducing direct procurement costs has always been at the top of the purchasing agenda. As shown below, this is the prime target when relying on a low-involvement relationship strategy. But there are also a number of other costs that emanate from supplier relationships. Each purchasing transaction is associated with other expenses such as costs of transportation, handling of goods, ordering, and so on. These 'direct transaction costs' are generally more difficult to measure, but as a rule they can be traced both to the specific transaction and the specific supplier. Other costs cannot be directly related to specific transactions but can be traced to an individual supplier. Some relationships require substantial investments in terms of the adaptations undertaken among the parties. Other relationships demand continuous interaction for maintaining the relationship—although the transactions may be quite infrequent. These costs are thus dependent on the extent of involvement with suppliers and are identified as 'relationship handling costs'. In high-involvement relationships these costs are considerable. In most cases, however, their sizes are unknown because they only partly show up in company accounts. Finally, the customer may sustain substantial costs that cannot be directly attributed either to specific transactions or to individual suppliers. The 'supply handling costs' are structural costs and are common for the purchasing organization as a whole, including communication and administrative systems, warehousing operations, and general process adaptations, etc.

Some relationship costs are difficult to measure. When it comes to the relationship benefits, the problems are even greater. Most often, considerable resources must be used even to identify them. According to Table 8.1, two types of relationship benefits can be distinguished. 'Cost benefits' represent cost savings in the operations of the buying company that can be related to relationships with suppliers. Numerous examples illustrate supplier contributions to efficiency improvements in customers' operations. Joint efforts in product development and integrated logistics operations are two significant examples, which appeared in the description of Kodak's hidden costs (Figure 2.2). Cost benefits are tricky to measure, owing mainly to the interdependencies between various types of costs and benefits in—and between—relationships.

The second type of relationship benefits—the 'revenue benefits'—represent the impact on the income side of the buying company. These benefits arise when a solution in a supplier relationship affects the revenues of the buying company. The effects can be linked to improvements in product quality or process performance that affect the competitiveness of the customer. It goes without saying that they are extremely difficult to assess owing to the fact that they are indirect. There is little systematic evidence of these benefits. However, there are many examples of companies that have achieved substantial product innovation and quality improvements by making better use of suppliers (see, e.g. Davis 1993, Lewis 1995, Gadde and Håkansson 1994, Quinn 1999, Carlisle and Parker 1989).

It is apparent that the economic consequences cannot be evaluated only in the content of the individual relationship. The value of a supplier relationship stems to a large extent from how it fits into the operations of the customer and its other relationships. The economic consequences of one and the same solution from a supplier may differ among various customers and change over time, as the company's operations and its other relationships change.

High- and Low-involvement Relationships

A review of the literature clearly illustrates a shift in the view of what should be considered efficient relationships. Historically, it was recommended that buying firms avoid too much involvement with individual suppliers—customers should not become overly dependent on a specific vendor. There are three rational arguments for such an approach to suppliers (Figure 8.1).

First, dependence on one source may increase transaction uncertainty, the uncertainty as to whether or not the supplier will be able to fulfil its obligations. By having a number of alternative suppliers to rely on, the buying firm can reduce this uncertainty. The second argument is also about avoiding being locked into a specific relationship. However, in this case it is more the long-term flexibility in terms of technology that is considered. The technical capability of a supplier can take a direction that is not advantageous for the customer. If the customer is too deeply involved with this supplier—and has no alternatives—the situation can become problematic. The third advantage of low involvement relationships is that they make it possible to encourage competition among a group of suppliers. Primarily, the opportunities for playing off suppliers in terms of price have been considered an important determinant of efficient purchasing.

Avoiding dependency on individual suppliers leads to so-called 'arm's length relationships'. These relationships can be handled with limited co-ordination, adaptations and interaction. No specific product or service adaptations are needed, thus minimizing resource ties. Activity links are weak owing to standard-ized order processing and shipments from centralized inventories. In such cases, the interaction among the individuals in the two companies can be contained to sales and purchasing administration, implying few and limited actor bonds. Therefore, the low-involvement relationship is characterized by low relationship handling costs. Furthermore, we have argued that it may affect direct procure-ment costs positively because it increases price competition among suppliers. On the other hand, splitting orders among vendors may affect direct procurement costs negatively. In the same vein, switching from one supplier to another makes it difficult to routinize exchange activities, which probably increases the direct transaction costs. The low-involvement approach may also lead to substantial 'hidden' costs in other activities of the company. There may be costs for adapting internal resources to fit with what suppliers have to offer. In the absence of tight co-ordination the buyer might be obliged to create a buffer against possible risks.

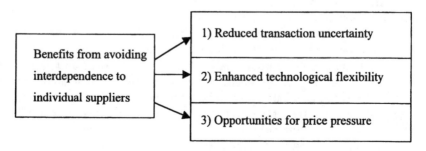

FIGURE 8.1 Arguments for avoiding supplier dependence.

Furthermore, in order to assure availability of supplies the customer might tend to use many suppliers, thus increasing supply handling costs. When it comes to the relationship benefits the low-involvement approach offers minimal opportunities for reaping cost benefits, and is not likely to contribute to revenue benefits.

The economic consequences of a high-involvement relationship show a very different pattern. The main rationale for high involvement is associated with the relationship benefit side. By extending involvement it may be possible to attain cost benefits in terms of reduced costs in production processes and material flows as well as improved service levels and flexibility. Furthermore, it is possible for the customer to take advantage of supplier skills and capabilities to improve the quality of its own products and services which, in turn, has revenue benefits. However, high-involvement relationships are costly. The gains of the benefits cannot be attained without substantial co-ordination, adaptation and interaction, which entail costs. In particular, high involvement increases relationship-handling costs. Therefore, increased involvement only makes sense when the consequently increased relationship costs are more than offset by relationship benefits. Reaping these benefits most often requires non-standardized solutions and customer-specific adaptations. High-involvement relationships are thus associated with an investment logic, as further discussed in the next section.

Evaluating the merits of the two involvement approaches—and all combinations between these extremes—is an onerous task. The economic consequences are difficult to trace and quantify. Furthermore, some important factors are qualitative in nature and impossible to estimate. Sometimes, it may be problematic even to identify a clear direction of the effects. Applying the low-involvement approach implies limited adaptations to stay free to choose the 'best' supplier in each transaction. Adaptations would mean reducing this type of freedom. On the other hand, this behaviour leads to low freedom in another sense. The buying firm is forced to procure standardized products and services, which means disadvantages in terms of internal adaptations. However, by relying on a standardized product the buyer is provided with the opportunity to play suppliers off against one another. To decide on the level of involvement is thus a complex task for the buying company. We must also remember that a high involvement approach is never an outcome of a one-sided decision. It requires a similar interest on the supplier side.

As the discussion has shown, there is a relationship between the level of involvement and the interdependence between the buyer and the seller. However, this relationship is not characterized by a straight trade-off because both involvement and interdependence are multidimensional. An arm's length relationship is a means of avoiding three types of dependency (Figure 8.1). A buying firm relying on an arm's length type of relationship may not give priority to all these three opportunities offered. For example, having a number of alternative suppliers to secure supply (option 1) does not necessarily imply that those vendors are aggressively played off against one another to minimize direct procurement cost (option 3). On the contrary, transaction uncertainty may be reduced by long-term relationships with a number of suppliers where the customer deliberately avoids price chasing. The same arguments hold for option 2. A buying firm with the aim of staying flexible in the long term, thus favouring a low-involvement relationship, can make use of this situation in two ways. One is to switch among different suppliers to try to increase the degrees of freedom for future action. The other is to stay with one supplier over a long time, in spite of the fact that no major adaptations—or interdependencies—are at hand.

In all three situations the customer chooses a low-involvement approach, thus avoiding adaptations and interdependencies. What differs among the three cases is how the customer makes use of the potential for switching among different suppliers. This is the second important dimension of a relationship. It is related to the continuity of the relationship. There is a link between the level of involvement and the continuity of a specific relationship. High-involvement relationships take time to develop, which calls for continuity. On the other hand, we have seen that continuity is not necessarily accompanied by high involvement and that low-involvement relationships may be long term. The degree of continuity thus deserves a more thorough discussion.

Relationship Continuity

The foregoing section revealed that the degree of continuity is an important dimension of supplier relationships. High-involvement relationships are time con-suming to develop because they follow investment logic. Investment logic implies that costs precede revenues. Some of the main costs associated with a high-invol-vement relationship are substantial from the beginning. The adaptations that are necessary for reaping relationship benefits tend to come early. Some of the benefits may appear from day one, but generally they tend to come with time. Therefore, once the adaptations have been made both buyer and supplier have an interest in keeping the relationship ongoing. Another reason for high-involvement relation-ships to be long lasting is that buyer and seller need to know a lot about each other before establishing this type of relations. For example, co-operation in R&D requires a common history, trust and commitment, which takes time to develop. Numerous examples of long-term buyer–seller relations in industrial networks have been reported (see, e.g. Håkansson 1982, Gadde and Mattsson 1987). However, when the whole supplier base of a company is considered it becomes clear that there are also many short-tem supplier relationships (Table 8.2).

This data comes from a longitudinal study of the supplier relationships of a forklift manufacturer. The suppliers represent components and systems which together account for about one-third of the total costs of purchased goods. Table 8.2 illustrates that out of 52 suppliers no less than eight had delivered for more than 25 years, and six of them were still being used at the time of the study. But we also find that no less than 31 companies had supplied for a period of less than nine years. Some of these suppliers had been used in parallel with others for a few years. Others had been tested, but had not lived up to expectations. None of these relationships were of the high-involvement type. It would be very unlikely for a high-involvement relationship to be characterized by a low degree of continuity in this type of production structure.

Where it comes to the low-involvement approach the situation is less clear cut. As discussed above, this approach can be combined either with a low or a high degree of continuity. The price pressing behaviour, which is a primary driving force in the historical view of efficient purchasing, relies on low continuity, where

TABLE 8.2 The duration of 52 supplier relationships of a forklift truck producer. Source. Dubois and Gadde 1996, p. 5.

Number of years as a supplier	Number of suppliers
1–4	21
5–9	10
10–14	6
15–19	4
20–24	3
25–29	4
30–33	4

the lack of involvement makes it possible to change supplier without problems— the switching costs are low. By shopping around, a buying company may benefit in terms of lowered direct procurement costs. Therefore, many supplier relationships are characterized by low continuity, as can be seen in Table 8.2, where around 40% of the relationships lasted less than four years.

The buying firm may argue the contrary as well. Even in the absence of specific adaptations to a certain supplier it might be advantageous to stay with one and the same vendor to simplify administrative routines such as ordering. It has been empirically confirmed that 'durable arm's length relationships' exist (Dyer et al. 1998). These relationships are characterized by 'less face to face communication, less assistance, and fewer relation specific investments'. This means that even long-lasting relationships can be effectively managed with limited involvement. Furthermore, shopping around requires an extensive search for information, which may be avoided by sticking to the same supplier. Another reason for this behaviour is that by concentrating the whole volume of business on one vendor the customer might be perceived as a more interesting business partner than if switching among various suppliers. On the other hand, the buyer avoids involvement—either because the costs of involvement are higher than the corresponding benefits or to have the option of changing supplier. There are thus certain advantages related to the combination of low involvement/high degree of continuity. Concerning the supplier relationships in Table 8.2, it is evident that some of the most long-lasting relationships were to be characterized as low-involvement ones.

The main conclusion to be drawn up to this point is that different types of relationships in terms of involvement and continuity can each provide its benefits to a customer. Figure 8.2 summarizes the characteristics of the four combinations obtained when combining the involvement dimension with the continuity dimension.

The Need for Variety in Relationships

There are clearly good arguments for a buying firm to develop relationships of various types. Suppliers offer different contributions in terms of benefits—their costs also vary. Above, we dealt with the involvement of the parties and the

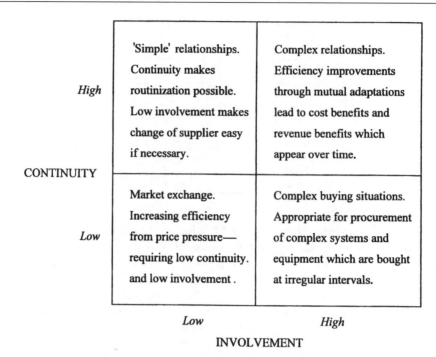

	Low	High
High	'Simple' relationships. Continuity makes routinization possible. Low involvement makes change of supplier easy if necessary.	Complex relationships. Efficiency improvements through mutual adaptations lead to cost benefits and revenue benefits which appear over time.
Low	Market exchange. Increasing efficiency from price pressure— requiring low continuity. and low involvement .	Complex buying situations. Appropriate for procurement of complex systems and equipment which are bought at irregular intervals.

CONTINUITY

Low   *High*

INVOLVEMENT

FIGURE 8.2   Relationship involvement and continuity.

length of the relationship as dimensions of differentiation, but there is more variety to exploit. Bensaou (1999) reports on a study of 447 purchasing managers where the objective was to analyse the performance of different types of relationships. One variable of particular interest to Bensaou was the extent to which buyer and supplier made specific investments related to the counterpart. Buyer specific investments included tangible ones like buildings, tooling and equipment dedicated to a specific supplier or products and processes customized to the components procured from the supplier. The investments of the buyer also involved intangible resources in people or in time and effort spent on learning about the supplier's business practices and routines, exchange of information and development of knowledge for nurturing the relationship. On the supplier side, the specific investments take similar forms and include both tangible and intangible resources. The relationships in the sample could then be classified according to Figure 8.3.

Cell A in the figure represents the typical 'market exchange' type of relationship, while D is classified by Bensaou as a 'strategic partnership'. Those two types correspond to the core illustrations of low- and high-involvement relationships. Cell B represents the case where the supplier has made specific investments while the buyer hasn't. The supplier is thus more dependent on the customer than vice versa. In cell C the opposite situation occurs—the customer is more dependent on the supplier. This is thus also an illustration of high involvement from the buying firm. The figures in the cells represent the frequency of the relationships in the two samples that belong to each respective combination of counterpart

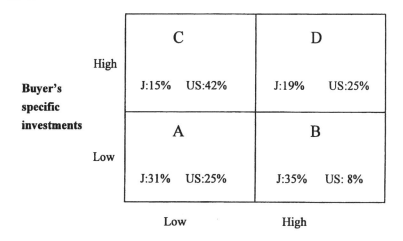

FIGURE 8.3   Frequency of supplier relationships with different types of customer-supplier specific investments. Source: Bensaou 1999, p. 36. Copyright © Sloane Management Review Association. All rights reserved.

specific investments. The study was carried out in Japan (J) and the United States (US).

There are some notable differences between the countries. Relationships in Japan are characterized by a larger share of supplier specific investments, while the opposite situation prevails in the US. There is also an unexpected similarity between the two samples. The occurrence of market exchange and strategic partnership is about the same in both countries. In fact, the US scores higher on partnerships and lower on market exchange, which is contradictory to expectations, based on popular beliefs. However, for our purpose this is not the most important finding of this study. What is more interesting is that in both samples we can observe a considerable variety in the supplier portfolios of the buying firms. The Japanese sample shows an especially even balance between the four different combinations, with 35% as the top score and 15% as the lowest.

What is even more interesting is the performance of different types of relationships. According to Bensaou's observations there were major performance differentials between the various relationships. But the differences in performance were not related to where in the matrix the relationship belonged. There were no statistically significant differences among the four cells in Figure 8.5. Bensaou comments (ibid., p. 37):

> No one type of relationship, not even the strategic partnership, is inherently superior to the others. Each cell contained low- and high-performing relationships, suggesting that each type of relationship can be well or poorly managed.

We return to the managerial issues in the sixth section, but first we discuss some other dimensions of a relationship where variety may be important. It is generally suggested that high involvement is preferable in supplier relationships that represent major volume of business for the buying company, and that low involvement can be practised in minor volume relationships. However, it should be observed that both low-involvement relationships to major suppliers and high involvement with minor suppliers might be viable and effective strategies. Firstly, high involvement in relationships with minor volumes of business is an appropriate approach when the supplier has particular skills and capabilities that are critical to the buying company's own offerings. The supplier may also represent great development potential. This situation is well illustrated by large pharmaceutical companies that establish high-involvement relationships with small innovative companies in biotechnology (Ford *et al.* 1998). Secondly, a buying company can handle only a limited number of high-involvement relationships because they are resource intensive. Therefore, it might not be possible to be highly involved with all suppliers representing major business volumes. A customer is thus faced with the necessity of determining which of its major relationships should be of the high-involvement type and which must be handled in other ways (Gadde and Snehota 2000). Low involvement with major suppliers is appropriate when the potential gains from further involvement are limited, which is often the case where standardized products and solutions are concerned. Savings from reducing the level of involvement in a large volume relationship may be substantial in some cases.

Variation Among High-involvement Relationships

So far, we have considered the high-involvement relationships of a company as a homogeneous group. However, there is great diversity among these close relationships. As we described in Chapters 4–6, there are some important differences in the content of relationships. We used the three concepts activity links, resource ties and actor bonds to distinguish among different dimensions of the content. From a relationship management point of view there is a need to adapt the managerial actions in accordance with these dimensions. Below, we take up the three dimensions of the content and try to identify typical problems in the corresponding type of relationships.

The first type of content is the links among the activities. Linking has to do with creating efficiency in the activity structure. It is about finding ways to take advantage of relating what is done by the supplier in terms of production and handling to what is done by the buying firm. This linking has very much to do with the procedures, routines and systems in the two companies. Relationships where the content is dominated by activity links will be very much directed towards successive improvements in these repetitive processes. Now and then, radical transformations are undertaken—e.g. in terms of business process re-engineering—but most changes take place through day-to-day rationalizations. The main objective is to make the relationships as 'lean' as possible, mainly reducing resource utilization in relation to all activities. Depending on the frequency of transactions and volumes of the products subject to exchange, the effects can be mainly directed towards either the physical flow (production and logistics) or the paper flow (administration).

Changes in the resource ties have to do with finding new ways to make use of resources. It is about creating more value in the supplier relationships. Every supplier has a set of resources, including some particular knowledge. In order to take advantage of these resources in the best way, the buying company must find ways to bind these resources to its own. This might be done by adapting one's own products or production facilities or by developing certain knowledge to be able to make use of the supplier's resources. Of course, resources have to match— in order to make use of resources you also need to have resources. Matching of resources is crucial for the efficient utilization of suppliers. In order to be good at this matching the buying company must be very knowledgeable both regarding its own resources and those of the supplier. Depth of technical knowledge is thus a main requirement. Most of the joint activities take place in terms of development projects similar to those described in Chapter 5. The projects have to be both designed and conducted in a way that is in accordance with the relationship. Learning and teaching are central tasks and relationships have to function in both ways. The buying company has to learn, as does the supplier. The buying side has to help the supplier learn through various teaching activities, which are discussed in Chapter 10.

Actor bonds represent the third type of content. Bonds have to do with attitudes, trust and commitment. In the product development case study where Toshiba was working together with Cummins the two companies experienced many problems in the first phase owing to mistakes caused by misunderstanding. Many relationships fail primarily for such reasons. Just as companies work internally to build efficient and creative organizations they should do so in the organizing of the relations with suppliers, as suggested in Chapter 6.

Managerial Tasks

It is necessary for any company to actively manage its supplier relationships. Managing is required to make the best use of the resources of suppliers. There are two different dimensions regarding what is the best use. Managing is about using each individual supplier in the most appropriate way and about using the combined potential contribution from all suppliers in the network in the best way. This section deals with the first of these tasks, while the second is discussed in Chapter 9. The core of our argument is that contributions from suppliers will depend on how they are handled. In particular, decisions concerning the extent of involvement are highly important strategic matters.

We bring up three managerial issues in our discussion. Firstly, there is a continuous need to monitor relationships to ensure that benefits keep pace with costs. Secondly, it is necessary to keep in mind that buyer—seller relationships are two-sided. What is available from suppliers depends to a large extent on the way the customer intervenes in the operations of suppliers. Thirdly, any supplier must be motivated to enter a high-involvement relationship and then receive support to continue to be a resource provider for the buying firm.

Monitoring and Modifying Relationships

The level of involvement is a crucial issue in any relationship. High-involvement relationships may provide substantial benefits, but they also entail substantial

---

Kodak's Criteria for Evaluation of Partnerships

1. Amount of technical support.
2. Number of innovative ideas.
3. Supplier's ability to communicate effectively on important issues.
4. Flexibility shown by supplier.
5. Cycle time, responsiveness, and improvements shown.
6. Supplier identification with Kodak goals; are our goals common?
7. Level of trust that exists in dealing with the supplier.
8. Strength of the relationship at each plant.

Source: Ellram and Edis 1996, p. 25.

---

costs. Therefore, the first managerial issue is about assessing these costs and benefits. In many cases, these assessments take the form of evaluation of the supplier rather than the relationship. For example, the Box below shows the criteria used by Kodak for evaluation of the performance of the supplier partnerships they have developed.

Evaluations of this type are rare. Many firms tend to enter high-involvement relationships and, accordingly, reduce the supplier base without analysing the prerequisites and consequences of these strategic changes. For example, one study revealed that firms 'appear to be pursuing supplier reductions without a clear assessment of the costs and benefits involved' (Cousins 1999). Another study reports on a relationship that was characterized by the fact that the customer 'had been overpaying for services in the name of partnerships, the terms and benefits of which could not be identified, let alone quantified' (Kapour and Gupta 1997). Benefits from partnerships are thus not reaped automatically. Furthermore, the level of involvement must be continuously monitored and adapted to changing conditions. Modifying involvement in terms of what is justified in the specific relationship is one of the critical issues in supply network strategies. If this is omitted buying firms may end up in either over- or under-designed relationships, both of which have been found to be paths to failure (Bensaou 1999). Over-designed relationships evolve where the resources utilized in the relationship exceed the resource requirements. Over-designed relationships are not only unnecessarily costly, but also tend to be risky owing to the specific investments undertaken. In most relationships there are times when it becomes necessary to decrease the level of involvement. In some cases, substantial gains might be attained through a standardized low-involvement relationship. At the other end of the spectrum—under-designed relationships—the movement may need to go in the opposite direction, because there may be potential benefits from increasing involvement. Both increasing and decreasing the extent of involvement are thus always strategic options to be considered.

When supplier performance is perceived as inadequate there are two options. Traditionally, firms changed suppliers in these situations. Nowadays, the main effort seems directed towards assisting suppliers to enhance performance. For example, a representative of Harley Davidson states that if suppliers are not doing well 'we send resources to help them' (Milligan 2000). This way of dealing with suppliers' lacking performance is representative of a general shift in attitudes. This shift implies that making the most of supplier relationships has become a matter of using existing relationships in the best way rather than trying to find the 'best' potential partner.

To avoid low performing suppliers many firms develop training programmes that vendors are required to follow. Motorola was one of the pioneers in this field (Cayer 1988), the reason being that improving the quality of Motorola's products required extending quality assurance to suppliers. Company representatives argued that suppliers 'affect quality more than any factor in the equation except for design'. The most important of the training courses offered—and required— dealt with statistical process control, design for manufacturability and short-cycle management (including just-in-time techniques). More recent examples indicate that formal training programmes are no longer the most important means of enhancing supplier performance. In a survey in 1998 only 13% of respondents actually provided formal training to suppliers. The others stated that working closer together gave new insights through collaboration which supported performance improvements. For example, Harley Davidson explained the way they were dealing with the issue (Milligan 2000, p. 62):

> We have continuous improvements teams who go out to suppliers and review their supply processes. [...]
> We make suggestions to them because we have experts in a lot of fields. We will call in consultants if necessary. We will do a deep dive into their processes and make suggestions on how things can be improved.

Although we have so far discussed evaluation of the supplier, the most important thing is to monitor and evaluate the relationship. Lamming *et al.* (1996) present a useful model for relationship assessment. Without going into the details of this model we emphasize the fact that the supplier's contribution to the relationship is strongly conditioned by what is ongoing on the buyer side. This takes us to the second managerial issue dealing with the involvement of the customer in the operations of the supplier.

The Role of the Customer

The second issue in managing relationships is the need to consider that buyer– seller relations are two-sided. It is customer and supplier in interaction that determine the performance of the relationship. Therefore, any attempt from the buying firm to manage the relationship must take the interest of the supplier into consideration as well. Firstly, a buyer cannot decide in isolation about involve-ment and partnering—it takes two to tango. A seemingly interesting partnership from the customer point of view may be impossible to realize owing to supplier reluctance. Such imbalance in terms of interests and motives has been shown to be quite common (Krause and Ellram 1997). Secondly, in the ongoing relationship the customer may choose different approaches when it comes to supplier in-volvement. In many cases, the role of the supplier tends to be decided mainly from the internal perspective of the buying firm. This is witnessed by the atten-tion paid to supplier development programmes (see, e.g. Hahn *et al.* 1990, Krause and Ellram 1997). These programmes usually aim at directing supplier operations to fit better with those of the customer. There might be good reasons for a customer to help suppliers develop in this way, but there is some danger in pushing these efforts too far. In Chapter 7 we quoted Quinn (1999) on the potential problems with innovation when the buyer imposes overly detailed specifications. Quinn's opinion is that the most critical management issue is to shift the buyer outlook towards managing the desired output from the supplier rather than the operations of the supplier.

Similar arguments are advocated by Araujo *et al.* (1999). These authors analyse the consequences related to various types of customer intervention in the operations of suppliers—in particular, how intervention impacts on the resource utilization of the supplier. Quinn's analysis revealed two different types of cus-tomer prescriptions—*what* (i.e. prescribing the outcome) and *how* (prescribing the operations). These two options correspond to two of the resource interfaces identified by Araujo *et al.* 'How' is similar to what is referred to as a 'specified' interface. In these situations, the buying firm specifies in detail the characteristics of the object of exchange and/or how it is to be manufactured. Sub-contracting and traditional outsourcing of component manufacturing are examples of this type of interface. In these cases, the buyer uses the supplier as an extension of its own production structure. Such arrangements can be very effective. For example, a sub-contractor may be able to pool orders and reap economies of scale and scope beyond the reach of any of its customers.

Quinns's 'what' corresponds to a 'translational'—or functional—interface. In this case, the buyer informs the supplier of the function of the object of exchange—for example, in terms of speed, tensile strength, etc. Then the supplier can decide on its own the best way to supply this 'functionality'. Thus, even this case relies on directions given by the buyer. However, in the translation interface these directions leave a significant degree of freedom for the supplier to decide on the best way to meet the buyer's requirements.

Araujo *et al.* bring up a third type of interface, which is not contingent on customer directions. In 'interactive' interfaces buyer and supplier jointly develop the specification of the product subject to exchange. Buyer and supplier may, based on considerations of their joint set of resources, evaluate different solutions and the various trade-offs among them. Hence, this type of interface enables firms to consider productivity consequences for both parties as well as benefits that can be jointly developed *vis á vis* specific third parties, such as the buyer's customers and the supplier's suppliers.

The type of interface developed in a relationship will have direct consequences for the way the resources of suppliers are activated. Interfaces affect the extent to

TABLE **8.3** Characteristics of different types of interfaces. Source: Araujo *et al.* 1999, p. 505. Copyright ©1999, Elsevier Science.

Interface Category	Characteristics	Customer Benefits Productivity	Customer Costs Productivity	Customer Benefits Innovativity	Customer Costs Innovativity
Standardized	No directions. No specific connection between user and producer contexts.	Cost benefits from supplier economies of scale and scope, as well as learning curve effects.	Adaptation to standardized solutions may create indirect costs elsewhere.	None	No direct costs. Allows only indirect feedback to suppliers based on sales figures.
Specified	Precise directions given by customer on how to produce.	Supplier can pool together similar orders; economies of scale and scope can be attained.	Supplier's resource base 'locked in.' Limited possibilities to influence specifications.	Minimal (supplier can propose changes to blueprints).	Suppliers used as capacity reservoir. Development of supplier resources may suffer.
Translation	Directions given by customer based on user context and functionality required.	Supplier can propose efficient solutions that improve its own as well as the customer's productivity.	Supplier may reap benefits that are not shared with customer.	Supplier has some leeway to propose innovative solutions.	Supplier may not know enough about customer context to innovate radically.
Interactive	Joint development based on combined knowledge of use and production.	Open-ended exchange allows full consideration of direct and indirect costs for both parties.	Investments in knowledge of how best to make use of existing resources.	Supplier learning about user context opens up the gamut of solutions offered.	Requires investments in joint development and learning.

which a customer may access the resources of the supplier. Furthermore, the different types of interfaces differ in terms of the costs associated with using them and the benefits they provide. Araujo *et al.* analyse these costs and benefits in terms of how they contribute to productivity and innovativity on both sides of the focal dyad. In Table 8.3, the characteristics of these interfaces are compared with each other and the characteristics of a 'standardized' exchange, where the buying firm chooses its products from the general assortment of a supplier, thus giving no direction at all.

The main conclusion of the analysis conducted is that any buying firm needs a variety of interfaces, because each provides different contributions to productivity and innovation. A second conclusion is that changing interfaces is not a one-sided affair, no matter how powerful the customer—or supplier— may be. A supplier–buyer interface is always the outcome of decisions made on both sides of the dyad and is also strongly dependent on the interfaces with other firms. Finally, Araujo *et al.* point out the danger of focusing too narrowly on core competencies. The ability to analyse and develop complex interfaces requires the development of competencies that relate different but complementary specialities. By definition, these competencies then cannot be described as 'core'.

Mobilization and Motivation of Suppliers

One underlying theme of the book is that high-involvement relationships entail huge costs for buying firms because they require considerable and continuous investments. But these relationships impose costs on suppliers as well. Therefore, buying firms have to encourage and motivate suppliers to be able to mobilize them in high-involvement relationships because they need their assistance. Ellram and Edis (1996) illustrate how Kodak identifies the incentives and improvements offered to suppliers involved in partnerships. The first benefit for Kodak's suppliers is that they have secured Kodak's long-term business, which makes them better able to plan for the future investments and use of resources. The supplier can thus sharpen its resource utilization, and focus on meeting the specific needs of fewer, key, customers. Understanding the directions and needs of a demanding customer may, in turn, lead to new development opportunities. A supplier may, for example, be able to develop business with Kodak's OEM-suppliers, since Kodak requires them to work with the designated partner on new product development. The supplier also may reduce its administrative burden and improve its use of resources when it has lower bidding and quotation requirements. Furthermore, the supplier no longer has to 'hard-sell' at all Kodak's locations; Kodak's internal teams do the selling job for supplier partners. Finally, the dedicated Corporate Account Management System helps to build a strong international customer/supplier network among all of Kodak's facilities, supporting improved relationships.

Once suppliers have been mobilized they must be continuously encouraged to continue the relationship and contribute to performance enhancement. Beyond evaluation and monitoring discussed in relation to the first managerial issue, motivational aspects are also important. Being able to access supplier resources is not only a matter of customers' efforts to manage interfaces. It is also about getting supplier input in actual operations. Even in this respect Motorola was a forerunner. In the late 1980s, they established a number of activities to encourage supplier participation. The Communication Sector—Motorola's largest business—worked with four formalized functions in this respect. They formed a Supplier Advisory Board to improve two-way communication between Motorola and a core of selected suppliers. The Annual Supplier Conference provided exchange of information and insights into various business activities. At these conferences, top Motorola managers were involved, to indicate the importance of the conference and the desire to develop close relationships with suppliers. Technical symposia and Supplier Shows were two activities where suppliers were able to directly impact on Motorola. The Supplier Shows were forms of exhibitions where suppliers presented their products and services to Motorola—and other companies. The symposia took the form of in-depth technical seminars on topics presented by technical experts from supplier companies.

Some recent examples of motivational programmes can be found at Caterpillar and Cessna. Caterpillar uses three types of activities to strengthen relationships with suppliers (Millen-Porter 1997b). One of them is a business simulation game where representatives of Caterpillar and suppliers learn to identify potential benefits from high-involvement relationships. This is the most significant activity in trying to develop the contact pattern between the parties and establish a common perspective on the business operations. The two other building blocks in the supplier programme are a system for quality assurance and a supplier show similar to that of Motorola. Cessna has two main activities to support suppliers and strengthen relationships (Morgan 2000). First, are supplier conferences, which are perceived as strategic communication and learning vehicles and are run on an annual basis. Another part of the programme involves the setting up of a supplier advisory board, which makes it possible for suppliers to get their voices heard by the Cessna management.

All these efforts of mobilizing and motivating have an impact on—and are impacted on by—what we have identified as the relationship atmosphere. The programmes presented were aimed at developing trust and commitment, which are prerequisites for high-involvement relationships. These relationships build on mutual adaptations and investments, which is one of the reasons they tend to be of a long-term nature. But, as we argued in the section on continuity, the relationship needs to have a history before the partners become deeply involved with each other. It would be highly unlikely for a supplier to make considerable customer specific investments unless the firms are familiar with one another. But familiarity and absence of unpleasant experiences are not enough. The supplier also has to consider the future prospects of the potential partner and how the customer fits into the whole network of which the supplier is a part. Furthermore, engaging in a high-involvement relationship requires trust, because it is quite different to do business in terms of market exchange as compared with strategic partnerships, in the terminology of Bensaou (1999). In turn, these close relationships impose dependence on buying firms. The traditional approach of avoiding dependence must therefore be replaced by strategies to handle dependence.

When it comes to the relationship atmosphere in terms of co-operation and conflict we believe generally held attitudes need reconsideration. There is a tendency to portray arm's length relationships as conflictual, while partnerships are assumed to be more friendly and co-operative. In our experience, this is a misconception. All relationships are characterized by a mix of conflict and co-operation. In fact, high- involvement relationships usually involve more conflict than low-involvement relationships do. In the latter type of arrangements there may be frequent discussions about price levels, quality and delivery terms, but on the whole there is not so much more to argue about. In high-involvement relationships joint investments, product adaptations and other strategic issues require that customer and supplier agree on a common approach, in spite of the fact that their views may be quite different. The higher the involvement between the companies the greater the interdependence and the more pronounced the potential for conflict. This fact is illustrated by the way the IT-company Sun deals with suppliers (Carbone 1996, p. 44):

> While Sun works closely with suppliers involving them in product development and bringing them in-house it doesn't mean that the company isn't demanding. In fact, Sun has a reputation for being tough with suppliers on cost, delivery, and quality.

The main characteristic of the relationship atmosphere in high-involvement arrangement is thus the simultaneous occurrence of conflict and co-operation, as pointed out in Chapter 6. Owing to the mutual interdependence of the companies, conflicts have to be solved in one way or another before they escalate to confrontation. This does not mean that conflicts should be avoided. On the contrary, diversity of goals and convictions are prerequisites for innovation and dynamics. Therefore, it is necessary for each company to continue to emphasize its own objectives and interests. At the same time, it must be accepted that the counterpart has other interests and objectives that also need to be taken into consideration.

Key Issues

Supplier relationships are important resources for a company and take many various forms. The higher the involvement in a relationship the higher the potential for benefits of various kinds. However, there is a trade-off to consider because the higher the involvement the higher the costs and interdependencies. The most important issues to handle when developing appropriate relationships are the following:

- **Evaluating the economic consequences of relationships.** Supplier relationships represent major investments. Like all investments, they must be assessed in terms of benefits and costs. However, because relationships are connected these analyses must often concern the combined effects of several supplier relationships.
- **There is a need for relationship variety.** There is no such thing as *the* best type of relationship. Different suppliers provide benefits and costs of various kinds. For this reason, relationships must be managed in different ways.
- **Avoiding over- and under-involvement in relationships.** Over-involvement occurs when the customer's resource input to the relationship exceeds

the benefits gained. In this case, the customer must reduce its input or take efforts to improve the output. In an under-involvement relationship the customer has invested too little to take advantage of the supplier's potential.

- **Determining appropriate interfaces with suppliers.** The effect of a supplier relationship is contingent on the type of interface. In particular, the interface impacts on the opportunities for the supplier to make the best use of its own resources and those of its network partners.

- **Interdependencies should not be avoided, but must be handled.** Mutual adjustments are important means of increasing relationship benefits. These adjustments make the customer dependent on suppliers and should not be avoided, as was recommended in the past. Relationships among individuals in the two companies play an important role in handling these dependencies.

- **Partnerships require an interested supplier.** High-involvement relationships are costly for suppliers as well. Therefore, a key task for buying firms is to continuously mobilize and motivate suppliers to engage in relationships. This is important not only in the early phases of the relationship but has to be maintained during its total life-time to make the best use of the suppliers.

Chapter 9

DESIGNING SUPPLY NETWORKS

This chapter deals with the third of the strategies on the supply side of companies: designing supply networks. The issues analysed in Chapters 7 and 8 have profound implications for the supply base of a company. The supply base is the aggregate of all the supplier relationships of a company—the supplier portfolio in the terminology of Bensaou (1999). The increasing reliance on outsourcing discussed in Chapter 7 implies an increase in the number of suppliers. This, in turn, increases total supply costs because there are specific costs associated with the handling of each supplier. The main conclusion of Chapter 8 is that any company needs suppliers with various capabilities and resources. The supply base must thus be characterized by variety in terms of relationship involvement, which was clearly illustrated by the comparative study of supplier relationships in Japan and the US (Figure 8.3).

Designing supply networks involves the following sub-issues. First, a buying company may use either single or multiple sourcing. Single sourcing means relying on only one supplier in the acquisition of a specific item. Sometimes, a buying firm may prefer to use two or more suppliers—i.e. dual or multiple sourcing. In the first section we describe the pros and cons of these choices. The decision concerning sourcing policy impacts on the size of the supply base of the company—i.e. the number of suppliers to deal with—which is discussed in the second section. Managing the supply network in terms of the numbers of suppliers is an important strategic issue because handling many relationships is costly. In the third section we present some cases where the opportunities to combine the advantages of single and multiple sourcing are illustrated. The US footwear producer Nike has developed a supply network where suppliers contribute different types of capabilities and resources. In the fourth section we analyse this supply network. Nike is one of the 'strategic centres' directing their own networks, as mentioned in Chapter 7. We present the characteristics and consequences of these emerging networks in the fifth section. Then we bring up some important strategic issues in network building. Finally, the managerial implications are summarized.

Single and Multiple Sourcing

The choice between single and multiple sourcing is to some extent related to two issues brought up in earlier chapters. There is a connection between the extent of involvement with suppliers and the number of suppliers used. High-involvement relationships are resource demanding and costly and a company cannot handle too many of them. Traditionally, when the main objective of purchasing behaviour was to avoid too strong a dependence on individual suppliers, multiple sourcing was the recommended strategy in this respect. It helped companies in dealing with the negative consequences related to dependence on suppliers, illustrated in Figure 8.1. The second issue with implications for the supply base is the choice between centralized and decentralized purchasing. When single business units or plants are free to determine their own supplier choices it is most likely that the total supply base of a buying company will be larger than in a centralized purchasing organization. One of the main reasons for centralized purchasing is to exploit economies of scale by using fewer suppliers.

There are two main arguments in favour of multiple sourcing. One is that it reduces dependence on individual suppliers. By using alternative vendors a buying company is supposed to improve the reliability in the flow of goods on the supply side. If one supplier has a problem in delivering according to plan, an alternative source may be used at short notice. Problems in this respect include the negative impact stemming from strikes and natural disasters, etc. Multiple sourcing also reduces the risks associated with being locked into certain technical solutions, which later become outmoded. Puto et al. (1985) illustrate how multiple sourcing is an important strategy for buying firms to reduce some of their uncertainties. The second argument for multiple sourcing is the advantages of having competing suppliers. By stimulating competition among suppliers buying firms may be better off in terms of the input they receive. In particular, the positive impact on the price level has been emphasized. For a more comprehensive overview of the characteristics associated with each respective sourcing strategy, see Table 9.1.

Historically, the main advantage of single sourcing was perceived to be the increase in bargaining power. By concentrating its purchases on one supplier the buying firm was considered more interesting as a business partner. Over time, however, another aspect of single sourcing came into focus. When customers started to tackle the indirect costs associated with their purchasing behaviour, they realized that there was a need to reconsider what was an appropriate sourcing strategy. Reducing indirect costs requires high-involvement relationships with suppliers. These relationships call for investments which, in turn, necessitate a reduction of the supply base. When this is done and customer and supplier start to work more closely a number of ways to improve relationship performance might appear. For example, an American study revealed that purchasers considered it possible to accomplish efficiency improvements through co-operation with single sources that would have been impossible to obtain when multiple sourcing was used.

Figure 9.1 illustrates the main differences between single and multiple sourcing approaches. Håkansson and Wootz (1984) argue that extensive collaboration with one supplier leads to lower total costs than multiple sourcing in two

TABLE 9.1   Advantages of single and multiple sourcing. Source: Hines 1995, p. 19, based on Bailey and Farmer 1982.

Some advantages of single sourcing	*Some advantages of multiple sourcing*
1. The supplier ought to be able to offer price advantages because of economies of scale.	1. With several sources there is insurance against failure at one plant as a result of fire, strikes, quality, delivery problems, and so on.
2. Personal relationships can be more easily established, thus making communications more effective.	2. With more than one supplier a competitive situation can be developed; no one supplier can afford to become complacent.
3. Administration work in the buyer's office is reduced.	3. In cases of standard items, no tooling cost is involved and there are often no advantages for added volume.
4. Closer relationships and a reasonable tenure can result in mutual cost reduction efforts.	4. The buyer is protecting against a monopoly and may have the advantage of two sources of new ideas or new materials.
5. Buyer-tied research can be undertaken.	5. There is no moral commitment to a supplier as when the total quantity would be a considerable proportion of the supplier's total sales.
6. Tool and pattern or fixture costs are reduced and long-run tools may be used.	
7. Transportation costs can be lower, and where pallets are used common pools can be established.	6. Giving orders to a number of suppliers increases flexibility in case of large additional call-off or decreased needs.
8. Quality control is made easier, since there is only one location.	7. Part business can be used as a base load in conjunction with which a smaller supplier may be developed.
9. Scheduling is made easier.	8. With two suppliers holding stock, the buyer company can reduce inventory level.

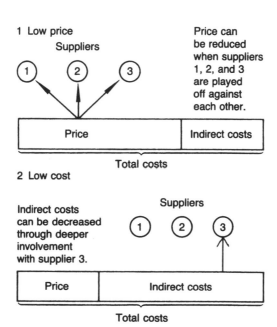

FIGURE 9.1   The impact of sourcing strategy on direct and indirect costs. Source: Asplund and Wootz 1986, p. 61.

situations. One situation is when the indirect costs associated with purchasing are substantial in comparison with price. For example, this is often the case with MRO-procurement. The second situation is when, for some reason, the indirect costs are more open to influence than price. This situation may arise with standardized items where, for example, costs of physical distribution may be affected through close collaboration. When neither of these conditions is at hand, the buying firm might be better off playing the market and relying on multiple sourcing.

The Size of the Supply Base

Traditionally, the size of the supply base was never, in itself, a key issue in purchasing strategy. When efficient purchasing was the same as optimizing the outcome of single transactions, the size and shape of the total supplier structure was not an interesting issue. Therefore, it was not uncommon in the past for management not to even know how many suppliers the firm used or who they were. When the view of efficient purchasing shifted, so did the view of sourcing strategies. The increasing reliance on single sourcing is one of the explanations for the reductions of the supplier bases of companies. Another reason is the enhanced awareness of the costs associated with handling a large number of suppliers. Some of the costs of handling the supply base are a function of the number of vendors rather than the volume of business. One of the purchasing managers interviewed for this book estimated the costs of keeping a supplier 'alive' in the company files to around USD5,000 per year—even if they bought nothing from the vendor.

Altogether, this means that companies have been eager to reduce the number of suppliers they use. In many cases the reductions have been dramatic, as illustrated by Table 9.2 showing the changes in a number of companies over a ten-year period (normally between 1985 and 1995). It is obvious that these figures overestimate the actual effects. To some extent, this is a result of excluding suppliers who might not have been used for a long time but who were still in the company's files.

These developments stand in marked contrast to what was traditionally considered effective purchasing. Newman (1988) states that the clear trend towards single sourcing that appeared at that time would have been considered 'an invitation to disaster' only one decade earlier. The main reason for such an

TABLE 9.2   Reduction of the supplier base in some US companies. Various sources.

	Changes in the number of suppliers	
	From	To
Xerox	5,000	500
Motorola	10,000	3,000
General Motors	10,000	5,500
Ford Motor	1,800	1,000
Allied-Signal Aerospace	7,500	6,000

attitude was that the buying firm, by applying a new view of sourcing, would lose the benefits of risk spread and price control, which stem from having many suppliers. However, it is by no means clear that multiple sourcing is the only means to achieve the objectives this strategy is supposed to support. In some cases, single sourcing might be an even better strategy than multiple sourcing, with regard to securing availability of supply. Single sourcing, in combination with a high-involvement approach, makes it possible to establish logistics facilities, which increase delivery reliability more than any multiple sourcing approach. Correspondingly, sticking to one supplier does not necessarily increase the likelihood of becoming locked into a specific technology. On the contrary, close co-operation and mutual openness regarding technical development may reduce the risks of these negative effects.

When it comes to the opportunities to play suppliers off against each other we have already mentioned that this is favourable only in terms of decreasing direct procurement costs. In cases where direct costs are relatively less important than the indirect costs, single sourcing may be a better way to deal with cost rationalization. Furthermore, what is often forgotten is that there is a cost of competition (Hahn *et al.* 1986). There are substantial costs associated with 'playing the market'. Prospecting for potential suppliers, tendering procedures and supplier evaluation are resource demanding. In many cases, the gains from price reductions owing to these competitive procedures are more than outweighed by the increasing administrative costs of handling these procedures. In some cases, the company may attain short-term benefits by playing the market. However, in the long run this short-sightedness might lead to increasing costs. It is difficult for the buying company to benefit from potential rationalizations in supply handling through a continuous search for lowest price. It also imposes restrictions in price negotiations because the bargaining power is to a large extent dependent on the total business volume with the supplier. Other implications are that the economies of scale of the supplier are negatively affected and that it becomes difficult to ask suppliers for solutions that are well adapted to the internal conditions of the buying firm.

Consolidation of the supply base has been a strong driving force for reduction of the number of suppliers. For example, in 1981 Motorola had 109 active suppliers of capacitors (Stork 1999). The central purchasing department installed a simple supplier rating system so they could inform the decentralized business units which suppliers actually offered the best business conditions. After a few years, three suppliers had won 95% of Motorola's capacitor business. The remaining 5% went for low volume and speciality capacitors not produced by the other three. A number of similar changes have been reported. For example, Harley Davidson has cut its supply base in half since 1990 (Milligan 2000). They did this in a conscious effort to eliminate the suppliers who were not 'up to meeting the new objectives of cost, quality, and timing'. In the area of original equipment purchases, Harley Davidson concentrates 80% of its purchases on a critical group of suppliers who willingly take part in the company's supplier strategies. This group consists of only 70 suppliers. HD is currently rationalizing its MRO-procurement. The company is on track to move from in excess of 3,000 MRO-suppliers to concentrating 80% to 90% of its buying on only three suppliers. The gains provided by consolidation are expressed in different ways. One is savings on direct cost. For example, Mercury Marine, a division of Brunswick Corporation, reports savings of more than 10% from consolidating the purchases of IT, telecom and copying (Avery 1999b). These experiences made the parent company interested in transferring the same ideas to other purchasing areas. The effects of three more consolidation efforts are reported ('non-traditional' purchases, travel management and MRO-supplies). The savings in these areas were all of the order of 10–13%. However, according to corporate management, these financial gains are only part of the advantages of consolidation. The new arrangements assure the company that it has 'sound written agreements developed upon which we have negotiated' (ibid., p. 38). Another advantage is that Brunswick achieves consistency in service levels across all its different divisions and companies, which is of help in controlling costs.

Similar developments are reported from the pharmaceutical industry where Welch Allyn, like many companies, has consolidated its supplier base (Milligan 1999). Today, 60 suppliers account for 80% of its supply dollars. This consolidation has allowed the company greater leverage, flexibility and cost savings. The focused cluster of suppliers has arranged for automated replenishment systems that keep supplies coming in and prevent the manufacturer from running out at inopportune times. One main advantage of the concentration of the supply base is the reduction in contact work. Purchasing prefers dealing with fewer people. Another company highlights the advantages associated with becoming an increasingly important customer to the suppliers who remain in the supply base. A third company reports that a consolidated supply base makes it easier for the company to manage its suppliers. However, there are downside effects as well. One representative states that if you have only one supplier 'they can hold tight on what they are charging you'. Another significant experience is that there are times when the suppliers are out of stock of a particular component, which causes severe problems in terms of factory lead times (ibid., p. 71).

Our discussion shows that single and multiple sourcing both have their pros and cons, as indicated in Table 9.1, and consolidation of the supply base is associated with advantages as well as disadvantages. The most appropriate strategy for a buying firm would therefore be to take advantage of both approaches, at the same time trying to avoid the main disadvantages. The next section outlines how a mixture in this respect might be developed.

Combining Single and Multiple Sourcing

The first observations of the supply systems in the Japanese auto industry indicated two characteristics of customer–supplier relationships. The relationships were closer than in the western world—there were stronger links, ties and bonds. Furthermore, it had been possible to establish those close relationships owing to the single sourcing strategy adopted by large buyers. However, the latter characteristic, that single sourcing was the underlying reason, was re-interpreted when more experience was gained. Richardson (1993) reports that Toyota used single sourcing for only 28% of its components, while the corresponding figure for Honda was 38%. This means that, on average, two-thirds of supply was not single sourced. The main characteristic of these firms' sourcing policy is what

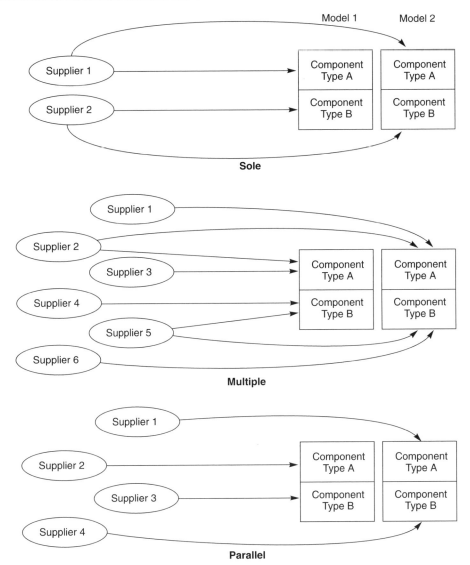

FIGURE 9.2   Alternative sourcing strategies. Source: Richardson 1993, p. 343. Copyright © John Wiley & Sons Ltd. Reproduced with permission.

Richardson labels 'parallel sourcing' (see Figure 9.2). According to Richardson parallel sourcing has the following characteristics (ibid., p. 342):

> A snapshot in time would show an assembler with many sole sources suppliers. But a closer look would reveal that there are several firms in the supplier group that are qualified to produce a component. Some are currently producing similar components for different models while others have done so in the past [. . .] The distinctive feature of parallel sourcing is that two or more suppliers with similar capabilities are concurrently sole-sourcing suppliers for very similar components. While using a sole source for a component, the assembler establishes parallel sources to provide performance comparisons and competitive bidding for the next model cycle.

Parallel sourcing is a way to combine the benefits of both single and multiple sourcing, and this strategy has now been adopted by firms in the western world as well. For example, Motorola's consolidation of its supplier base for capacitors relies on this logic. When the 109 suppliers were reduced to three, the supplier characteristics were as follows: 'One of them performed best in ceramic parts, one that performed best in tantalum parts, and one that was very good in both ceramics and tantalums' (Stork 1999). If one of the suppliers failed, business could quickly be shifted. Annually, the Motorola commodity team adjusted shares of business based on actual supplier rating results. The best performing supplier was given a larger market share than the poorer performing. That strategy was perceived as prompting 'considerable competition in quality, delivery, technology, pricing, and provided the administrative simplification benefits of single sourcing'.

Hines (1995) observed the same phenomenon and identified it as 'network sourcing'. The key issue related to network sourcing is to develop an 'inter-company environment where the creative tension between co-operation and competition is used to maximize the benefits to all supply sources, the customer, and ultimately the end-customer as well' (ibid., p. 22). The author illustrates the network sourcing approach with Mazda's sourcing strategy for seats for its domestic Japanese plants. At the time, Mazda split its seat purchases between two suppliers—Delta Kogyo and Toyo Seat. Each company was responsible for different models of seats and was used as a single source for the particular model over its lifecycle of three to five years. The seat business as a whole was thus dual sourced with a division of 60% to Delta and 40% to Toyo. Interviews with the companies involved revealed that both were informally assured of a certain percentage of Mazda's seat business at any one time. This percentage was approximately one- third to each of the companies (see Figure 9.3). This means that each firm had an assured long-term share of Mazda's seat business. According to a representative of Mazda, all supplier relationships (whether they are affiliates, sub-contractors or common parts suppliers) were established for an 'indefinite' period of time.

Delta and Toyo thus are both competing and co-operating. They compete over the remaining third of Mazda's total seat business. This competition is very intense, since both firms know that they have only one chance to take over the

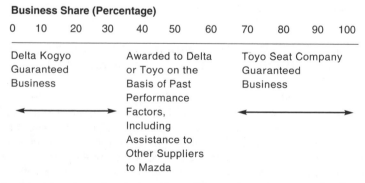

FIGURE 9.3   Mazda's seat sourcing strategy. Source: Hines 1995, p. 22. Reprinted with permission from the National Association of Purchasing Management.

order for a new car model every three to five years. The areas of competition involve design abilities, management strength, cost reduction progress, quality records, etc. However, the companies compete only for one-third of the total business. For the remaining two-thirds, they co-operate—there is a significant degree of openness between the two firms. In some cases, this openness takes the form of co-operation in solving mutual or individual problems, because the other seat supplier is often in a better position to give advice than Mazda itself. In fact, the amount of assistance the supplier has given its direct competitor is one of the performance measures that are evaluated when business is allocated among the vendors.

Strengthening the capabilities of suppliers is an important objective for the buying company as well. Dyer and Ouchi (1993) studied the buying behaviour of the main Japanese manufacturer in electronics—NEC. An interview with one of NEC's suppliers illustrates how this company perceived the situation (ibid., p. 57):

> We are always in competition with another supplier to produce the lowest-cost, highest-quality circuit boards. NEC would often provide assistance to both of us by sending in teams of engineers to help us improve. We usually won the competition but NEC didn't just give us all the business. Instead it seemed like they renewed their efforts to help the other supplier compete. They would send in people to help them improve production methods. They would buy our technology and then share it with them. In short, they would try to help them keep up with us. Of course, they praised and rewarded us for being their best supplier but they would always remind us that they could go elsewhere if we didn't continuously improve.

Dyer and Ouchi made similar observations regarding other Japanese customers. For example, a representative of Nissan stressed the importance of assisting weaker suppliers to improve their competencies. To have creative competition among suppliers requires that both have advanced capabilities. Therefore, providing support to suppliers is a highly effective method for both helping and forcing suppliers to continuously innovate and improve. These examples illustrate creative combinations of competition and co-operation.

We argued above that there is a connection between the nature of relationships with suppliers and their number. High-involvement relationships cannot be applied to too many vendors. There is therefore a connection between level of involvement and sourcing strategy. However, as indicated by the examples above, there is no straightforward association between the two. This finding contradicts a seemingly common view that close relationships go hand in hand with single sourcing and that multiple sourcing is accompanied by loose relationships. On closer examination, the relationship between the level of involvement and the sourcing policy appears more complex, as is discussed in relation to Figure 9.4.

The matrix illustration indicates that level of involvement and sourcing policy need to be seen as two independent dimensions of purchasing strategy. As mentioned above, it is generally cells 1 and 4 of this matrix that have been considered the appropriate combinations of involvement and sourcing policy. Furthermore, in recent decades the common recommendations for partnering have implied a movement from cell 1 to 4. It is one of the main themes of this book to illustrate the benefits a buying company may gain from high-involve-

Sourcing policy	Single	3	4
	Multiple	1	2
		Low involvement	High involvement

FIGURE 9.4   Combinations of relationship involvement and sourcing policy. Source: Gadde and Snehota 2000, p. 313. Copyright © 2000 Elsevier Science.

ment relationships. However, we also find it important to challenge the fairly one-sided recommendations of a general move from 1 to 4, which we think is an oversimplification of a complex strategic issue. Reality shows that buying companies in certain situations rely on a low involvement approach and apply multiple sourcing—and that they do so for good reasons. High-involvement relationships are costly and can be motivated only when relationship benefits outweigh costs. Furthermore, high involvement requires interested partners, who are not always available. Therefore, it is perfectly rational for a company to manage some of its relationships under the conditions in cell 1. One recent study clearly illustrates that many purchasing professionals 'continue to manage the process with a tactical price based mentality' (Purchasing 1998). From a rationality point of view we also suggest that changing situations might lead a buying company to move some of its transactions from cell 4 to cell 1. This occurs when conditions that once motivated a high involvement relationship no longer prevail. For example, a recent survey shows that 43% of the purchasing managers polled say they have been forced to change back from single to multiple sourcing arrangements (Purchasing 1999b) for two main reasons. The first is a fear of supplier complacency (creeping inflation, deteriorating quality or delivery performance). The second is a fear that emergencies or natural disasters could occur, disrupting supplies with serious long-term consequences. Therefore, our conclusion is that buying companies need supplier relationships both in both cells 1 and 4, depending on prevailing conditions.

However, it is important to observe that cells 2 and 3 also provide strategic options, which have been relatively neglected. Effective purchasing needs to take these alternatives into account. A buying company may develop high-involvement relationships even when more than one source is used for an item (cell 2). Furthermore, it is also an option to avoid high involvement when a sole source is used (cell 3). Starting with cell 2, it is obvious from the examples of parallel sourcing that it is possible to be highly involved with more than one supplier. Other examples favouring this strategic option include, for instance, when the customers of the buyer prescribe different sub-suppliers.

In cell 3 we find relationships characterized by a low-involvement approach with a single source. Several rationales underpin this option. For example, Dyer et al. (1998) argue that 'traditional' arm's length relationships—buyers who frequently rotate purchases across multiple sources—are no longer an economically sensible approach. Firstly, the administrative costs associated with managing a large number of vendors easily outweigh the benefits associated with switching among suppliers and by using single sourcing the supply handling costs can be reduced. Secondly, dividing purchases across multiple sources reduces both the potentials for suppliers to achieve significant economies of scale and the bargaining power of the customer. If the buying firm is small it may try to be perceived as a more interesting business partner by allocating the whole of its business to one supplier. By avoiding adaptations to this supplier, the customer retains the option of changing to another vendor.

The four combinations of involvement and sourcing policy provide very different opportunities for improving purchasing performance. Each of them has its specific advantages. Companies considering only the traditional dichotomy founded in cells 1 and 4 are unnecessarily delimiting their strategic scope. Again, variation is prescribed as a powerful recipe for effective purchasing. A buying company needs a bundle of supplier relationships with different, complementary characteristics. One crucial issue is how these different relationships can be appropriately combined. This leads us in the direction of supplier networks and their organization. The section below describes the Nike network, a perfect illustration of complementary capabilities of different suppliers.

Nike's Supplier Network

Nike is one of the major US athletic footwear producers. This case study deals with their supplier network structure and strategy. It is based on information in an article written by Donaghu and Barff (1990). We have included this old example for two reasons. It is one of the few examples that are available of a properly designed supply network. Further, Nike's production system is an example of the way western companies deal with developing countries. The developments of the international networks we discuss clearly have political consequences. They are controversial from a societal point of view. This aspect is not discussed in the book but it is an issue that companies and politicians must deal with in the future.

Nike's supplier network is described in Figure 9.5. The first thing to observe is that Nike's production system was in 1990, and still is, entirely based on outsourcing to independent suppliers—they manufacture no shoes in-house. First-tier suppliers are considered 'production partners', rather than sub-contractors. Many of their supplier relations are of a long-term nature and suppliers are given various kinds of responsibilities within the Nike production system.

Three types of first-tier suppliers can be identified. One of them is the 'developed partners'. These firms are responsible for the production of Nike's latest and most expensive products. Their factories are located in Taiwan and South Korea. In these countries, production costs have risen substantially over the years and so production of price-sensitive products has been moved elsewhere. The shoes produced by developed partners are characterized by fairly low price elasticity, however, which means that they can absorb increasing production costs. Nearly all the developed partners manufacture Nike shoes exclusively. These relations are therefore characterized by strong mutual dependence, thus making it important for both parties that stability and trust are promoted. These

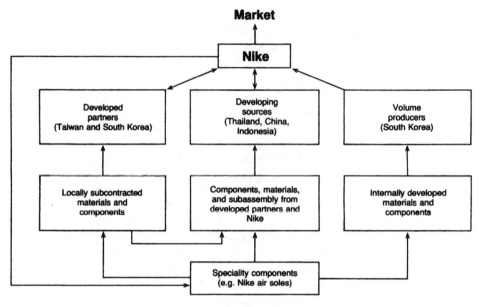

FIGURE 9.5   Nike's system of first- and second-tier subcontracting. Source: Donaghu and Barff, 1990, p. 545. Reproduced by permission of Taylor & Francis Ltd. www.tandf.co.uk/journals

firms are typically characterized by vertical disintegration. Their factories are usually supplied by local sub-contractors.

'Volume producers' are suppliers of more standardized footwear. They generally manufacture a specific type of footwear (e.g. football shoes, athletics shoes, etc.). They tend to be more vertically integrated than developed partners, often owning leather tanneries, rubber factories and assembly plants. Volume producers have a production capacity four or five times that of developed partners. Their customer relations are not exclusive. Instead, they have ten or more separate customers for whom they produce shoes. Therefore, neither Nike nor the competitors develop or manufacture any of their high-end and innovative products in these plants, where other brands are produced. Rather, volume producers are used to balance demand and supply in various phases of the business cycle. Developed partners, owing to their limited capacity, can only marginally absorb the cyclical variations in demand, which may be considerable. Monthly orders to individual volume producers may fluctuate by 50% or more. Therefore, Nike makes rather limited efforts to stabilize and deepen its relationships to the volume producers, as their strategy is to utilize them for cyclical sub-contracting.

The third supplier group is represented by 'developing sources'. Producers in this group are attractive owing to their low costs (especially labour) and their potential to diversify assembly location. Almost all the developing sources are exclusive Nike manufacturers. Nike is very active in assisting these firms in their capability development. At the beginning of the collaboration, the product and production standard of these firms may be comparable to the situation 40 years ago in the US. Nike, therefore, concentrates on increasing the production capability of these factories to meet the global production standard of Nike. The long-term goal is for a significant proportion of the developing sources to become developed partners.

Nike's supplier network, as described, is a mixture of relationships with different levels of involvement. Some of them are long term while others change from year to year. Some are characterized by high involvement while others are more 'arm's length'. Long-term, intimate partnerships with suppliers must somehow be promoted, maintained, and developed by the customer. Nike uses three main strategies to do this. Firstly, Nike operates what it calls an 'expatriate program' wherein Nike expatriate technicians become permanent personnel in factories producing Nike footwear, where they function as liaison between Nike headquarters and suppliers' R&D to help ensure smooth product development processes and maintain quality control. Secondly, Nike encourages its partners (particularly the more established ones) to participate in joint product development activities. Most basic research is performed at Nike's Beaverton facilities, but responsibility for the development of new footwear is shared with its production partners. The partners are especially important in the search for new material inputs and the implementation of improved production processes. These close ties also serve to keep the production partners abreast of the directions Nike intends to take in the marketplace. Thirdly, Nike places a monthly order with those factories that manufacture only Nike products (over half of all the partners), seeing to it that production does not vary more than 20% per month. These efforts to stabilize the production of Nike shoes take place both with those factories that have been with Nike for many years and with newer producers.

It is interesting to observe the activities undertaken by Nike to increase the capability of their developing sources. The developed partners also participate and play an important role in this process. The establishment of developing sources often takes the form of joint ventures between local factories in China or Indonesia and a Nike exclusive developed partner in South Korea or Taiwan. Owing to this arrangement, the developed partners have a direct economic interest in the development of the new sources, and will be interested in transferring and sharing their capabilities with these partners. In this way, all three actor groups benefit from increasing involvement. Developed partners are able to move production of the price sensitive part of the product programme to locations where cost is lower. They concentrate their own manufacturing activities on the more expensive, image creating products, where price is less important. Developed partners will also be able to supply developing sources with both components and materials. Developing sources will clearly be able to benefit from the joint venture. The transfer of various capabilities (from Nike and the developed partner) will accelerate the development of these firms as compared to a situation without these links with the larger network. Advantages will be obtained in terms of manufacturing techniques, owing to the demands from competent customers and the availability of important input resources.

Finally, Nike also stands to benefit from the new structure of the production system. The diversified structure of production hedges against currency fluctuations, tariffs and duties. The joint venture arrangements seem to be an efficient means of transfer of capabilities, which is efficient for the entire network. But the system also keeps the pressure on the developed partners at the first tier. They need to keep production costs low, as developing sources might otherwise mature into full-blown developed partners.

Strategic Centres and Webs of Partners

Nike is one example of what has been identified as 'strategic centres' (Lorenzoni and Baden-Fuller 1995). A strategic centre is a firm that takes a hub role in a network structure. Lorenzoni and Baden-Fuller argue that the business conditions of the late 20th century require alliances and networks that are strategically directed by a central firm. The strategic centre is responsible for the value creation for its partners as well as being 'a leader, role setter and capability builder' (ibid., p. 147).

The strategic centres studied (see Table 9.3) all represent businesses characterized by rapid growth. The primary reason for the success of these central firms is that they organize and manage networks different from common arrangements. According to Lorenzoni and Baden-Fuller most organizations continue to use their suppliers as sub-contractors, which makes partners behave as passive doers. Typically, these buying firms specify exactly what they want suppliers to do and leave little to the creative skills of others. Relating to the discussion in Chapter 8, this corresponds to a specified interface in the terms of Araujo *et al.* (1999). The strategic centres, on the other hand, rely on 'strategic outsourcing', which means that each of the relationships extends beyond simple sub-contracting. Central firms expect their partners to do more than follow the rules. They expect them to take—and reward them for taking—initiatives and for being creative on their own.

Strategic centres generally outsource more activities than most organizations, which is clearly illustrated by the Nike case study. To keep its position, a central firm needs to control some particular capabilities and resources—they have to develop some core competencies. Interestingly, the central firms define core competence not in terms of what is inside the ownership boundary of the strategic centre, but as what keeps the network together. Lorenzoni and Baden-Fuller identify four particular agendas for the central firms related to this 'glue' (ibid., p. 152):

- the idea
- the investment
- the climate
- the partners

The firms in the study demonstrated an unusual ability to conceptualize a business idea that can be shared not only internally, but also with other partners. These business ideas included specific aspects such as 'mass fashion for young people' (Benetton) and 'creation of user friendly computers' (Apple). In addition to these individual dimensions of the business ideas there was also a strong general dimension. All the business visions studied had a 'notion of partnership, which includes the creation of a learning culture and the promotion of systems experiments' (ibid., p. 153). The strategic centres tend to view their role as one of

TABLE 9.3 Main characteristics of strategic centres. Source: Lorenzoni and Baden-Fuller 1995, p. 148.

Name of company and its industry	Activities of strategic center	Activities of the network
Apple (Computers)	Hardware Design Software Design Distribution	Principal subcontractors manufacture 3,000 software developers
Benetton (Apparel)	Designing Collections Selected Production Developing New Technology Systems	6,000 shops 400 subcontractors in production Principal joint ventures in Japan, Egypt, India and others
Corning (Glass, Medical Products and Optical Fibers)	Technology Innovation Production	More than 30 joint ventures worldwide
Genenteche (Biotechnology/DNA)	Technology Innovation	JVs with drug companies for production and distribution licensing in from universities
McDonald's (Fast Food)	Marketing Prototyping Technology and Systems	9,000 outlets, jcount ventures in many foreign countries
McKesson (Drug Distribution)	Systems Marketing Logistics Consulting Advice	Thousands of real drug outlets and ties with drug companies and government institutions
Nike (Shoes and Sportswear)	Design Marketing	Principal subcontractors worldwide
Nintendo (Video Games)	Design Prototyping Marketing	30 principal hardware subcontractors 150 software developers
Sun (Computers and Computer Systems)	Innovation of Technology Software Assembly	Licensor/licensees for software and hardware
Toyota (Automobiles)	Design Assembly Marketing	Principal subcontractors for complex components Second tier for other components Network of agents for distribution

Copyright © 1995, The Regents of the University of California

leading and orchestrating systems. Their distinctive characteristics reside in their ability to perceive the full business idea and understand the role of the different partners in many different locations. Many of the central firms admit the business idea was not an outcome of strategic thinking in terms of a 'work of a moment' of one company. On the contrary, it is obvious that their vision emerged over long time and in co-operation with suppliers. The vision is dynamic because as their networks grow and as the context changes, the organizational vision also changes.

There are two main types of investments in the strategic centre. The first is the development of a brand name and the second is the establishment of the system that integrates the network. Control over these investments and activities gives the central organization a pivotal role and allows for the exercise of power. The most important means by which a strategic centre retains its power is to ensure that the information between partners flows freely and is not filtered. In many cases the strategic centres are best seen as hubs in a communication network. As illustrated in earlier chapters of this book, exchange of information is an essential task in supply networks. We showed the relevance and characteristics of the information exchange in all the three network structures. Communication is a costly activity and developing effective communication systems is always the responsibility of the strategic centres. Depending on the type of information and the intended role of communication these systems take different shapes.

When it comes to the third dimension of the glue—the climate—strategic centres' main task is to 'develop a sense of trust and reciprocity in the system' (ibid., p. 154). Doing this is important because it takes many partners operating efficiently to make the system work, 'but the negative behaviour of only a few can bring the whole system to a halt'. Lorenzoni and Baden-Fuller argue that the typical organizations' main response to this need is to enter into contracts with other firms in a formal legalistic manner. However, the strategic centres usually do not apply to this approach, because formal contracts are relatively inflexible and are suitable only when behaviour is easy to describe. The relationships in strategic networks have to be creative and flexible and are therefore very difficult to capture and enforce contractually. Instead, the approach of central firms is to develop a sense of reciprocity and trust in the system. Trust and reciprocity are dynamic and allow for tight co-ordination. This tightness is apparent in each actor's agreement to its known obligations, similar to contracts in the sense that obligations are precisely understood. However, there is a major difference as well. According to Lorenzoni and Baden-Fuller, Anglo-Saxon contracts typically delimit behaviour in the sense that partners are not expected to go beyond the contract. Strategic networks, on the other hand, prescribe behaviour for the unknown. Each partner is expected to work in a particular manner to resolve future challenges and difficulties as they arise. The most extreme version of this trusting behaviour is the Benetton franchising system. In Europe, Benetton does not use legal contracts, but relies on unwritten agreements. The company claims that these working rules focus everyone's attention on making the expectations clear. However, in other geographical areas Benetton uses formal contracts to supplement the trust system, mainly owing to local emphasis on law and contracts.

The partners of the central firm are extremely important in strategic networks. When discussing the characteristics of the relationships with these partners Lorenzoni and Baden-Fuller bring up aspects which have been highlighted throughout this whole book: co-ordination among all partners, a common long-term perspective, an acceptance of mutual adaptations, and incremental innovation (ibid., p. 156). In building a strong and prosperous network it is crucial to consider which partners become involved. Even in this important aspect, the strategy has changed over time. Initially, central firms tended to use trial and error, since it is difficult to know in advance which partners are most appropriate. The many styles of doing things are not easy to grasp and they are quite difficult to codify. However, over time, a partner profile emerges together with a selection procedure aimed at finding what is missing in the network structure.

Building Supply Networks

The central concepts derived in Chapters 4–6 can be used for analysing network positions and as a basis for systematic network building. Networking relates relationships to each other by finding and utilizing connections. These network connections may be links, ties and/or bonds in relationships. A supply network should be evaluated in terms of how efficient the activity pattern is, how innovative and value creating the resource constellation is and how powerful the established actor web is. These three dimensions are also clearly closely interrelated. The complexity in building as well as evaluating the existing supply network is obvious. However, some key issues can be identified.

The first has to do with the activity structure. Over the last decade, a lot of purchasing attention has been focused on efficiency in supply chains. These chains are certainly important but the network model suggests that there is a risk in overemphasizing the chain aspect. There are good reasons to include all the other branches in the network (that go out in other directions) in the analysis. If the chain is focused on in isolation, the companies may again start to build the kind of integrated company that was once so popular. So, when the activity structure is organized, supply chain aspects must be included, but it might cause problems if they are stressed too much.

The second issue relates to the central role of the information flows in the activity structure. The only way to control activities is by controlling the information flow. There are always problems in the information flows when boundaries are passed, when one system is left and another entered. This was the reason the automotive industry established a standardized system for exchange of information as the starting point in the development of the Odette delivery system. It is necessary to have such an internal information system to which important suppliers can easily be connected. If the buying company is powerful—as in the automotive industry—it may force the other party to adapt, but in most situations the buying company itself has also to adapt. It is critical to find adaptations in single relationships that can be interrelated—to establish network connections.

The third issue has to do with the resource constellation and the need to stimulate experimentation with resource combinations. The development of knowledge can never be just an intellectual exercise. The physical interaction between technical items such as products and facilities is equally important. Accordingly, development projects should take their point of departure both in ideas coming from the theoretical sphere and from problems and/or observations in the physical world.

The fourth issue is the number of participants in development projects. To date, there has been a clear tendency for one single supplier to be involved in each project. These efforts have been difficult enough to handle, but in the future we can expect to see more network development projects where three or more companies get together so as to be able to find new solutions where several resources are combined. These projects are challenging from a management point of view because they require much more of both balancing and mobilizing actions than projects with two parties only. One possibility might be to use special organizational forms such as virtual companies to handle such projects.

The fifth and final issue has to do with the creation of powerful supply networks.

A number of companies have tried to develop supplier associations with the ambition of getting the suppliers committed and connected to the buying company. Such general types of organizations can probably be useful in some situations, but they have very little to do with building networks. Functioning networks require unique combinations of activities and resources and, in this respect, general supplier associations have little to offer. They may even be dangerous as they may become too focused on relationships in general and, in particular, the balance of power between suppliers and the buying company, in which case the supplier association might develop into a bargaining organization. If the buying company wants to work with several suppliers at the same time, one crucial issue is the decision as to who should take part. In some cases, partners other than suppliers may be important—for example, customers of the buying company or even someone buying the same product.

Managerial Tasks

In Chapter 3, we analyse the characteristics of what we perceive as a new type of economy. We argue that its most prominent ingredient is an industry structure that is network-like, in which individual firms must be capable of managing in networks. Managing in networks is not about being a giant powerful actor forcing other firms to behave in a desired way but, to a large extent, about relating to the rest of the network and trying to adjust operations in accordance with the conditions. This chapter shows that managing is about active strategizing. The cases presented concern large firms, but the same principles hold for small companies—the main issue is to establish a position in the network. Irrespective of whether there is a large or a small 'hub' firm some general managerial issues should be considered.

Toyota's production system was probably the first example of a visible network structure. The characteristics of the system were illuminated by a spokesman for Toyota (Nishiguchi 1986, p. 348):

> In order for the Toyota production system to be truly effective, the individual effort of Toyota Motor alone, a mere assembler, would be insufficient. We can approach the completion of the system only when we establish a destiny-sharing community with our satellite suppliers and subcontractors.

In the early 1980s, Toyota was using a total of more than 40,000 suppliers in its production system (see Figure 9.6). However, only a marginal number of these (168) were in direct contact with Toyota. The others were organized in a hierarchical structure where primary suppliers were responsible for structuring the rest of the supply system.

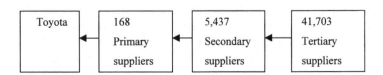

FIGURE 9.6   Toyota's hierarchical supply structure. Source: Berry 1982, p. 25.

The first managerial issue for the 'hub' firm is to consider which partners are needed in the network. The most important determinants in this respect are the resource and capability requirements on the supply side of the buying firm. These issues need continuous attention because the problems and opportunities change constantly. Sometimes, it might be difficult to decide which supplier should be on the primary level. An example from Harley Davidson illustrates (Milligan 2000, p. 62):

> The challenge for buyers at Harley is choosing the suppliers who can provide all the necessary technology for various motorcycle systems, while maintaining the 'art form' of the motorcycle. As systems become more electronic, that is a problem because suppliers who were competent at the art form sometimes are not up to date with the technology.
>
> Example: lighting systems. In the past we have had lighting suppliers who were not necessarily experts in lighting, but in die-casting. [...] Our motorcycles are art forms and lighting has been part of our art form. What we found was our lighting suppliers could do the art form, but could not keep up with producing the lighting. The bike looked great in the daylight but when you were on the road at 60 mph at night you didn't care about the art form if you couldn't see.

Lighting on a motorcycle is more complex than it may seem. Brighter lights require more energy and generate more heat. This is a tricky issue and involves complex photometrics. Harley Davidson analysed the situation carefully and discussed it with many potential suppliers. They decided to change suppliers to one who had the technical capability, but lacked the art form expertise. The purchasing director concluded: 'They do not have experience with the art form, but we are managing the supply chain and are working with them on that'.

The second managerial issue concerns co-operation among the various suppliers combined in the network. Pedersen (1996) illustrates benefits that can be obtained by exploiting couplings among supplier relationships. The Nike case study provides some examples of substantial benefits stemming from such arrangements. By combining suppliers' capabilities and stimulating interaction among the vendors Nike is able to take advantage of the optimum configuration regarding product development and product quality (through developed partners), capacity balance (volume producers) and low cost (developing sources). For this co-operation to function both formal and informal organizational arrangements are needed. Various kinds of formal arrangements may support and promote interaction. The joint ventures between Nike and different supplier constellations are important to stimulate technology transfer among the suppliers. In Chapter 6, we illustrated how the organizational structure of the individual firms either promotes or impedes interaction with external partners. The informal organizational aspect, in terms of the atmosphere in the network, also has a profound impact on the level of effective co-working. In the analysis of relationship involvement, we discussed the need for trust and commitment as well as the simultaneous occurrence of conflict and co-operation. These aspects of the atmosphere are no less important when we deal with network efficiency, while handling them is even more difficult, as complexity increases when more actors become involved.

Another managerial issue is concerned with the information exchange in the network. Establishing efficient communication structures is a prerequisite for well functioning networks. Part of this communication structure is about building 'formal' structures for the exchange of information needed to co-ordinate activities and combine resources. EDI-systems and integrated CAD-CAM networks are examples of formal communication structures. But there is also a strong need to stimulate the 'informal' exchange of information. This type of communication is essential to the future development of the network, because it provides opportunities for identifying new combinations of actors, activities and resources. One problem with exchange of information of this type is that it cannot be planned, but has to emerge. Lorenzoni and Baden-Fuller (1995) found that the 'strategic centres' were better at promoting this kind of information exchange than the less prosperous firms in the control group of the study. The strategic centres actively tried to provide a breeding ground for information generation and exchange. In this way, their behaviour contrasted sharply with the firms in the control group. In these companies, Lorenzoni and Baden-Fuller found that critical information was guarded rather than shared. The hub firms in the control group had not been able to establish a structure where information sharing was considered a natural ingredient.

Key Issues

The relationship with a supplier needs to be seen in its network context. It is the total supplier network that determines the efficiency and the effectiveness of the operations on the supply side of companies. The capability of an individual supplier is important, but even more important is that this capability is combined and integrated with those of other suppliers. In these efforts there are some important factors to consider:

- **A company cannot handle too many high-involvement relationships.** High-involvement relationships are resource demanding and must be limited in number. Low-involvement relationships also incur costs—even when they are used only to a limited extent. Any company, therefore, needs to avoid too large a supplier base.
- **The customer must encourage co-operation among suppliers.** The examples of the different strategic centres illustrate the benefits that can be gained from actively supporting supplier co-operation. Joint actions in terms of activity co-ordination and resource combining are means of enhancing performance.
- **Exchange of information plays a significant role for network efficiency.** Efficient information flows are prerequisites both for co-ordination of activities in a network and for the exchange of information needed for resource development. Parts of the total information flow may be formalized and exchanged through standardized information systems, while informal channels still probably are the most important ones because they are required for more advanced tasks.
- **A supply network view is required for performance enhancement.** The supply chain perspective must be complemented with a network view. Focusing too much on single chains might make the buying firm overlook opportunities and constraints residing in the intersection with other relationships of suppliers and customers.

Chapter 10

NETWORK STRATEGIES AND NETWORKING

This book is about supply network strategies. In the first three chapters, we illustrated the increasing importance and changing roles regarding what is happening on the supply side of companies. We analysed the key issues in today's operations and related them to some important changes in the overall industry structure and conduct. We arrived at the conclusion that in the new type of economy, a network approach provides appropriate analytical tools for better understanding of purchasing and supply issues.

In Chapters 4–6, the tools for network analysis were presented. The industrial network approach and the ARA-model were applied to purchasing and supply issues. In Chapters 7–9, we returned to the three main supply issues already identified, dealing with:

- the boundaries of the company's own activities
- the nature of relationships with individual suppliers
- the total supply base and the connections among the suppliers.

The concepts developed in Chapters 4–6 were used to identify, analyse and reflect on significant problems and questions related to each of these three overall issues.

The basic idea underlying the ARA-analysis is to improve the overview of a complex reality. Interpretation of each separate structure increases our understanding of reality because each perspective helps us to explore different features. However, the three ARA-structures only represent partial views of reality. They are also completely intertwined, because activities are undertaken by actors, who control the resources that are prerequisites for their activities. Therefore, any analysis needs to return to the 'overall' network level. A first step in this direction was taken in Chapters 7–9 and continues in this chapter.

Chapter 10 deals with network strategies and networking. It is most likely that firms' strategies reflect their ambition to improve performance. Strategies, therefore, have to be seen in relation to some performance criteria. Therefore, we begin the chapter with a discussion of efficiency and effectiveness in networks. The rest of the chapter is devoted to analysis and implementation of strategies in networks. The second section, about network strategies, is a basic building block connecting Chapter 10 with the rest of the book. From that section, we then derive three important aspects of networking: network thinking, network organizing and network acting.

We conclude by commenting on the development potential on the supply side of companies. We also make a few remarks concerning the relevance of a network approach for analysis of industry structure and firm behaviour. Historically, markets and hierarchies have been perceived as the appropriate governance forms in industry. However, over time, relational exchange and network governance have received increasing interest from a theoretical point of view. We think our analysis of the supply side of companies provides a further argument for the need for a complementary approach.

Efficiency in Networks

One of the explanations for the complexity of strategizing in networks is related to their multidimensionality. A fundamental point of departure for network analysis is that any action undertaken by one actor impacts on others in several different ways. This makes it tricky to interpret the total consequences of various actions. Any change has some direct effects—but it also has a number of indirect effects, on other firms, that, in turn, impact on the actor's performance.

To be able to move the analysis further, we narrow the scope substantially. Our interest is in the direct impact on the efficiency of an individual actor. The first consideration relates to what kind of efficiency we want to explore. Efficiency can only be measured for something with a clear boundary, because it is defined as the ratio between output and input. In order to define and/or measure these two constructs there is an obvious need for a boundary around the entity that is subject to scrutiny (Torvatn 1995). One particular feature of networks is that it is possible to identify different entities that need to be considered in terms of efficiency. Examples of such entities are a single transaction, a series of transactions with a specific supplier (a relationship), and all the transactions a buying firm conducts with its total supply base. The view of efficient behaviour differs depending on which of these boundaries is applied. These three situations are explored below.

Efficiency in a Single Transaction

The first situation is when the boundary is drawn around a single transaction, which can be evaluated in terms of its benefits and costs. This is done in transaction cost analysis where efficiency is defined in terms of the most cost efficient way of dealing with each transaction. As discussed in Chapter 8, there are many reasons for conducting this type of analysis in order to increase the awareness of the cost and benefit drivers directly related to each transaction. Such an analysis may concern the content of the transaction, or how the transaction is carried out.

There are considerable differences among single transactions. For example, large numbers of frequent, small transactions have their logic while major, occasional, investments have other characteristics. Numerous models of organizational buying behaviour have been developed to explore these differences in terms of 'new task buying' versus straight or modified re-buy (see, e.g. Robinson, Faris and Wind 1967 and van Weele 2000).

Efficiency in a Series of Transactions With a Specific Supplier

The boundary can be drawn around a relationship—i.e. a series of transactions with one supplier. The most important feature of a relationship is that activities appearing over time are related. Consequently, when the efficiency of a relationship is considered, we have to relate costs and benefits to time. In a relationship, we can expect that there will be costs early in the relationship that need to be regarded as investments while the benefits are expected to appear later. One important consequence—which has often been discussed in relationship literature—is that relationships are only profitable over time. The received picture is illustrated in Figure 10.1(a). There is clearly an important message in this picture—raised in Chapter 8—relationship benefits take time to exploit, while relationship involvement is always costly.

However, as shown in Chapter 8, relationship benefits and relationship costs are characterized by variety. In Figure 10.1(b)–(c) we give a glimpse of the variation by illustrating two alternative outcomes. Let us compare the three curves from the viewpoint that they describe three supplier relationships. In the first relationship, a large effort to improve performance is made in the early stage. For some time, this solution pays off in a very nice way, but successively the benefits decrease when conditions gradually change.

The second case describes a relationship where the initial efforts are the same as in case (a) but where new efforts are also made after some time in order to exploit changing opportunities. The benefit curve follows the same pattern as the costs, but with a time lag. The third relationship differs considerably. In this case, the parties seem to fit well together from the beginning, but the benefits successively drop despite efforts to keep them up. Example (c) indicates that short-term relationships can also be profitable and that there is no guarantee that relationships will always develop in a positive financial sense. Thus, the continuous monitoring and evaluation of relationships proposed in Chapter 8 is of great importance.

The curves in Figure 10.1 require some additional comments. The first concerns the difficulties associated with estimating costs and benefits. As we showed in the first section in Chapter 8, both include a number of indirect and 'soft' effects that are difficult to quantify. Owing to these problems, there are seldom reasons to try to make exact and detailed estimates of the financial effects. The main objective of the analysis should be to identify the most important drivers of costs and benefits, which may then be used in attempts to improve efficiency. The second comment relates to the allocation of costs and benefits among the two parties, which is a most crucial issue because it affects the future ambitions about the relationship. Certainly, fairness and honesty in economic terms is a breeding ground for the interaction atmosphere as well as for the development of trust and commitment.

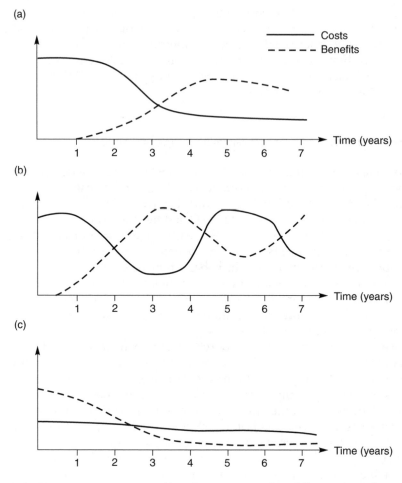

FIGURE 10.1 Buyer's costs and benefits over time in three different relationships.

The variation indicated above is related partly to the ambitions of the parties involved—a relationship has important psychological dimensions—and partly to other factors such as the characteristics of what is exchanged and the type of counterpart. A relationship based on procurement of large quantities of raw materials is different from a relationship where the object of exchange is a service or an advanced technological system. A component produced in accordance with the buyer's own drawings will form a different type of relationship than supply of standardized maintenance products. The large variation is contingent on the multifaceted benefits available. Relationship benefits are often indirect and, as we have described above, they can be related to changes in activities or in resources. There is large variation in what can be achieved, as well as in the way it can be done. Relationships should, accordingly, always be seen as unique, and there are good reasons for never trying to find just one relationship form. On the contrary, analyses of efficiency in relationships should focus on finding opportunities to exploit uniqueness.

Efficiency in Transactions With All Suppliers

Primarily, there are two main aspects that are important in any network of relationships. One has to do with how the threads in the network (the relationships) are connected and the other with the number of relationships and the variation among them. The first aspect to consider is to what extent, and in which forms, the different relationships are connected. The more the parties involved have made use of their relationships in a systematic way in technological or organizational development, the more extensive the connections will be. These connections make the network efficient in terms of transmitting and absorbing changes. The second aspect has to do with the ramifications of the network. If a network is well developed it can relate what is going on in one part of the network to other parts—and to other networks as well. In this way, the network can be seen as a 'root system', and the better its branches cover the area, the better it can utilize all the potential resources.

Network Efficiency

To develop effective supply strategies means to work with all the different types of efficiency simultaneously, because they are often contradictory—at least to some extent. The network efficiency will not be optimized even if each transaction is conducted in an optimal way. In the same way, too strong a relationship focus will lead to sub-optimization. The same problem will appear if a specific sub-network is optimized on behalf of the totality. Every network of business relationships is built up of a number of different dimensions, all of which are important from an efficiency point of view. Thus, every actor has to consider all these efficiencies when behaving as a network actor, and every company interested in developing its supply has to combine a number of efficiency criteria and find ways to achieve compromises among them. Figure 10.2 illustrates the discussion.

Figure 10.2(a) is focused on a single transaction. There is every reason to try to make each transaction as efficient as possible. Every transaction includes a number of activities, which activate various resources. The activities can be performed in different ways and the better they are adapted to the characteristics of the single transaction, the higher the efficiency. Thus, there are individual activities that need to be undertaken more efficiently and there are single resources that must be utilized better.

Figure 10.2(b) illustrates series of transactions within a relationship. These transactions can be made more efficient through finding and exploiting the interdependencies among them. It is the interdependence among activities and the potential for combinations of single resources that should be dealt with in the most efficient way here. The particular consideration concerns the activities and resources related to an individual counterpart. By relating transactions to one another new opportunities to improve on performance may be exploited. However, there is also a downside. By relating transactions more and more, certain restrictions are imposed on the performance of individual transactions. Sometimes, the losses in this respect may be larger than the benefits, and in such situations a high involvement relationship should not be considered at all.

FIGURE 10.2(a)   Efficiency in single transactions.

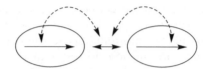

FIGURE 10.2(b)   Relationship efficiency.

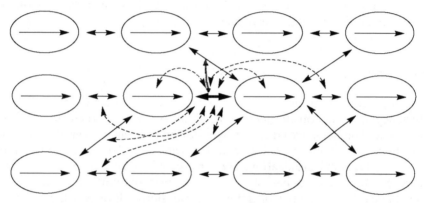

FIGURE 10.2(c)   Network efficiency.

However, as we argued in Chapter 8, the benefits from increasing co-operation are more substantial than the costs in many situations, and that is the reason for the increasing interest in developing close business relationships. As Figure 10.2(b) indicates, there are possibilities to relate what takes place in the transactions to what is going on within the two companies. The relationship provides opportunities to adapt and to utilize specific interdependency in all the activities of the two companies in relation to each other.

Figure 10.2(c) illustrates a transaction connected to a series of transactions within a relationship, which are 'in turn' connected to transactions within six other relationships. By adapting the focal transaction to the interdependencies with all these other transactions some benefits will be achieved—but again the benefits are accompanied by increasing costs in other dimensions. Every transaction within any network may be improved in a number of ways. New technical solutions can be developed as well as new ways to handle resources or activities. Resources can be used in a more efficient way and there are always new ways in which resources can be combined. Any transaction can be changed and adapted in order to increase the network efficiency. But there is also always a negative side to these modifications. There is a price to be paid in terms of reduced efficiency from a strict transactional or relationship view.

In each step we take from analysing the utilization of a single activity or a single resource in itself, towards analysing the use of them in a wider network, new opportunities emerge. The total number of possibilities is always infinite if analysing the supply network of any producing company. This is even more obvious if we consider an extended network and also include the customers and other external parties of the buying company. But again, there is always a cost side to take into consideration. To identify and exploit connections reduces the possibilities of conducting each individual transaction optimally. The more restrictions imposed in terms of connections—the greater the losses. However, from an analytical point of view it would be possible to find an optimal solution provided we could define a clear-cut network with one specific boundary. But network boundaries are always arbitrary—they are based on perceptions and are continuously changed.

In this section, we have shown why companies always need to use several efficiency measures to explore the benefits and costs associated with various strategic options. There is also another important aspect to consider in relation to a company's network strategy. For any company, it is important to try to achieve a central position in a network. In general, the most active companies gain central positions. The most active companies can develop most connections, given that they work in such ways that they are able to involve others. Action creates attention and direction, which means to become in the middle of the process, to be central. Furthermore, it means that the company's own resources are used by the others, which will increase their value. Thus, efficiency for one company is related not only to what it does itself, but also to the extent others are basing their actions on the focal company's activities and resources.

The consequences for purchasing are considerable and demanding. Purchasing can play a key role for all companies—small and large—by continuously finding new ways to approach suppliers, new ways to combine the resources and the skills of the suppliers and the customers with the companies' own resources. This requires a constant search for increasing efficiency in single activities, in combining activities and in establishing new activity patterns. It also means constantly trying to find new ways to use individual resources as well as exploring better ways to make use of combinations of resources and to identify more efficient utilization of constellations of resources. A prerequisite for successful implementation is variety in the way purchasers work. Some purchasers have to be very narrow-minded, while others have to be very broad-minded. In other words, purchasing today is a very demanding task that requires an organizational design of quite a new type.

Network Strategies

Forming and implementing adequate supply network strategies is a difficult and highly complex task. To illuminate this inherent complexity we return to an example we discussed briefly in Chapter 5. Figure 5.2 illustrates the components forming the instrument panel of a car and also how the instrument panel is related to other systems and their components. The picture is a representation of the combined efforts of a large number of actors. The finished car is the outcome of the actual division of labour among the actors involved. The perspective of our interest is the supply side of the assembly firm. Consciously or unconsciously, this firm has used a network strategy when allocating the total efforts to the different actors.

The instrument panel is a result of operations in an activity structure. The allocation of tasks to the various actors has obviously taken the similarity among activities into consideration. In some cases, the assembly firm decided to keep activities in-house, while in other cases suppliers were found to be in better positions to exploit economies of scale. Some of the activities are closely complementary—meaning that the output of a certain operation must be used as input in another specific operation. Closely complementary activities may occur in the manufacturing operations of one component or when different components in the instrument panel are assembled to form the system. They may also occur in relation to components in other systems of the car. As illustrated in Figure 5.2, some components are parts of more than one system, for example pipes and hoses are physically located in the instrument panel, but are important components in the climate system as well.

The instrument panel can be regarded also as a combination of resources. Some of these resources reside in the assembly firm, while others are controlled by suppliers. The resulting resource combination is determined by the characteristics of the individual resource elements, but also by the opportunities and difficulties in combining them. From Chapter 5, we recall the simultaneous need for co-operation and confrontation among the individual resource elements.

Finally, the instrument panel results from substantial interaction among large numbers of actors. The relationships formed to develop, manufacture and assemble the instrument panel have different characteristics. Some of them are high-involvement relationships, while others are subject to market exchange. The atmospheres of the relationships differ considerably in terms of power and dependence, conflict level, trust and commitment. Some of the suppliers involved in the manufacturing of the instrument panel are connected in a sub-network. The same goes for components of other systems, for example the electrical system.

In this way, the activated network structure can be seen as a realization of the network strategy of the assembly firm. This strategy is identified by the firm boundaries that have been determined, the level of involvement with suppliers, and the connections among these suppliers. However, as we have tried to show, the immense complexity of reality makes it impossible ever to try to develop an 'optimum' strategy. In the foregoing section, we showed the difficulties associated with determining an appropriate view of efficiency. In this section, we illustrate how the three network structures provide the buying company with multiple opportunities for improvement. Furthermore, deciding on the level of involvement with suppliers and the extent of connection among suppliers requires careful consideration. Finally, there is no simple way to determine the relevant boundaries of the buying firm. In Chapter 3, we concluded that the traditional focus on the ownership boundary needs to be supplemented. In the new type of economy it is meaningful to make a distinction between four perspectives of a firm—the production unit, the knowledge unit, the communication unit and the capital-earning unit. Each of these perspectives implies its own logic where boundaries are concerned.

Any buying firm is thus embedded in an extremely complex network structure. For this reason it is impossible to come up with a 'master network strategy' taking every aspect into consideration. Still, any company needs strategies—in many different dimensions. However, these strategies are always partial and they are valid only for the time being, and must continuously be changed and altered. This is accomplished through 'networking'. Strategizing through networking involves three important lessons.

The first lesson is concerned with the importance of thinking and planning in network terms. Buying firms increasingly have to formulate their strategies in relation to others and to their resources and activities. The thinking must be in terms of activity patterns and resource constellations and how single activities and single resources can be developed within these overall structures.

The second lesson is about the importance of organizing. All networks are organized webs of actors, activities and resources. Organizing is the breeding ground for development and can be discussed in strategic terms. Organizing includes efforts to position the own company in relation to others through relationship building. It also includes organizing each of these relationships and connecting them into networks.

The third lesson is focused on acting in networks. One of the key features of networks is that actions can most often be seen as reactions to the actions undertaken by others. Therefore, strategies for interacting units have to include plans for network acting. Furthermore, the reactions come not only as one reaction from one counterpart, but more in terms of patterns. Even if the original action is directed toward a specific actor, the reaction might come from someone else and in another dimension than expected. Acting within a network requires skills in predicting and understanding these complex reaction patterns.

These three lessons are so important that they deserve a section each. Network thinking is discussed in the following section, while network organizing and network acting are treated in the fourth and fifth sections.

Network Thinking

The discussion of network strategies illustrates that purchasing managers have a complex reality to handle. However, network analysis not only reveals complexity —it also offers help in handling complexity. Clearly, thinking in network terms makes it possible to capture the most important structural and processual aspects of reality. Furthermore, network thinking can be used as a mental model for identifying strategic alternatives and—even more—for evaluating potential consequences. Because it can be used for structuring the thinking of managers, it can also be used for formulating strategies. In this section, we identify some key aspects when using the network model.

The main issue in all network thinking is that 'others' need to be included. One aspect of this thinking is to see one's own activities and resources as parts of a larger structure, as we showed in Chapters 4–6. Doing this provides the company with a better understanding of its problems and opportunities. There is a second aspect of network thinking as well. Thinking in network terms must always involve an attempt to step out of one's own position and look at oneself from the outside. There is no point in having a specific ability, if others do not utilize it. There is no point in being knowledgeable if this knowledge can not be used in relationships with others or by these others. It is of utmost importance to realize that there is not only one map of reality. On the contrary, it is obvious that a company looks quite different from various outside positions. Above, this was encapsulated by the conclusion that every network is built up around several different dimensions. When multiple dimensions exist in the network there are several different pictures or images of the company. In turn, this gives rise to a duality between the actual resources and abilities of a company and those which are appreciated and used by the counterparts. Therefore, it is necessary for the company to learn about its counterparts, but it is equally important that the counterparts learn about the company.

The second key aspect is related to time. The network is never stable or in balance. It is always in transition because of developments in resource and activity combinations. The existence of long-term relationships is a response to this fact. Relationships create stability and are important when time matters. Thus, networks have not only a space dimension including certain actors but also a time dimension. Networks are a way to relate what is done today with what has been done earlier—but also to what is anticipated to be done later. Network thinking always has to include history as well as expectations—it cannot be reduced to a matter of structure. Networks must be thought of as processes where yesterday is related to tomorrow by what is done today. The more of yesterday that can be activated in relation to what happens tomorrow, the better the network will work. This important aspect has been more or less neglected in some of the unrealistic predictions about the new economy and the potential effects of information technology. In network thinking, the basic point of departure must always be the existing resource structure, while the question of how to use this resource structure must constantly be asked. No one can foresee what will happen—the outcome of any effort to combine and recombine resources and activities is always impossible to predict—but it is obvious that most of the resources that are important today will also be used tomorrow.

The importance of others and the crucial time dimension indicate that boundaries are key issues in all network thinking. In Figure 10.3 a sub-net is identified within a larger network structure. The figure illustrates that there is no natural network boundary—any boundary is arbitrary. All boundaries are created by someone and there are always reasons to question and to change these boundaries. This is one of the most important network features—networks are 'in principle' always border-less, which is probably the reason for their importance from a development point of view. Dynamics stem from continuously questioning boundaries. Moving boundaries is about including resources and activities that have previously been perceived as being outside the network or through exploring new ways to combine separate sections of the network. This is illustrated in Figure 10.3(b), where we have eliminated the 'core' network in order to identify its environment. The environment consists of a number of cut-off relationships. Thus, even the environment has a very clear structure, consisting of individual relationships. It is easy to change the boundary by including one more relationship. The boundary is thus extremely flexible and the actors can change the boundary in any situation. They can always include someone

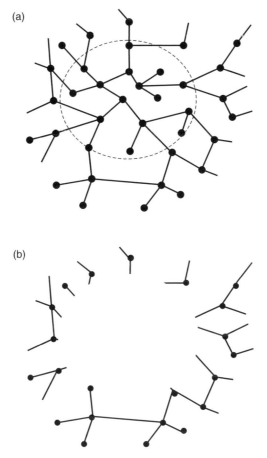

FIGURE 10.3   A network and its environment.

else and they can easily extend what is seen as the relevant network in any direction.

According to Johanson and Mattsson (1992), the perceptions and actions of firms in this respect are formed by their 'network theories'. It is through their network theories that actors determine, for example, what relationships are considered complementary and what resources will be crucial in the future. It is clear that the network theories held by other firms are important for the outcome of the supply network strategies of a buying firm. Therefore, one important task is to influence the network theories of others (ibid., pp. 214–15):

> Such action may aim at influencing the 'network theories' of a specific actor or a specific set of actors in a network. It may also aim at influencing or creating a dominant 'network theory' in the network. This may imply attempts to make the 'network theories' of different actors more consistent. It may, however. also represent efforts to disconnect the network into two or more separate nets, where, for instance, the focal actor is the only link between the nets or where the focal actor has a strong position in one of the nets. Alternatively it may aim at connecting different sections more closely or connecting different networks with each other.

Consequently, there is never a 'one and only' network. This is also the reason for the statement above that it is impossible to identify an optimal balance among the different efficiency measures.

Network strategies thus have to consider different dimensions of efficiency. In particular, efficient utilization of the existing network structure may counteract its future development. Short-term productivity and long-term dynamics very seldom go well together. Therefore, we can expect that firms apply different network strategies when it comes to handling complex issues. Again, we return to the instrument panel in Figure 5.2. In the foregoing section, we illustrated the magnitude of issues to be handled when developing a network strategy for supply in that system. However, every car manufacturer has to solve this problem for each car model that is launched. Doing this involves lots of network thinking.

The first thing to consider is what should be included in the instrument panel (IP). The IP can be seen as a system consisting of a number of components (air conditioner, speedometer, glove boxes, etc.). For the carmaker, the first crucial decision is to set the boundaries of the IP-system—i.e. to determine what components are to be parts of this system and which should be parts of other systems. This stage also involves the specification of the interfaces among components and systems. The second decision—related to the first—is whether to make the IP in-house or outsource it to a supplier. Owing to the complexity of this decision, it will come as no surprise that carmakers have applied quite different strategies in this respect (*Purchasing* 1999c). General Motors uses Magna as a system supplier of IPs, while Honda of America has adopted another strategy. According to the purchasing manager, Honda has historically preferred to make IPs in-house. This is in contrast with Honda's normal procurement activities which, to a large extent, rely on system suppliers. The reason for Honda's keeping IPs in-house is that there are mixed technologies involved and 'no one supplier can be an expert on all of them', the purchasing manager argues. Many other factors affect this decision as well, for example the production capabilities of customer and supplier and the logistics arrangements (Jellbo 1998).

In cases where the system is outsourced, a third decision becomes important—the responsibility of the supplier. According to *Purchasing* (1999c), Honda makes a distinction between three levels of system (or modular) supply:

1. The system is assembled by the supplier. The buying firm stays responsible for system design, component sources and technical development.
2. The customer firm retains control of sourcing and development, the assembler takes responsibility for part of the quality assurance and ordering of parts.
3. Full turn-key supply. Tier-one supplier assembles the system and has full sourcing and development responsibility.

There are thus a huge number of different possible combinations available for the buying company. The strategies applied are primarily determined by the network thinking of the various actors. The choices made, in turn, impact on the opportunities for the future as discussed in Chapter 8. The type of relationship developed impacts on productivity and innovation, for both customer and supplier. The capabilities established and maintained by the various suppliers are strongly dependent on what responsibilities they are given by the buying company. On the other hand, the responsibilities they are given reflect the capabilities they are perceived to have and what they have been able to achieve historically. This illustrates the importance of the time dimension of network thinking and network strategies.

Network Organizing

The reasons for firms (like Honda and GM in the foregoing section) to come up with different supply strategies are related to differences in network thinking. In turn, this follows from the need to apply different types of efficiency measures owing to a 'rugged economic landscape'. There are several, partly contradictory, dimensions that must be considered to determine the network strategy. These considerations also affect the implementation of network thinking. There is no way to find a simple decision rule, or other general mechanism that can capture the various dimensions simultaneously. Therefore, handling this issue is a matter of organizing. In Chapter 9, we analysed the characteristics of supply networks like Nike and how these networks can deal with the organizing issues raised in Chapter 6.

For the discussion of network organizing, we return to the 'strategic centres' presented in Chapter 9. Conventional literature on strategies of the firm advocates Chandler's famous *dictum* that 'structure follows strategy'. According to Lorenzoni and Baden-Fuller (1995), the strategic centres they studied were not established in that way. When the capabilities of the partners are crucial for the development of the hub firm, then strategy and structure must be built simultaneously. This is to say that the network strategy is as dependent on the capabilities of others and the connections to these capabilities, as on internal capabilities. Lorenzoni and Baden-Fuller argue that novel forms of strategic thinking are required (ibid., p. 157):

> When each partner's resources and competencies are so essential to the success of the enterprise, new forms must be designed. To achieve this, structuring must come earlier, alongside strategizing and both require an interaction among partners to create a platform of flexibility and capability. This behaviour challenges much of what is received managerial practice and avoids some of the traps that webs of alliances face.

Lorenzoni and Baden-Fuller found that strategic centres differed from the firms in the control group, in terms of organizing. The strategic centres had adapted their way of working in accordance with the requirements on a central firm, 'whereas the losers are signing agreements without changing their organizational forms to match them' (ibid., p. 157). There are several examples in this book that highlight the importance of appropriate organizing. The Cummins-Toshiba case study illustrates aspects related to organizing individual relationships. The IKEA case study takes us a step further and shows the benefits of network organizing.

Most examples provided are associated with large firms—in this book and elsewhere. However, it must again be emphasized that the underlying principles are applicable not only for global players. For example, Powell (1987) shows the significance of these ideas among small and medium-sized firms. One example is the German textile industry, which is characterized as a craft industry relying on 'a highly refined system of production that links small and medium-sized firms with a wide range of institutional arrangements that further the well-being of the industry as a whole' (ibid., p. 70). Most textile producers are highly specialized, and the more distinctive each firm is 'the more it depends on the success of other firms' products that complement its own'. The organizational arrangements are important means of assuring collaboration in technical development. These arrangements, in turn, 'strengthen the social structure in which textile firms are embedded and encourage co-operative relations that attenuate the destructive aspects of competition'.

Information sharing is a crucial issue in all types of networks, as described in Chapter 3. Both the strategic centres discussed in Lorenzoni and Baden-Fuller and the small and medium-sized firms analysed by Powell are heavily dependent on exchange of information. Furthermore, the discussion of the new economy in Chapter 3 revealed, in particular, that the firm as a knowledge unit and the firm as a communication unit are completely dependent on well functioning information flows. Part of this information exchange concerns 'hard data' but also 'ideas, feelings, and thoughts' (Lorenzoni and Baden-Fuller 1995, p. 158). However, in a network context, the design of appropriate information systems is a problematic task (Imai 1987, quoted in Lorenzoni and Baden-Fuller, p. 158):

> One of the basic premises in our network view is that new information leading to new ways of doing things emerges in a process of interaction with people and real-life situations. It follows that the 'information ability' of the firm depends critically on a scheme of inter-actions. The difficulty is that the generation of new information cannot be planned, but has to emerge. Thus the task of the manager is one of designing a structure, which provides an environment favourable for interactions to form and for new information to be generated.

The conclusion of this statement is that effective information exchange among network actors is more a question of appropriate organizing arrangements than of well-designed information systems.

The organizing of relationships and networks is directly related to the internal organizing of companies. The pros and cons of centralization and decentralization discussed in Chapter 6 impact on the organizational arrangements. One of the main recommendations today is to use a 'team-approach', which is meant to improve the conditions for collaboration among the different functional depart-ments in the buying firm. However, this approach is not without its drawbacks. In Chapter 6, we discussed the problems associated with different role perceptions of the various functions involved.

The team approach is associated with other problems as well. According to Sobek et al. (1998), establishment of cross-functional teams has resulted in substantial improvements of company operations. But the new organizational solutions also created new problems. First, the improvements in cross-functional co-ordination were gained at the expense of decreasing depth of knowledge within functions, the simple reason being that people spend less time within their functions because they are primarily allocated to projects. Toyota has tried to solve that problem by avoiding assigning engineers to dedicated project teams. Most people reside within functional areas and are hired by projects. By rooting engineers in a function, Toyota ensures that the functions develop deep specialized knowledge and experience.

The second problem relates to learning. Cross-functional teams tend to work well within individual projects, but the temporary personal nature of the teams makes it hard for them to transmit information to other project teams. Sobek *et al.* (1998) argue that US companies, through a single-minded focus on bringing functions together within projects, have created other information-sharing problems. Similar problems with project organizations have been identified elsewhere as well. For example, von Krogh (1998) observed these effects in R&D projects. He found that in most cases too little effort is devoted to transmitting knowledge and experience from one project to another. O'Dell and Grayson (1998) argue that the present reliance on decentralization and projects means that within each company and organization 'lies unknown and untapped a vast treasure house of knowledge, know-how and best practice' (ibid., p. 157). According to O'Dell and Grayson, the main reason is the lack of contact relationships and common perspectives among people who do not work side-by-side. The authors have found that in most organizations the left hand does not know what the right hand is doing. However, the problems become even greater in cases where 'the left hand may not even know that there is a right hand'. Obviously, these conditions are particularly problematic for the firm as a knowledge unit. According to Nonaka and Konno (1998), new knowledge is generated through a spiralling process of interactions between explicit and tacit knowledge (Figure 10.4). If transmission of information between different parts—or projects—in a firm is hindered, then the four conversion processes are not likely to generate the knowledge that could have been developed.

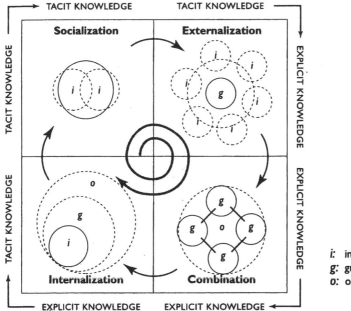

FIGURE 10.4   The knowledge creation process. Source: Nonaka and Konno 1998, p. 43. Copyright ©, by the Regents of the University of California.

Organizational learning across projects has also dropped because people rotate rapidly through positions and functions (Sobek *et al.* 1998). Again, Toyota uses a contrasting approach, tending to rotate most engineers within only one function. For example, body engineers work on different auto body sub-systems for most of their careers. They thus gain the experience that encourages standardized work (the lack of which is a problem in the fully decentralized corporation). This consistency over time means that the engineers in the manufacturing division need to spend less time and energy in communicating and co-ordinating with their colleagues in design, because over time they learn what to expect from them. Of course, this approach has its drawbacks if not properly handled. There is an obvious risk that it may conserve behaviour and thus hamper innovation and development.

At the beginning of this section, we argued that 'organizing' is a means of handling the complexity arising from the different dimensions of network efficiency. During the last decade, one of these dimensions has been particularly focused. The increasing attention to 'key account management' is an attempt to integrate business relationships into the internal organization. Obviously, a key account specialist working with a single supplier may contribute substantially to improving efficiency in dealing with that supplier over time.

The efforts of a key account manager cover the second of the efficiency dimensions identified in the first section. The organizational structures of companies should also pay attention to the two other dimensions. Therefore, buying firms also need people who are very focused on the productivity of individual transactions. It is important to maintain and improve efficiency in these operations. For example, some procurement situations require very little communication and information exchange among buyer and seller. In these cases, the buying firm should use what we identified in Chapter 8 as a 'low-involvement approach'. Performance improvements in these operations might be gained, for example, by development of systems for e-procurement (Avlonitis and Karyanni 2000, and Lancioni *et al.* 2000). The transactions suitable for this approach cover various items and various suppliers. Therefore, a buying company may benefit from assigning this task to dedicated people.

Finally, there is a need for managers responsible for network structures— i.e. parts of the total network in which the buying company is embedded. These structures can be identified in different ways. A system approach like the instrument panel described in the foregoing section is one example—but there are other alternatives as well. For example, a company heavily dependent on procurement of plastic moulding of different types may assign a person as responsible for structuring the plastic moulding supply of the company. Other companies may rely extensively on supply from specific parts of the world—such as specialized raw materials. In these cases a geographical network view may be appropriate.

The key issue in network organizing is to assign responsibilities in all the three efficiency dimensions. By authorizing representatives advocating the efficiency of transactions, relationships and networks the buying company may improve its total supply performance. The task is to continuously try to develop solutions where the opportunities residing in one dimension are confronted with the costs and problems that are caused in the other dimensions and vice versa. In this way, each of the three sub-units has to fight for the efficiency of its own dimension and try to convince the others, with good arguments, i.e. to advocate appropriate solutions.

Network Acting

Acting in networks is a reflection of network thinking and network organizing and there are some specific considerations related to network acting. Networks have important dynamic features. They are never in equilibrium—they are always in a state of flux. Furthermore, they are complex with a number of inter-related relationships. All this makes them difficult to manage, but at the same time great reservoirs for learning.

At the beginning of this chapter, we argued that network organizing is a governance mechanism complementing markets and hierarchies. These three governance modes have quite different characteristics when it comes to managing and acting. In Chapters 7–9, we brought up some important managerial issues related to our view of supply strategy. However, when it actually comes to 'managing'—i.e. to acting in networks—the degrees of freedom in managing may be severely restricted. A hierarchy can—and should—be managed. In fact, the raison d'être for the firm resides in the opportunities provided for managing the various operations under common ownership. Reliance on market governance imposes quite different situations. In a pure market, all external conditions are, by definition, given and cannot be managed. In a network context the situation is less clear-cut. A network actor can influence what is going on. At the same time, these influencing actions have to be adjusted in accordance with what is appropriate for other actors. If an actor is too much of a 'manager', then the network develops into a hierarchy. On the other hand, if the actor avoids influencing—then the network becomes a market from the perspective of this firm. These characteristics of managing opportunities are very important features of a network. Thus, a 'good' network should be difficult to manage—but still possible to influence.

One of the most important reasons for the problems with managing in net-works is the complexity in terms of reaction patterns. All actions lead to reactions, and in a network these reactions can be difficult to predict as the various parties are interrelated. The continuous development makes these reactions more impor-tant—any action must thus be seen in relation to development processes. The reaction might appear in another dimension and at another place than expected. Therefore, appropriate acting is conditioned by its perceived reactions of others as much as by its direct benefits for the acting firm. The differences concerning acting in hierarchies and networks are nicely illustrated in a study by Langlois and Robertson (1992). They show the consequences arising from various ways of acting. The study deals with innovation and technical development and builds on two cases—the developments of the stereo components industry and the micro-computer industry. In both cases, the industries were re-engineered through the development of modular systems. Firms in the industries used different strategies to exploit modularity. In both cases, some companies tried to develop proprietary systems which were incompatible with other systems (for example, RCA and Digital Equipment). However, these 'hierarchical' efforts were less successful than another approach (ibid., p. 311):

But these [proprietary] attempts ultimately failed, and companies who relied heavily on an external network of competitors and suppliers were clearly more successful. Columbia encouraged the production of 33-rpm records and players, and IBM allowed Microsoft to license MS-DOS widely. These firms became significant players in networks that were not under their control, thereby garnering larger payoffs than if they had attempted to market a proprietary product.

Further analysis sheds some additional light on our discussion in Chapter 3 on the different views of the firm in the new economy. Langlois and Robertson discuss the consequences of vertical integration and argue that this approach may have its benefits (or at least relatively few disadvantages) for the manufacturing of the components of the system. This is because a hierarchy may have some advantages in co-ordinating systemic innovation of the internal sub-components of the modular system. However, when it comes to co-ordination across the capability boundaries of the larger system, 'large size and vertical integration are of little benefit'. Their conclusion is that particularly in the early stages of development 'experimentation is a much more important concern than co-ordination' (ibid., p. 311).

Returning to the problems related to 'managing' networks in an appropriate way, the solution is not to do less because of these difficulties, but to do more. Our conclusion is in line with that of Langlois and Robertson: the network complexity in combination with the need to act makes experimentation extremely important. There is need for a continuous experimentation in a number of dimensions. These experiments might be related to specific transactions or relationships. They might concern a technical solution or the way logistics are handled for a certain category of products or how two suppliers can be combined. Experimentation can thus be done in relation to various issues. 'Experimentation' indicates that it is important to map and analyse reactions and to reflect on and adjust to these findings. It also indicates that it is more important to reflect on the results than to try to predict them beforehand.

The word 'experimentation' is also a good indication of the importance of learning and teaching in networks. Learning has been stressed by so many people and in so many ways that there is no need to repeat them here. Teaching has not been as often recommended but in business networks teaching is as important as learning. The significance of both activities is illustrated in a case study of Matsushita (Lincoln *et al.* 1998). It is shown that, on the one hand, Matsushita has successfully been able to absorb new technologies from the most advanced suppliers. On the other hand, they actively assist, motivate and encourage suppliers to develop in specific directions. A representative of Matsushita pointed out the importance of continuously 'reversing the role of teacher and student'. We concluded above that efficiency can be increased either by adaptations by the buying company or by others adapting to it. This is an indication of the importance of teaching. Interaction is concerned with double directional learning—or at least there is a potential for it. A buying company can learn from all its suppliers, but it can also teach them. It can teach them about its own resources and activities, and it can teach them about its customers and their resources and activities. It can teach supplier A about the activities and resources of supplier B, as well as teach a group of suppliers about important characteristics of the buying company or the potential of a certain technology. The relevance of teaching is an indication of the importance of always trying to facilitate learning for others. The opportunities for teaching and learning are substantially impacted on by the interaction atmosphere, discussed in Chapter 6.

The word experimentation also gives an indication of the importance of signalling, of telling others about the ambitions of the company. In a network building on business relationships, it is crucial to be seen and to be prioritized by others. In this way, every form of experimentation is not just an action but also a signal to the others, showing what and who are important. In this way, experimentation is part of forming the identity of the company, as discussed in Chapter 6. From this point of view, it is important to have a set of experiments going on where different parties are involved. Thus, experimentation has a political dimension that must be considered.

Finally, acting within networks seems to have a lot in common with what is described within the literature of complexity theory (Waldrop 1992). Two concepts that have been used there—simplexity and complicity—are relevant for network acting as well. Both concepts are used to show that the characteristics of a general pattern can be created by mechanisms that are of opposite types. Simple patterns can be created by very complex mechanisms and very complex patterns by simple mechanisms, which is very much the same in networks. In some situations, a very simple act can result in a very complex reaction pattern, while what appears to be complex acting may be followed by a rather 'simple' reaction pattern.

Final Comments

This chapter discussed a number of key areas in relation to the development of supply network strategies. We started with efficiency where three different dimensions were identified, each capturing important aspects of what is going on in a network. All these dimensions can and should be developed to improve on purchasing performance. We then illustrated the complex context in which a network strategy has to be developed, and commented on the immense problems in analysis and implementation. This complexity calls for what we identified as network 'thinking'. One specific aspect of network thinking is the need to actively explore the network boundaries in order both to develop the thinking and to formulate new strategies. With regard to this aspect, too, there is reason to believe that there is great development potential. The same is true for 'organizing'. There are probably companies that are fairly good at both external and internal organizing, but most companies have a lot of development potential in these respects. Finally, we discussed network 'acting' and how this must be considered as a way to create reactions.

In all these areas, from efficiency considerations to action, there is great potential for further development on the supply side. In spite of the major changes and developments reported in this book, there is still much more benefit to gain. Companies have started to develop the supply side of their operations— but most of the gain is still to come.

The framework of this book is the industrial network model. We have used this model because the network form seems to be a viable and growing means for firms to relate to each other. This way of relating companies to each other affects both the use of resources and their development. Network organizing makes it possible to identify rationalization opportunities across firm boundaries and to combine external and internal resources in innovative ways, affecting both efficiency and effectiveness. In our view, these are the most significant characteristics of the evolving economy.

The analysis of recent developments on the supply side of companies also has some theoretical implications. The findings cast some doubts on the relevance of the established view of markets and hierarchies as the basic forms of governance. The changes on the supply side of companies indicate a transition away from the hierarchy. Buying firms are increasingly becoming dependent on resources controlled by others. They also outsource activities to suppliers more and more frequently. However, these movements away from the hierarchy are not going in the direction of enhanced reliance on market exchange. On the contrary, the findings indicate that buying firms tend to form closer relationships with suppliers than they used to. Therefore, we think it is time to acknowledge relational exchange and network organizing as a governance form on its own merits— not only as a second best alternative when markets and hierarchies for some reason cannot be utilized. In this respect we agree with Piore (1992, p. 443) and his conclusion that 'it may be that what we think of as networks are a natural form of organization and that markets and hierarchies are two extremes'.

REFERENCES

Abernathy, W. and Clark, K. (1982) *Notes on a Trip to Japan*. Graduate School of Business Administration, Harvard University, Boston.

Alchian, A. and Demsetz, H. (1972) Production, Information Costs, and Economic Organization. *The American Economic Review*, **62**, pp. 777–795.

Araujo, L., Dubois, A. and Gadde, L.-E. (1999) Managing Interfaces with Suppliers. *Industrial Marketing Management*, **28**, pp. 497–506.

Asplund, E. and Wootz, B. (1986) En inköpsstrategisk omorientering. *Purchasing Magazine*, No. 1, pp. 60–64.

Avery, S. (1996) Standardization of Controls Melts 'Iceberg' Costs at Kodak. *Purchasing*, March 7, pp. 44–46.

Avery, S. (1999a) Team Approach to Buying Improves Process Efficiency. *Purchasing*, April 22, pp. 55–58.

Avery, S. (1999b) Brunswick Saves Big Bucks by Centralizing Services Buy. *Purchasing*, March 25, pp. 38–41.

Avlonitis, G. and Karayanni, D. (2000) The Impact of Internet Use on Business to Business Marketing. Examples from American and European Companies. *Industrial Marketing Management*, **29**, pp. 441–459.

Axelsson, B. and Håkansson, H. (1984) *Inköp för konkurrenskraft*. Liber, Stockholm.

Bailey, P. and Farmer, D. (1982) *Materials Management Handbook*. Gower, Aldershot.

Baldwin, C. and Clark, K. (1997) Managing in an Age of Modularity. *Harvard Business Review*, September–October, pp. 84–93.

Barney, J. (1991) Firm Resources and Sustained Competitive Advantage. *Journal of Management*, March, pp. 99–120.

Barreyre, P. (1988) The Concept of 'Impartition' Policies: A Different Approach to Vertical Integration Strategies. *Strategic Management Journal*, **9**, pp. 507–520.

Bensaou, M. (1999) Portfolios of Buyer-supplier Relationships. *Sloan Management Review*, Summer, pp. 35–44.

Bergman, B. and Johanson, J. (1978) Inköp och produktutveckling. In Håkansson, H. and Melin, L. (eds.) *Inköp*. Norstedts, Stockholm.

Berry, B. (1982) Is Detroit Prompting a Shake-Out in the Supplier Network. *Iron Age*, July 14, pp. 25–28.

Blau, P. (1964) *Exchange and Power in Social Life*. John Wiley and Sons, New York.

Blois, K. (1971) Vertical Quasi-Integration. *Journal of Industrial Economics*, Vol. 20, No. 3, pp. 33–41.

Bonoma, T. and Zaltman, G. (1976) Organizational Buying Behavior. Proceedings of Workshop on Industrial Marketing, University of Pittsburg.

Brandes, H. (1993) Inköp i förändring. Licentiate dissertation. Linköping University, Linköping.

Brown, J. and Duguid, P. (1998) Organizing Knowledge. *California Management Review*, Vol. 40, No. 3, pp. 90–111.

Brunelli, M. (1999) What Buyers Want From Web Sites. *Purchasing*, December 16, pp. S6–S42.

Burt, D. and Sukoup, W. (1985) Purchasing's Role in New Product Development. *Harvard Business Review*, September–October, pp. 90–97.

Carbone, J. (1996) Sun Shines by Taking Out Time. *Purchasing*, September 19, pp. 34–45.

Carbone, J. (1999) Reinventing Purchasing Wins the Medal for Big Blue. *Purchasing*, September 16, pp. 38–62.

Carlisle, J. and Parker, R. (1989) *Beyond Negotiation. Reedeming Customer-supplier Relationships.* John Wiley & Sons, Chichester.

Cayer, S. (1988) World Class Suppliers don't Grow on Trees'. *Purchasing*, August 25, pp. 45–49.

Chandler, A. (1977) *The Visible Hand: The Managerial Revolution in American Business.* Harvard University Press, Cambridge.

Clarke, K. and Fujimoto, T. (1991) *Product Development Performance. Strategy, Organization and Management in the World Auto Industry.* Harvard Business School Press, Boston.

Cole, R. (1998) Introduction to Special Issue on Knowledge and the Firm. *California Management Review*, Vol. 40, No. 3, pp. 15–21.

Cousins, P. (1999) Supplier Base Rationalization—Myth or Reality? *European Journal of Purchasing & Supply Management*, **5**, pp. 143–155.

Culliton, J. (1942) Make or Buy. Graduate School of Business Administration, Harvard University, Boston.

Curry, J. and Kenney, M. (1999) Beating the Clock: Corporate Responses to Rapid Changes in the PC Industry. *California Management Review*, Vol. 42, No. 1, pp. 8–36.

Davis, T. (1993) Effective Supply Chain Management. *Sloan Management Review*, Summer, pp. 35–46.

Dion, P., Banting, P. and Hasey, L. (1990) The Impact of JIT on Industrial Markets. *Industrial Marketing Management*, **19**, pp. 41–46.

Donaghu, M. and Barff, R. (1990) Nike just did it: International Subcontracting and Flexibility in Athletic Footwear Production. *Regional Studies*, **24.6**, pp. 537–552.

Drucker, P. (1990) The Emerging Theory of Manufacturing. *Harvard Business Review*, May–June, pp. 94–102.

Dubois, A. (1998) *Organizing Industrial Activities Across Firm Boundaries.* Routledge, London.

Dubois, A. and Gadde, L.-E. (1996) Purchasing Behaviour During Three Decades—Some Reflections on the Variety of Supplier Relationships. Proceedings of the 12th IMP-conference, Karlsruhe Universität, Karlsruhe.

Dyer, J. and Ouchi, W. (1993) Japanese-style Partnerships: Giving Companies a Competitive Edge. *Sloan Management Review*, Fall, pp. 51–63.

Dyer, J., Cho, D. and Chu, W. (1998) Strategic Supplier Segmentation: The Next 'Best Practice' in Supply Chain Management. *California Management Review*, Vol. 40, No. 2, pp. 57–76.

Ellram, L. and Billington, C. (2001) Purchasing Leverage Considerations in the Outsourcing Decision. *European Journal of Purchasing & Supply Management*, **7** pp. 15–27.

Ellram, L. and Edis, O. (1996) A Case Study of Successful Patnering Implementation. *International Journal of Purchasing and Materials Management*, Fall, pp. 20–28.

Emerson, R. (1962) Power-dependence Relations. *American Sociological Review*, **27**, pp. 31–41.

Fitzgerald, K. (1999) Purchasing Unlocks Supply Treasures. *Purchasing*, March 11, pp. 50–57.

Ford, D. (ed.) (1997) *Understanding Business Markets.* Dryden Press, London.

Ford, D. and Saren, M. (1996) *Technology Strategy for Business.* International Thomson, London.

Ford, D., Cotton, B., Farmer, D., Gross, A. and Wilkinson, I. (1993) Make-or-Buy Decisions and their Implications. *Industrial Marketing Management*, **22**, pp. 207–214.

Ford, D., Gadde, L-E., Håkansson, H., Lundgren, A., Snehota, I., Turnbull, P. and Wilson, D. (1998) *Managing Business Relationships.* John Wiley & Sons, Chichester.

Gadde, L.-E. (2000) From Marketing Channels to Differentiated Networks—Distribution Dynamics in a Historical Perspective. In Dahiya, S. (ed.) *The Current State of Business Disciplines.* Spellbound Publications, Rohtak, pp. 2641–2662.

Gadde, L.-E. and Håkansson, H. (1993) *Professional Purchasing.* Routledge, London.

Gadde, L.-E. and Håkansson, H. (1994) The Changing Role of Purchasing: Reconsidering Three Strategic Issues. *European Journal of Purchasing & Supply Management*, Vol. 1, No. 1, pp. 27–36.

Gadde, L.-E. and Mattson, L.-G. (1987) Stability and Change in Network Relationships. *International Journal of Research in Marketing*, **4**, pp. 1, 29–41.

Gadde, L.-E. and Snehota, I. (2000) Making the Most of Supplier Relationships. *Industrial Marketing Management*, **29**, pp. 305–316.

Gemünden, H. G. (1985) Coping with Inter-organizational Conflicts. Efficient Interaction Strategies for Buyer and Seller Organizations. *Journal of Business Research*, **13**, pp. 405–420.

Gilbert, J. (1990) The State of JIT Implementation and Development in the USA. *International Journal of Production Research*, Vol. 28, No. 6, pp. 1099–1109.

Gillett, J. (1994) The Cost-benefit of Outsourcing: Assessing the True Cost of Your Ownership Strategy. *European Journal of Purchasing & Supply Management*, Vol. 1, No. 1, pp. 45–48.

Granstrand, O., Bohlin, E., Oskarsson, C. and Sjoberg, N. (1992) External Technology Acquisition in Large Multi-technology Corporations. *R&D Management*, Vol. 22, No. 2, pp. 111–133.

Greco, J. (1997) Outsourcing: The New Partnership. *Journal of Business Strategy*, July–August, pp. 48–54.

Hahn, C., Kim, K. and Kim, J. (1986) Costs of Competition: Implications for Purchasing Strategy. *Journal of Purchasing and Materials Management*, Vol. 22, No. 4, pp. 2–7.

Hahn, C., Watts, C. and Kim, K. (1990) The Supplier Development Program: a Conceptual Model. *International Journal of Purchasing and Materials Management*, Vol. 26, No. 2, pp. 2–7.

Hartley, J., Zirger, B. and Kamath, R. (1997) Managing the Buyer-supplier Interface for On-time Performance in Product Development. *Journal of Operations Management*, Vol. 15, pp. 57–70.

Hayes, R. and Pisano, G. (1994) Beyond World Class: The New Manufacturing Strategy. *Harvard Business Review*, January–February, pp. 77–86.

Helper, S. (1986) Supplier Relations and Technical Progress: Theory and Application to the Auto Industry. Department of Economics, Harvard University.

Helper, S. (1991) How Much has Really Changed between US Automakers and their Suppliers? *Sloan Management Review*, Summer, pp. 15–28.

Helper, S. and Sako, M. (1995) Supplier Relations in Japan and the United States: Are They Converging? *Sloan Management Review*, Spring, pp. 77–84.

Hines, P. (1995) Network Sourcing: A Hybrid Approach. *International Journal of Purchasing and Materials Management*, Spring, pp. 18–24.

Håkansson, H. (ed.) (1982) *International Marketing and Purchasing of Industrial Goods—An Interaction Approach*. John Wiley & Sons, Chichester.

Håkansson, H. (ed.) (1987) *Industrial Technological Development. A Network Approach*. Croom Helm, Beckenham.

Håkansson, H. (1989) *Corporate Technological Behaviour—Cooperation and Networks*. Routledge, London.

Håkansson, H. (1993) Networks as a Mechanism to Develop Resources. In Beije, P., Groenewegen, J. and Nuys, O. (eds.) *Networking in Dutch Industries*. Garant, Apeldorn, pp. 207–273.

Håkansson, H. and Snehota, I. (1995) *Developing Business Relationships*. Routledge, London.

Håkansson, H. and Waluszewski, A. (1997) Recycle Fibres Turning Green. In Gemunden, H.-G., Ritter, T. and Walter, A. (eds.) *Relationships and Networks in International Markets*. Pergamon Press, Oxford.

Håkansson, H. and Wootz, B. (1975) *Företags inköpsbeteende*. Studentlitteratur, Lund.

Håkansson, H. and Wootz, B. (1984) Låga priser eller låga kostnader? *Purchasing Magazine*, No. 2, pp. 83–84.

Imai, K. (1987) A Network View of the Firm. Hitotsubashi-Standford Conference, March.

Imai, K., Nonaka, I. and Takeuchi, H. (1985) Managing the New Product Development Process: How Japanese Companies Learn and Unlearn. In Clark, K., Hayes, R. and Lorenz, S. (eds.) *The Uneasy Alliance: Managing the Productivity-technology Dilemma*. Harvard Business School Press, Boston, pp. 337–376.

Itami, H. (1987) *Mobilizing Invisible Assets*. Harvard University Press, Cambridge.

Jauch, L. and Wilson, H. (1979) A Strategic Perspective for Make or Buy Decisions. *Long Range Planning*, **12**, pp. 56–61.

Jellbo, O. (1998) Systemköp—en definitionsfråga. Licentiate dissertation. Chalmers University of Technology, Department of Industrial Marketing, Gothenburg.

Johanson, J. and Mattson, L.-G. (1992) Network Positions and Strategic Action—An Analytical Framework. In Axelsson, B. and Easton, G. (eds.) *Industrial Networks—A New View of Reality*. Routledge, London.

Kapour, V. and Gupta, A. (1997) Aggressive Sourcing: A Free Market Approach. *Sloan Management Review*, Fall, pp. 21–31.

Kinch, N. (1987) Emerging Strategies in a Network Context—The Volvo Case. *Scandinavian Journal of Management Studies*, **3**, pp. 167–184.

Kraljic, P. (1982) Purchasing must Become Supply Management. *Harvard Business Review*, September–October, pp. 109–117.

Krause, D. and Ellram, L. (1997) Critical Elements of Supplier Development. The Buying Firm Perspective. *European Journal of Purchasing & Supply Management*, Vol. 3, No. 1, pp. 21–32.

Laage-Hellman, J. (1997) *Business Networks in Japan. Supplier-customer Interaction in Product Development*. Routledge, London.

Lambert, D. and Cooper, C. (2000) Issues in Supply Chain Management. *Industrial Marketing Management*, **29**, pp. 65–83.

Lamming, R. (1993) *Beyond Partnership. Strategies for Innovation and Lean Supply*. Prentice Hall, Hemel Hempstead.

Lamming, R. C., Cousins, P. D. and Notman, D. M. (1996) Beyond Vendor Assessment. Relationship Assessment Programmes. *European Journal of Purchasing & Supply Management*, **2**, 4, pp. 173–181.

Lancioni, R., Smith, M. and Oliva, T. (2000) The Role of the Internet in Supply Chain Management. *Industrial Marketing Management*, **29**, pp. 45–56.

Langlois, R. and Robertson, P. (1992) Networks and Innovation in a Modular System: Lessons from the Microcomputer and Stereo Computer Industries. *Research Policy*, **21**, pp. 297–313.

Leenders, M. and Nollet, J. (1984) The Grey Zone in Make or Buy. *Journal of Purchasing and Materials Management*, Fall, pp. 10–15.

Lewis, J. D. (1995) *The Connected Corporation*. The Free Press, New York.

Lincoln, J., Ahmadjian, C. and Mason, E. (1998) Organizational Learning and Purchase-supply Relationships in Japan: Hitachi, Matsushita, and Toyota Compared. *California Management Review*, Vol. 40, No. 3, pp. 241–264.

Lorenzi, G. and Baden-Fuller, C. (1995) Creating a Strategic Center to Manage a Web of Partners. *California Management Review*, Vol. 37, No. 3, pp. 146–163.

Lundvall, B.-Å. (1988) Innovation as an Interactive Process: From User–producer Interaction to the National System of Innovation. In Dosi, G., Freeman, C., Nelson, R., Silverberg, G. and Soete, L. (eds.) *Technical Change and Economic Theory*. Pinter Publishers, London, pp. 349–369.

Madsen, P. T. (1999) Den samarbejdende virksomhed: Mönstre i Produktudviklingen for Danske Fremstillingsvirksomheder. Disko-projektet: Rapport nr. 6, Aalborg University, Aalborg.

Miles, G., Miles, R., Perroni, V. and Edvinsson, L. (1998) Some Conceptual and Research Barriers to the Utilization of Knowledge. *California Management Review*, Vol. 40, No. 3, pp. 281–288.

Millen-Porter, A. (1997a) The Problems with JIT. *Purchasing*, September 18, pp. 18–23.

Millen-Porter, A. (1997b) At Cat they're Driving Supplier Integration into the Design Process. *Puchasing*, March 7, pp. 37–40.

Milligan, B. (1999) Buyers face new supply challenges. *Purchasing*, November 4, pp. 63–72.

Milligan, B. (2000) Harley Davidson Wins by Getting Suppliers on Board. *Purchasing*, September 21, pp. 52–65.

Minahan, T. (1995) Can't Get a Handle on Freight Costs? Give Up Trying. *Purchasing*, November 23, pp. 35–36.

Minahan, T. (1996a) Xerox Plots a Logistics Plan Worth Copying. *Purchasing*, July 11, pp. 90–91.

Minahan, T. (1996b) JIT. How Buyers Changed It. *Purchasing*, September 5, pp. 37–38.

Minahan, T. (1996c) World Class Suppliers: General Motors. Is Harold Kutner GM's Comeback Kid? *Purchasing*, August 15, pp. 40–47.

Minahan, T. (1997) JIT. A Process with Many Faces. *Purchasing*, September 4, pp. 42–49.

Monczka, R. and Morgan, J. (2000) Competitive Supply Strategies for the 21st Century. *Purchasing*, January 13, pp. 48–59.

Morgan, J. (1999) Purchasing at 100. Where It's Been, Where It's Headed. *Purchasing*, November 18, pp. 72–94.

Morgan, J. (2000) Cessna Charts a Supply Chain Flight Strategy. *Purchasing*, September 7, pp. 42–61.

Newman, R. (1988) Single Source Qualification. *Journal of Purchasing and Materials Management*, Summer, pp. 10–17.

Nishiguchi, T. (1986) Strategic Dualism: A Japanese Alternative. Unpublished Ph.D. thesis draft.

Nonaka, I. (1991) The Knowledge-creating Company. *Harvard Business Review*, November–December, pp. 96–104.

Nonaki, I. and Konno, N. (1998) The Concept of 'Ba': Building a Foundation for Knowledge Creation. *California Management Review*, Vol. 40, No. 3, pp. 40–54.

Nonaka, I. and Takeuchi, H. (1995) *The Knowledge-creating Company*. Oxford University Press, New York.

O'Dell, C. and Grayson, J. (1998) If Only We Knew What We Know: Identification and Transfer of Internal Best Practices. *California Management Review*, Vol. 40, No. 3, pp. 154–174.

Pedersen, A.-C. (1996) Utvikling av leverandörrelasjoner i industrielle nettverk—en studie av koblinger mellom relasjoner. Doctoral dissertation 1996:107, Norges teknisk-naturvitenskapelige universitet, Trondheim.

Penrose, E. (1959) *The Theory of the Growth of the Firm*. Basil Blackwell, Oxford.

Piore, M. (1992) Fragments of a Cognitive Theory of Technological Change and Organizational Structure. In Nohria, N. and Eccles, R. (eds.) *Networks and Organizations. Structure, Form and Action.* Harvard Business School, Boston.

Porter, M. (1985) *Competitive Advantage.* The Free Press, New York.

Porter, M. and Millan, V. (1985) How Information Gives You Competitive Advantage. *Harvard Business Review,* July–August, pp. 149–160.

Powell, W. (1987) Hybrid Organizational Arrangements: New Form or Transitional Development? *California Management Review,* Vol. 30, No. 1, pp. 67–87.

Powell, W. (1998) Learning from Collaboration: Knowledge and Networks in the Biotechnology and Pharmaceutical Industries. *California Management Review,* Vol. 40, No. 3, pp. 228–240.

Purchasing (1995) Compaq uses world class suppliers to stay #1. *Purchasing,* August 17, pp. 34–45.

Purchasing (1997) Suppliers: The Competitive Edge in Design. *Purchasing,* May 1, pp. 32S5–32S23.

Purchasing (1998) OEM-buyers Are Up to the Same Tricks. *Purchasing,* June 4, pp. 68–69.

Purchasing (1999a) Who Spends How Much on What? *Purchasing,* November 4, pp. 52–57.

Purchasing (1999b) Single Sourcing—Some Love It, Most Fear It. *Purchasing,* June 3, pp. 22–24.

Purchasing (1999c) For Automotive Purchasers: The System is the Thing. *Purchasing,* February 11, pp. 60–66.

Puto, C., Patton, W. and King, R. (1985) Risk Handling Strategies in Industrial Vendor Selection Decisions. *Journal of Marketing,* Vol. 49, Winter, pp. 89–98.

Quinn, J. (1999) Strategic Outsourcing: Leveraging Knowledge Capabilities. *Sloan Management Review,* Summer, pp. 9–21.

Quinn, J. and Hilmer, F. (1994) Strategic Outsourcing. *Sloan Management Review,* Summer, pp. 43–55.

Ragatz, G., Handfield, R. and Scannell, T. (1997) Success Factors for Integrating Suppliers into New Product Development. *Journal of Product Innovation Management,* Vol. 14, No. 3, pp. 190–202.

Raia, E. (1991), Taking Time Out of Product Design. *Purchasing,* April 4, pp. 36–39.

Reese, J. and Geisel, R. (1997) JIT Procurement. A Comparison of Current Practices in German Manufacturing Industries. *European Journal of Purchasing & Supply Management,* Vol. 3, No. 3, pp. 155–164.

Richardson, G. B. (1972) The Organization of Industry. *The Economic Journal,* **82**, pp. 883–896.

Richardson, J. (1993) Parallel Sourcing and Supplier Performance in the Japanese Automobile Industry. *Strategic Management Journal,* **14**, pp. 339–350.

Robertson, D. and Ulrich, K. (1998) Planning for Product Platforms. *Sloan Management Review,* Summer, pp. 19–31.

Robinson, P., Faris, C. and Wind, Y. (1967) *Industrial Buying and Creative Marketing.* Allyn & Bacon, Boston.

Ruggles, R. (1998) The State of Notion: Knowledge Management in Practice. *California Management Review,* Vol. 40, No. 3, pp. 80–89.

Schwartz, M. and Fish, A. (1998) Just-in-time Inventories in Old Detroit. *Business History,* Vol. 40, No. 3, pp. 48–71.

Scherer, F. M. (1970) *Industrial Market Structure and Economic Performance.* Rand McNally and Company, Chicago.

Sobek, D., Liker, J. and Ward, A. (1988) Another Look at How Toyota Integrates Product Development. *Harvard Business Review,* July–August, pp. 36–49.

Stork, K. (1999) Single Sourcing Part II. *Purchasing,* November 4, p. 32.

Stundza, T. (1999) Aerospace Purchasing Gets Overhauled. *Purchasing,* June 5, pp. 66–73.

Stundza, T. (2000) It's Still Steel's Game to Lose. *Purchasing,* February 10, pp. 40B1–11.

Takeuchi, H. and Nonaka, I. (1986) The New New-product Development Game. *Harvard Business Review,* January–February, pp. 137–146.

Tan, K. (2001) A Framework of Supply Chain Management Literature. *European Journal of Purchasing & Supply Management,* **7**, pp. 39–48.

Teece, D. (1998) Capturing Value from Knowledge Assets: The New Economy, Markets for Know-how, and Intangible Assets. *California Management Review,* Vol. 40, No. 3, pp. 55–79.

Thompson, J. (1967) *Organizations in Action.* McGraw Hill, New York.

Torvatn, T. (1996) Productivity in Industrial Networks—A Case Study of the Purchasing Function. *Doctoral dissertation.* Norges teknisk-naturvitenskapelige universitet, Trondheim.

Trent, R. and Monczka, R. (1998) Purchasing and Supply Management: Trends and Changes Throughout the 1990s. *International Journal of Purchasing and Materials Management,* Fall, pp. 2–11.

Turnbull, P. and Valla, J.-P. (eds) (1986) *Strategies for International Industrial Marketing*. Croom Helm, London.

van Weele, A. (2000) *Purchasing and Supply Chain Management. Analysis, Planning and Practice*. Thomson Learning, London.

Venkatesan, R. (1992) Strategic Sourcing: To Make or not to Make. *Harvard Business Review*, November–December, pp. 98–108.

Vigoroso, M. (1999) Electronic Commerce—Lots of Interest, Little Action. *Purchasing*, March 25, pp. 43–48.

von Hippel, E. (1990) Task Partitioning: An Innovation Process Variable. *Research Policy*, Vol. 19, pp. 407–418.

von Hippel, E., Thomke, S. and Sonnak, M. (1999) Creating Breakthroughs at 3M. *Harvard Business Review*, September–October, pp. 47–55.

von Krogh, G. (1998) Care in Knowledge Creation. *California Management Review*, Vol. 40, No. 3, pp. 133–153.

Waldrop, M. (1992) *The Emerging Science at the Edge of Order and Chaos*. Touchstone, New York.

Webster, F. E. (1991) *Industrial Marketing Strategy*. John Wiley & Sons, Chichester.

Wernerfelt, B. (1984) A Resource-based View of the Firm. *Strategic Management Journal*, Vol. 5, pp. 171–180.

Womack, J., Jones, D. and Roos, D. (1990) *The Machine that Changed the World*. Macmillan Publishing Company, New York.

Wynstra, F. (1998) Purchasing Involvement in Product Development. Dissertation. Eindhoven Center for Innovation Studies. Eindhoven University.

INDEX